Between Pagan and Christian

Between Pagan and Christian

Christopher P. Jones

Harvard University Press

Cambridge, Massachusetts
London, England
2014

Printed in the United States of America

Library of Congress Cataloging-in-Publication Data

Jones, Christopher P.
Between Pagan and Christian / Christopher P. Jones.
pages cm
Includes bibliographical references and index.
ISBN 978-0-674-72520-1
1. Church history—Primitive and early church, ca. 30-600.
2. Christianity and other religions—Paganism—History—Early church, ca. 30-600. 3. Paganism—Relations—Christianity. I. Title.
BR162.3.J66 2014
270.1—dc23 2013027065

Contents

Note on Authors

This list contains editions and (where available) translations into a modern language of works mentioned more than once in the notes: works mentioned only once are indicated in their place. All volumes in the Budé series, the Loeb Classical Library, and Sources Chrétiennes contain translations, and for these I have indicated only the name(s) of the editor(s). I have not indicated original texts of works in Coptic or Syriac. (For Abbreviations, see pages 163–165.)

Aeneas of Gaza, *Theophrastus*	*PG* 85.865–1004; M. E. Colonna, ed., *Eneo di Gaza: Teofrasto* (Naples: S. Iodice, 1958), with Italian translation
Aeschylus, *Agamemnon*	E. Fraenkel, ed., *Aeschylus: Agamemnon* (Oxford: Clarendon Press, 1950)
Ambrose, *Letters*	O. Faller and M. Zelzer, eds., *Sancti Ambrosii epistulae et acta, CSEL* 82.1–4 (Vienna: Hoelder-Pichler-Tempsky and Verlag der Österreichischen Akademie der Wissenschaften, 1968–1996). Translation: M. M. Beyenka, *Saint Ambrose: Letters* (New York: Fathers of the Church, 1954)
Apostolic Constitutions	M. Metzger, ed., *Les Constitutions apostoliques,* SC 320, 329, 336 (Paris: Éditions du Cerf, 1985–1987)
Arnobius, *Against the Gentiles*	H. Le Bonniec et al., eds., *Arnobe: Contre les Gentils,* Budé (Paris: Les Belles Lettres, 1982–2010)
Augustine, *City of God*	G. E. McCracken et al., eds., *Augustine, The City of God: Against the Pagans,* LCL (Cambridge: Harvard University Press, 1957–1972)

Augustine, *Confessions*	J. J. O'Donnell, ed., *Augustine, Confessions* (Oxford, UK: Clarendon Press; New York: Oxford University Press, 1992). Translation: H. Chadwick (Oxford: Oxford University Press, 2008)
Augustine, *Letters*	A. Goldbacher, ed., *Augustinus: Epistulae, CSEL* 34, 44, 57, 58 (Vienna: F. Tempsky and other publishers, 1895–1898); J. H. Baxter, *Augustine: Select Letters,* LCL (London: Heinemann; New York: Putnam, 1930)
Bede, *Ecclesiastical History*	B. Colgrave and R. A. B. Mynors, eds., *Bede's Ecclesiastical History of the English People* (Oxford: Clarendon Press, 1969)
Besa, *Life of Schenoute*	D. N. Bell, transl., *Besa: The Life of Shenoute* (Kalamazoo: Cistercian, 1983).
Caesarius of Arles, *Sermons*	M.-J. Delage, ed., *Césaire d'Arles: Sermons au peuple,* SC 175, 243, 330 (Paris: Éditions du Cerf, 1971–1986)
Chronicle of Zuqnîn	A. Harrak, transl., *The Chronicle of Zuqnîn, Parts III and IV, A.D. 488–775* (Toronto: Pontifical Institute of Medieval Studies, 1999) [The *Chronicle,* preserved in a single ninth-century manuscript, begins with Creation and ends in 775/76. The third part, going from 480 to 577/78, preserves much of the lost second part of John of Ephesus's *Ecclesiastical History* (see below).]
Clement, *Letters*	B. D. Erdman, ed., *The Apostolic Fathers* 1, LCL (Cambridge: Harvard University Press, 2003)
Cyril, *Against Julian*	P. Burgière and P. Evieux, eds., *Cyrille d'Alexandrie: Contre Julien,* SC 322 (Paris: Éditions du Cerf, 1985) [first two books only; complete work in *PG* 76.509–1064]
Damascius, *Life of Isidore*	P. Athanassiadi, *Damascius: The Philosophical History* (Athens: Apamea Cultural Association, 1999)
Eugippius, *Life of Severinus*	Eugippius: H. Sauppe, ed., *MGH AA* 1.2 (Berlin: Weidmann, 1877); T. Mommsen, ed. (Berlin: Weidmann, 1898), with useful map. Translation: L. Bieler, *Eugippius: The Life of Saint Severin* (Washington, DC: Catholic University of America Press, 1965)
Eunapius, *Lives of the Philosophers*	G. Giangrande, ed., *Eunapii vitae sophistarum* (Rome: Publica Officina Polygraphica, 1956). Translation: W. C. Wright, *Philostratus and Eunapius,*

	LCL (Cambridge: Harvard University Press; London: Heinemann, 1921)
Eusebius, *Life of Constantine*	F. Winkelmann, ed., *Über das Leben des Kaisers Konstantin,* GCS (Berlin: Akademie-Verlag, 1975, rev. 1992). Translation: A. Cameron and S. G. Hall, *Eusebius: Life of Constantine* (Oxford: Clarendon Press, 1999)
Eusebius, *Ecclesiastical History*	E. Schwartz, ed., 2nd ed. F. Winkelmann, *Eusebius: Die Kirchengeschichte,* GCS (Berlin: Akademie Verlag, 1999). Translation: K. Lake and J. E. L. Oulton, LCL (Cambridge: Harvard University Press; London: Heinemann, 1926–1932)
Gelasius, *Against Andromachus*	G. Pomarès, ed., *Gélase Ier: Lettre contre les Lupercales,* SC 65 (Paris: Éditions du Cerf, 1959)
Gerontius, *Life of Melania*	D. Gorce, ed., *Vie de Sainte Mélanie,* SC 90 (Paris: Éditions du Cerf, 1962)
Gibbon, *Decline and Fall*	D. Womersley, ed., *Edward Gibbon: The History of the Decline and Fall of the Roman Empire,* 3 vols. (London: Allen Lane; New York: Penguin, 1994)
Gregory of Nyssa, *Life of Gregory the Thaumaturge*	*PG* 46, 893–958. Translation: M. Slusser, *St. Gregory Thaumaturgus: Life and Works* (Washington, D.C.: Catholic University of America Press, 1998)
Gregory of Tours, *History of the Franks*	B. Krusch and W. Levison, eds., *Gregorii Episcopi Turonensis historia Francorum, MGH, SRM* 1.1 (Hannover: Hahn, 1951)
Gregory of Tours, *Miracles*	B. Krusch, ed., *Gregorii Episcopi Turonensis miracula et opera minora, MGH, SRM* 1.2 (Hannover: Hahn, 1969)
Gregory the Great (Pope), *Letters*	P. Ewald and L. M. Hartmann, eds., *Gregorii I Papae registrum epistolarum,* 2 vols., *MGH, Epist.* 1–2 (Berlin: Weidmann, 1887–1899)
Isidore of Pelusium, *Letters*	P. Évieux, ed., *Isidore de Péluse: Lettres,* SC 422, 454 (Paris: Éditions du Cerf, 1997–2000), Letters 1214–1700 only. Complete edition: *PG* 78. [I have used Migne's pagination.]
Jerome, *Life of Hilarion*	P. Leclerc et al., eds., *Jérôme: Trois vies de moines (Paul, Malchus, Hilarion),* SC 508 (Paris: Éditions du Cerf, 2007)
John of Ephesus, *Ecclesiastical History*	E. W. Brooks, trans., *Johannis Ephesini historiae ecclesiasticae pars tertia, CSCO* 106 (Paris: Firmin-Didot, 1936). See also *Chronicle of Zuqnîn*

John of Ephesus, *Lives of the Eastern Saints*	E. W. Brooks, ed., *Lives of the eastern Saints, Patrologia orientalis* 17.1, 18.4,19.2 (Paris: Firmin-Didot, 1923–1925)
Julian, *Against the Galilaeans*	M. Stern, *Greek and Latin authors on Jews and Judaism* 2 (Jerusalem: Israel Academy of Arts and Sciences, 1980); E. Masaracchia, *Giuliano Imperatore: Contra Galilaeos* (Rome: Edizioni dell'Ateneo, 1990)
Julian, *Hymn to the Sun*	W. C. Wright, ed., *The Works of the emperor Julian* 1, LCL (London: Heinemann; New York: Macmillan, 1913), 348–435
Latin Panegyrics	É. Galletier, ed., *Panégyriques Latins,* Budé (Paris: Les Belles Lettres, 1949–1955); C. E. V. Nixon and B. S. Rodgers, *In Praise of Later Roman Emperors: The Panegyrici Latini* (Berkeley: University of California Press, 1994)
Libanius, *Autobiography*	A. F. Norman, ed., *Libanius: Autobiography and Selected Letters,* LCL (Cambridge: Harvard University Press, 1992)
Libanius, *Orations*	A. F. Norman, ed., *Libanius: Selected Works,* LCL (Cambridge: Harvard University Press, 1969–1977)
Macarius of Magnesia, *Discourse in Reply*	R. Goulet, ed., *Macarios de Magnésie: Le Monogénès,* 2 vols. (Paris: J. Vrin, 2003)
Macrobius, *Saturnalia*	R. A. Kaster, ed., *Macrobius: Saturnalia,* LCL (Cambridge: Harvard University Press, 2011)
Malalas, *Chronography*	I. Thurn, ed., *Ioannis Malalae chronographia* (Berlin: de Gruyter, 2000). Translation: E. Jeffreys, M. Jeffreys, and M. Scott, *The Chronicle of John Malalas* (Melbourne: Australian Association for Byzantine Studies and Sydney, University of Sydney, 1986)
Marinus, *Life of Proclus*	H. D. Saffrey and A.-P. Segonds, *Marinus ou Sur le Bonheur,* Budé (Paris: Les Belles Lettres, 2001)
Mark the Deacon, *Life of Porphyry*	H. Grégoire and M.-A. Kugener, eds., *Marc le Diacre: Vie de Porphyre, Évêque de Gaza* (Paris: Les Belles Lettres, 1930)
Martin of Braga, *On the Correction of the Peasants*	C. W. Barlow, ed., *Martini Episcopi Bracensis opera omnia, Papers and Monographs of the American Academy in Rome* 12 (1950): 159–203
Maximus of Turin, *Sermons*	A. Mutzenbecher, ed., *Maximi Episcopi Taurinensis sermones,* Corpus Christianorum, Series Latina 23

	(Turnholt: Brepols, 1962). Translation: B. Ramsey, *The Sermons of St. Maximus of Turin* (New York: Newman Press, 1989)
Nilus of Ancyra, Letters	*PG* 79.81–582
Orosius, *History*	M.-P. Arnaud-Lindet, ed., *Orose: Histoires,* Budé (Paris: Les Belles Lettres, 1990–1991)
Philostratus, *Life of Apollonius*	C. P. Jones, ed., *Philostratus: Apollonius of Tyana,* 2 vols., LCL (Cambridge: Harvard University Press, 2005)
Philostorgius, *Ecclesiastical History*	J. Bidez, ed., 3rd ed., rev. F. Winkelmann, *Philostorgius: Kirchengeschichte,* GCS (Berlin: Akademie-Verlag, 1981). Translation: P. R. Amidon, *Philostorgius: Church History* (Atlanta: Society of Biblical Literature, 2007)
Rufinus, *Ecclesiastical History*	T. Mommsen, ed., in F. Winkelmann, ed., *Eusebius: Die Kirchengeschichte,* GCS (Berlin: Akademie Verlag, 1999). Translation: P. R. Amidon, *The Church History of Rufinus of Aquileia, Books 10 and 11* (New York: Oxford University Press, 1997)
Rutilius Namatianus, *On His Return*	É. Wolff et al., eds., *Rutilius Namatianus: Sur son retour,* Budé (Paris: Les Belles Lettres, 2007)
Shenute, *Letters and Sermons*	J. Leipoldt, ed., *Corpus Scriptorum Christianorum Orientalium, Scriptores Coptici,* ser. 2, vols. 4–5 (Paris 1908–1936), with translation by H. Wiesmann (Paris 1908–1936) [Since it is often impossible to distinguish sermon from letter, I have referred to each item as "L. 1," etc.]
Socrates, *Ecclesiastical History*	P. Maraval et al., ed., *Socrate de Constantinople: Histoire ecclésiastique,* SC 477, 493, 505, 506 (Paris: Éditions du Cerf, 2004–)
Sozomen, *Ecclesiastical History*	J. Bidez et al., eds., *Sozomène: Histoire ecclésiastique,* SC 306, 418, 495, 516 (Paris: Éditions du Cerf, 1983–2008)
Sulpicius Severus, *Life of Martin*	J. Fontaine, ed., *Sulpice Sévère: Vie de Saint Martin* SC 133–135 (Paris: Éditions du Cerf, 1967–1969)
Symmachus, *Letters*	O. Seeck, ed., *Q. Aurelii Symmachi quae supersunt, MGH AA* 6.1 (Berlin: Weidmann, 1883); Callu, J.-P., ed., *Symmaque: Lettres,* Budé (Paris: Les Belles Lettres, 1972–2002)
Symmachus, *Reports* and *Panegyrics*	Callu, J.-P., ed., *Symmaque: Discours, Rapports,* Budé (Paris: Les Belles Lettres, 2009); R. H. Barrow, ed.,

	Prefect and Emperor (Oxford: Clarendon Press, 1984; *Reports* only)
Tertullian, *Apology*	T. R. Glover, ed., *Tertullian: Apology, De Spectaculis*, LCL (London: Heinemann; New York: Putnam's Sons, 1931)
Themistius, *Orations*	G. Downey and A. F. Norman, eds., *Themistii orationes* (Leipzig: Teubner, 1965–1974)
Theodoret of Cyrrhus, *Cure of Pagan Maladies*	P. Canivet, ed., *Théodorèt de Cyr: Thérapeutique des maladies helléniques*, SC 57 (Paris: Éditions du Cerf, 1958)
Theodoret of Cyrrhus, *Ecclesiastical History*	J. Bouffartigue et al., eds., *Théodoret de Cyr: Histoire ecclésiastique*, SC 501, 530 (Paris: Éditions du Cerf, 2006–2009)
Theodoret of Cyrrhus, *Letters*	Y. Azéma, ed., *Théodorèt de Cyr: Correspondance*, SC 40, 98, 111, 429 (Paris: Éditions du Cerf, 1955–1998)
Theodosian Code 16	T. Mommsen and J. Rougé, *Les Lois religieuses des empereurs romains I: Code Théodosien, Livre XVI*, SC 497 (Paris: Éditions du Cerf, 2005)
Zacharias of Mytilene, *Life of Severus*	M.-A. Kugener, ed. and trans., *Vie de Sévère, par Zacharie le Scholastique, Patrologia Orientalis* 2.1 (Paris: Firmin-Didot, 1907)
Zacharias of Mytilene, *On the Creation of the World*	*PG* 85.1011–1144
Zosimus, *New History*	F. Paschoud, ed., *Zosime: Histoire nouvelle*, Budé (Paris: Les Belles Lettres, 1971–1989)

Preface

Books with titles such as *Pagans and Christians, Christians and Pagans, Païens et Chrétiens* tumble from the presses. A related topic, the "last pagans," has been no less fertile. Gaston Boissier's *The End of Paganism: Study of the Last Religious Struggles in the West in the Fourth Century* (*La fin du paganisme: Étude sur les dernières luttes religieuses en Occident au quatrième siècle*) came out in 1891, went through three editions in his lifetime, and was reprinted as recently as 1987. Pierre Chuvin's *Chronique des derniers païens* has now also gone through three editions, with translations into English in 1990 and Italian in 2012, and Alan Cameron's *The Last Pagans of Rome* appeared in 2011.

Despite having learned much from these and similar works, I decided to contribute to what might seem an inexhaustible discussion by asking how far paganism was a construct that, while it certainly had a correlative in "reality," was also something perceived or imagined by those opposed to it, notably Christian authorities both secular and ecclesiastic. The word usually denotes those who did not accept the Christian god (though Trinitarian Christians, for example, could accuse their Arian opponents of pagan tendencies). But the word also has an element of the subjective: paganism could exist only because for Christians it represented one form of otherness, while Judaism, though another form of otherness, could never be thought of as pagan.

Another problem was that of "last pagans." Certainly there were fewer and fewer "pagans" after the conversion of the emperor Constantine to Christianity in 312; by the year 600, within what had been the borders of the Roman Empire, they were mainly confined to remote regions such as

Sardinia and Britain. But within those same borders the transition from a minority of Christians to a majority was gradual and uneven, differing from place to place and from one social level to another. Outside those borders, it sometimes occurred much later, as among the Saxons east of the Elbe, or not at all; and with the advent of Islam, Christianity was displaced even over a large part of the old Roman Empire.

It therefore seemed worth exploring, even in a brief compass, what might be called the ground between pagan and Christian. "Between" implies not only that Christianity and paganism had much in common, with Christianity drawing heavily on the beliefs and practices of paganism: it also refers to the ways in which Christians such as St. Paul could use the traditional culture of Greeks and Romans to build a bridge from their own side to the other. At the same time, the Judaism out of which Christianity grew had been familiar to many Greeks and some Romans long before Christianity entered their ken, and hence "pagans" could recognize concepts such as that of a single, creator God and practices such as observation of the Sabbath, even when they did not accept them. Conversely, Christians claimed that Greek thinkers, especially Plato, had been dimly aware of the Jewish and Christian truths even before the revelation brought by Christ's Incarnation.

I begin by discussing the language with which Christians referred to "pagans" in the eastern, mainly Greek-speaking portion and in the western, Latin-speaking portions of the empire (Chapter 1). I then consider the first Christian emperor, Constantine (Chapter 2), and then his successors (Chapter 3) in their relation with pagans. In the next chapter, I consider the similarities and dissimilarities in the pagan, Jewish, and Christian conceptions of godhead (Chapter 4), and how these differences were crystallized in discussions of "idolatry" (Chapter 5) and sacrifice (Chapter 6). I then consider the ways in which Christians and pagans defended their respective positions (Chapter 7), and the meaning of "conversion" and the different forms that it took (Chapter 8). Since the transformation of the pagan Roman empire into a web of diplomatically connected and largely Christian states occurred differently not only between the Latin-speaking West and the mainly Greek-speaking East, but also between different social levels, I consider town and country in West (Chapter 9) and East (Chapter 10). Finally, I ask in which sense paganism persisted both in reality and in perception (Chapter 11). An appendix examines the religious position of the author Macrobius. All translations, including biblical ones, are my own unless otherwise indicated.

The seeds of this book were planted in the 1970s, when I became interested in inscriptions whose character, Christian or non-Christian, was ambiguous. I had the privilege of giving seminars on this subject at the École Normale Supérieure, Paris, in 1979. In my last years at Harvard, I taught a course with a title "The Christian Revolution," in which I developed certain of the ideas that now appear here. I am grateful to the students in that course for their interest, and especially to my teaching assistants, Kyle Harper and Liz Mellyn, for many fruitful conversations and exchanges. Among institutions, I am indebted to Harvard University for allowing me in retirement full access to its unparalleled resources, and I am no less indebted to the Institute for Advanced Study, Princeton, which has given me the advantage of its own superb resources and support.

Two friends have read a draft of this book. Peter Brown's writings I have followed since his seminal articles published in the *Journal of Roman Studies* in the 1960s and since the first edition of his *Augustine*. Glen Bowersock has been my friend, guide, and thoughtful critic since we were both students at Oxford more than fifty years ago. To these two great historians of Late Antiquity I owe much more than the inspiration of their work.

CHAPTER ONE

The Perception of Paganism

In one of his great missionary journeys, Paul of Tarsus, a Jewish convert to Christianity, came to Athens. Now far declined from its days of imperial greatness, the city was still the heart of Hellenic culture, and Paul found it to be "full of idols" *(kateidôlos)*. He began to preach in the public space of the Agora, where certain of the philosophers for which the city was renowned considered him "an announcer of strange divinities *(daimonia)*." They brought him before city's senior and most exclusive body, the Areopagus, and asked him to explain his teaching, "since you bring certain strange things to our ears." As recounted by Luke, the presumed author of Acts, Paul's speech begins: "Men of Athens, in general I see that you are very devout. For as I went along and surveyed your cult-objects, I found an altar on which was written, 'To an Unknown God.' Him therefore whom you venerate without knowing I announce to you." Paul goes on to expatiate on this god in terms that pagans could understand, quoting as he does so a half line from the Greek poet Aratus referring to Zeus, "For of him we are descended." "As God's descendants," he continues, "we should not think that the divine *(theion)* resembles gold, silver or stone, something carved by art and by human imagination." Only at the end of his speech does he allude to Jesus, not by name or even as the son of God, but as "a man that God has determined, giving a pledge to all by raising him from the dead." Some of his hearers mocked him, others promised to hear more, but others "believed," among whom Luke names Dionysius the Areopagite and a woman called Damaris. Centuries later, a Christian using the pseudonym of Dionysius the Areopagite wrote a synthesis of Neoplatonic and Christian philosophy that was to have an enormous influence on

Christian thought, in part because its author seemed to have been one of the first converts to the new faith.[1]

Luke uses this event to illustrate an attempt of the first missionaries to reach out to Greeks *(Hellênes),* for whom Athens was still a focal point of history and culture, "the most ancient, wise and devout city, loved equally by gods and men." The Athenians, Paul suggests, are worshiping the Christian god without knowing it, and hence for them he is an "unknown god." Yet for the Athenians, Paul is the herald of divinities *(daimonia)* of whom they have never heard. Though he is concerned to minimize the distance between Greeks and Christians, the gap remains: it is crossed only when some of his hearers "believe."[2]

This incident is a harbinger of issues that were to prove crucial in later centuries. One is the possibility of compromise between non-Christian Greeks and Christians: perhaps both shared the same god, even if one of the two parties did so "without knowing." Behind this idea is another and more profound one: while knowledge of the true God had existed since the formation of mankind, and certain virtuous men such as Socrates had already had a partial glimpse of Him, the possibility of full knowledge had come with the advent of Jesus Christ. Another concept important in Luke's account is that of creatures below the level of God or of gods, *daimonia;* long familiar to Greeks as a word for minor divinities, this was eagerly caught up by Christians to designate all the supposed gods of paganism, and passed into modern languages as "demon." A third issue is conversion: some of Paul's hearers "believed" on the strength of his arguments alone, and thus were converted. To modern ears, "conversion" suggests a turn from one system of thought to another: though early Christians also talked of "turning," for them conversion was more a matter of passing from unbelief to belief, from blindness to seeing, or of ceasing to "wander" and finding "the Way."

When Paul talks of "one of your poets," he implicitly places the Athenians in the community of "Hellenes." The Christian New Testament several times uses this word alongside "Jews" *(Ioudaioi)* to refer to the two most conspicuous groups of nonbelievers in Jesus as the Messiah: thus Paul in Corinth tries to convince "both Jews and Hellenes" and in Asia causes "both Jews and Hellenes" to hear the word of the Lord. Jews writing in Greek had used "Hellenes" in the sense of "nonbeliever" or "idolater" from the later Hellenistic period, and from them it passed into the first

Christian Greek authors, and persisted well into Late Antiquity. With the growth of the Greek-speaking church, "Hellene" came also to characterize those who were not true Christians in the eyes of the speaker. It could designate those who represented a "split" *(schisma)* within the community of believers, for example by lapsing in time of persecution, or by slipping into pagan practices after baptism, or worse, who had made a "choice" *(hairesis)* that shut them off altogether. Thus the term "consubstantial" *(homoousios),* chosen by the Council of Nicaea to represent the relation between God the Father and God the Son, failed to end the controversy: according to the historian Socrates, "one party considered those who accepted this to be blasphemers, for they considered the Son as without a beginning and held the beliefs of Montanus and Sabellius, while the other side shunned their opponents as pagans *(Hellênes)* and accused them of introducing polytheism." "Hellene" thus has a variety of senses according to the context, and it is not always possible to determine if a person was a devotee of traditional religion, a Christian rightly or wrongly suspected of "paganism," or merely a suspected heretic. Moreover, many Christians of undisputed orthodoxy were Greek by birth or culture, and Gregory of Nazianzus among others vigorously denied that Christians could not be "Hellenes."[3]

Hellên had not only the disadvantage of ambiguity, but was inappropriate to designate those pagans who were not ethnically Greek, though it was sometimes so used. For these a better term was *ethnikos,* "gentile." This adjective and its noun *ethnos,* "nation," were borrowed by Christianity from Greek-speaking Judaism, in which the words reflected the view of "the nations" as a sea of nonbelievers surrounding the Jewish "people" *(laos);* hence the resurrected Jesus bids the apostles to "instruct all the nations *(ethnê).*" In later Christianity, when the struggle with Hellenism was a thing of the past, *ethnikos* retained its usefulness to designate those such as Huns who stood outside the Christian pale, as once the "nations" hemmed in the Jewish people.[4]

When Greek-speaking Christians wished to refer to nonbelievers in terms of their beliefs, the richness of their language gave them several other designations. "Idolater" (*eidôlolatrês,* literally "image-worshiper"), another borrowing from Jewish Greek, in Christian usage marked an essential difference between both Jews and Christians on one side, and nonbelievers on the other, since the Jewish abhorrence of graven images went back to the First and Second Commandments and passed directly into Christianity. In

Acts, the Council of Jerusalem, the first-ever meeting held to define the basic laws of Christianity, made "avoiding the pollution of idolatry" the first of its new rules. A similar term was "polytheist" *(polytheos),* since the rejection of multiple gods, like that of idolatry, derived from the First Commandment, "You shall have no other gods but me," and hence *polytheos* served to characterize one of the most obvious features of paganism. Though Christians sometimes took the view that pagan gods were really deified mortals, they often did not deny their continuing existence, but maintained that they were malign incorporeal beings, "demons" *(daimonia)* and not gods. Paradoxically, the refusal of pagans to revere the true God caused them also to be labeled as "godless" *(atheoi),* since their supposed gods were no gods at all; Eusebius says of Constantine's father, Constantius, that "he condemned the polytheism of the godless *(atheoi)*" (pagans returned the compliment by calling Christians "godless" for not venerating the traditional gods). A less opprobrious term was those "outside" *(ektos, exô, exôthen),* and Eusebius famously reports Constantine's claim, "I am perhaps a bishop appointed by God over those outside," though the emperor's precise meaning is disputed.[5]

The Roman Empire down to the late fourth century had managed to remain an administrative unity, despite losses in both East and West, but not a cultural or linguistic one. As Greek was the dominant language in the East despite the existence of many other languages such as Syriac and Coptic, so Latin was dominant in the West despite the survival of languages such as Celtic and Punic. "East" and "West" are only approximate terms for these two divisions of the empire. The eastern Balkans, Asia Minor, the Levant, and North Africa as far as Cyrene were ruled from Constantinople after the division of responsibilities between Arcadius and Honorius in 395; the rest of the former empire, from Pannonia (roughly the recent Yugoslavia) round to Africa (roughly modern Tunisia), was ruled from Rome. The political situation was later to grow more complicated, with the Germanic and Hunnic occupations of central and western Europe and of Africa in the fifth century, and the Byzantine reconquests of Italy, Africa, and a part of Spain in the sixth. Yet these did not immediately alter the linguistic divide at the level of secular and ecclesiastical administration. The churches of East and West continued largely to use Greek and Latin, and in the West the Germanic kingdoms such as those of the Franks and the Visigoths adopted Latin for administrative and legal purposes. Yet with all these qualifications, it is best to retain the terms "East" and "West" when talking of the linguistic and cultural traditions of the two parts.[6]

Since Christianity developed first in the East (though there were Latin-speaking Christians already in the time of the first apostles), Latin evolved a Christian vocabulary later than Greek, and its first surviving texts are not earlier than the late second century. Latin also reflects the spread of the new faith in a way different from Greek. The term "gentile" *(gentilis)* is a direct calque of the Greek *ethnikos,* but about the beginning of the fourth century this starts to lose ground to another term, apparently of popular origin, *paganus.* The etymological meaning of this is "belonging to a village" *(pagus),* from which develops a secondary one of "civilian" as opposed to "enlisted soldier." Some have derived *paganus* in the sense of "non-Christian" from the military sense, so that a *paganus* is one not enrolled in the army of Christ. Another view is that *paganus* denotes attachment to a single place of any kind, even within a city, but this view has little linguistic support.[7]

The Christian association of paganism with religious practices of the countryside is a recurrent theme of later antiquity. A law of 399 rules that "if there are any temples in the countryside *(in agris),* let them be destroyed without noise and disturbance; for once these are demolished and removed, the whole basis for superstition *(omnis superstitionis materia)* will be consumed." The Christian poet Prudentius imagines the emperor Theodosius urging Rome to "leave the gods of gentiles to barbaric villages" *(sint haec barbaricis gentilia numina pagis).* A few years later Augustine's associate Orosius affirms that pagans were so named "from the cross-roads and villages of country places" *(ex locorum agrestium conpitis et pagis),* and a pagan aristocrat, the senator Rutilius Namatianus, found "villages" *(pagi)* on the west coast of Italy joyfully celebrating the resurrection of Osiris "around the rustic cross-roads" *(per compita rustica).* In the late sixth century, Martin, bishop of Braga in Galicia, denounced the persistence of paganism in a sermon, *On the Correction of Peasants (De correctione rusticorum).* It seems therefore that Latin-speaking Christians first applied the term "villagers" *(pagani)* to peasants among whom the old beliefs and practices lingered on, and eventually extended the term to all "pagans." By a similar process, the German *Heide* and the English *heathen* were chosen to translate *paganus* because non-Christians belonged on the "heaths," in the untamed lands outside civilization; in French, *paganus* becomes *païen,* and *pagensis* becomes *paysan.* The fact that *Hellên* refers to high culture, and *paganus* to rusticity, is a reminder that the evolution of Christianity occurred in different ways in the two main divisions of the empire.[8]

Even among undoubted Christians there was a distinction between those who were Christians in the full sense and those who were not. Christianity soon developed an elaborate system of preparation for full initiation into the community, the "catechumenate" (from the Greek *katêchoumenoi,* "those undergoing instruction"). Adults wishing to be admitted as full Christians by the sacrament of baptism had to undergo a long period of instruction and preparation, and those not yet baptized were not true Christians: they were "faithful" *(pistoi, fideles)* but were not yet "illuminated" *(pephôtismenoi, illuminati).* Hence texts sometimes equate being Christian with being baptized. Caesarius of Arles in the early fifth century tells his hearers that anyone who consults a magician *(praecantator)* "immediately destroys his oath of baptism and straightaway becomes a sacrilegious pagan," and Pope Gelasius at the end of the same century rules that "no-one baptized, no-one who is a Christian" may celebrate the pagan festival of the Lupercalia.[9]

The word "pagan," when used by modern scholars of Christian history to designate those who were neither Christian nor Jew, is therefore inappropriate insofar as it borrows a Latin term used primarily by an in-group to denote an out-group, when the modern observer stands outside either group. This is even more of a drawback when applied to those whom Greek-speaking Christians called "Hellenes," since now it lumps into a single class people so different as Roman aristocrats fondly cherishing the religion and antiquities of their ancestral city, and Arabs and Germans worshiping gods outside the Greek and Roman pantheon. "Polytheist" might appear a possible alternative, but has the disadvantage of blurring the wide range of conceptions that "pagans" had about the divine: some are indeed polytheists, but others come close to monotheism, and yet others have a conception of a supreme being to whom all others are subservient or inferior (so-called "henotheism").[10] "Hellenism" has the advantage of being a word commonly used by Greek-speaking Christians to designate pagans, but has the disadvantage of ambiguity mentioned above, and is not applicable in the Latin West. "Paganism" is potentially misleading, but less so than the alternatives that have been proposed.[11]

In the following I shall use the term "pagan" for the whole body of those non-Jews who remained outside Christianity, whether by choice or in ignorance. I do so partly because the term points to an essential feature of paganism, its persistence in rural districts, but the distinction between city and country is not the only one. A city such as Carrhae (Harran) in Mesopotamia remained attached to its traditional religion while Edessa, scarcely more than a day's journey away, claimed that its Christianity went back to the time of Jesus. Language-groups also differ markedly in the way they react to Christianity: not only do Greek- and Latin-speakers develop a different vocabulary to designate non-Christians, but languages other than the classical ones become vectors for particular forms of Christianity, with their own vocabulary of "paganism." It is best therefore not to think of the distinction between pagans and Christians as a single spectrum running, like modern party-lines, from full or "committed" Christians at one end and "committed" pagans at the other, with "center-pagans" and "center-Christians" toward the middle. Who or what counts as "pagan" depends very much on the outlook of the contemporary observer. Thus for Augustine of Hippo, pagans might be unbelievers listening to one of his sermons, or they might be Roman aristocrats writing polite but faintly ironic letters to inquire about Christian doctrines. Paganism is always a blurred and shifting category that defies neat taxonomies.[12]

Some have talked of paganism as a "faith" or a "religion." It is often thought of as the opposite of Christianity, a rival or a parallel entity from which people could be converted, or to which they could return after being Christian. In the following, without abandoning the convenient term "paganism," I shall nonetheless explore the ways in which Christianity and paganism interpenetrate. Pagans can be monotheists, and Christians can be accused of polytheism or be branded as pagans because they cling to or revive old beliefs and practices. Zeus and the other deities of paganism are thought still to exist, but as demons and not as gods: demons can disguise themselves as the old gods in order to attract worshipers. Above all, since expanding Christianity was always coming into contact with peoples who did not share its beliefs, some of whom could be converted and others not, there could in one sense never be an end of paganism. Indeed, the propagation of a new religion by Muhammad and his followers had the consequence that Christians could be the new nonbelievers, somewhat as Jews or certain pagans had been for Christians—those who had received a partial revelation but not the full truth. At the same time, one of the first Christian critics of Islam, John of Damascus, considered the religion propagated by Muhammad a Christian heresy inspired by the doctrines of Arius.[13]

In modern times, Christians have not hesitated to use the word "pagan" or "gentile" to characterize the practices of churches other than their own.[14] Who counted as a "pagan" in antiquity cannot be determined merely from language, nor is a difference between pagans and Christians always observable in practice. The following chapters will explore the ways in which the varied beliefs of "those outside" interacted with those of the new religion, coloring and changing them in ways that make sharp distinctions impossible.

CHAPTER TWO

Constantine

PAUL'S SPEECH before the Areopagus represents the first attempt of a Christian to explain his faith to pagans. Both Paul and his fellow apostle Peter died in a persecution under Nero, and for another two and a half centuries Roman authorities tried to force Christians to sacrifice to the gods or to emperors, with imprisonment or grisly death as the penalty if they refused. The process of explaining the new belief nonetheless continued, and has left many works of literature from the second century down to the fifth or sixth. More effective than these, though now largely invisible, was the slow and patient work of teaching and example that turned nonbelievers into "faithful" and into full members of the Church.

Historically, the symbolic moment occurred in 312, when the emperor Constantine, not yet sole ruler of the Roman Empire, underwent a sudden and still mysterious conversion. His reign was to be a turning point in the relations of Christianity with the pagan world. From now on, with a conspicuous interruption in the person of the last emperor of the Constantinian house, Julian the "Apostate," Christianity occupied the seat of power, and the emperors began to evolve policies to deal not only with divisions within the Church itself, but with the nonbelievers outside it, principally pagans and Jews, two sets of nonbelievers who became more and more linked together in Christian thought.

Constantine was born at an uncertain date between 270 and 280, the son of a general and governor named Constantius and his "concubine" or common-law wife, Helena, the daughter of an innkeeper. In 293, the senior emperor, or "Augustus," Diocletian, made Constantius his junior partner, or "Caesar," in the West, while Constantine remained at the imperial court in Nicomedia as a hostage for his father's loyalty. When Diocletian began the last and fiercest persecution of Christians in 303, Constantius is said to have carried out the imperial orders only reluctantly. Two years later Diocletian promoted him to Augustus in the West while he and his coemperor Maximian abdicated, but he did not elevate Constantine to his father's old position of Caesar. Shortly afterward, Constantine escaped from Nicomedia in order to join Constantius in Britain, and soon after, on his father's death, the army proclaimed him Augustus. The next six years are among the most complicated of Roman imperial history, but by 311 the senior emperor Galerius, now dying of cancer, issued a deathbed edict of toleration toward the Christians, and so officially brought the Diocletianic persecution to an end. After his death, the two remaining rivals for power in the West were Maxentius, who held Italy and Africa, and Constantine, who held the northwestern provinces and Spain. When war broke out between the two in the summer of 312, Constantine moved rapidly from Gaul into northern Italy and, after heavy fighting, marched on Rome. He confronted the forces of Maxentius at "Red Rocks," several miles north of the city, and pushed the opposing forces back onto the line of the Tiber at the Milvian Bridge. The battle then became a rout, Maxentius was drowned, and Constantine entered the city as sole ruler of the West.[1]

Two writers contemporary with Constantine, the African Lactantius and Eusebius from Caesarea in Palestine, writing in Latin and Greek respectively, both affirm that while marching to confront Maxentius in 312, Constantine underwent a miraculous conversion to Christianity. The earlier of the two, Lactantius, reports that in a dream on the night before the battle Constantine received an order to put a Christian device on his soldiers' shields. Eusebius represents him when still in northern Italy as wondering what god to call to his aid against Maxentius. Since his father had always honored the God of the universe while polytheistic emperors had ended in ruin, his own inclination to do likewise was confirmed when he and his entire army observed a cross in the sky. The next night Christ appeared to him in a dream.[2]

Whichever version is closer to the truth (and Eusebius's version, written much later than the event, sounds like defensive panegyric), after the Battle of the Milvian Bridge Constantine began to act as a Christian emperor, though he was not baptized until the end of his life, and the depth of his faith is unclear. Some months after the battle he conferred with Licinius, then ruling Pannonia with the title of Augustus, and together they produced what is sometimes called the "Edict of Milan," though the document that survives is an edict issued by Licinius in 313. This went beyond the edict of the dying Galerius and granted full freedom of religion to all, with special privileges extended to the Christians. Licinius proceeded to eliminate the eastern Augustus, Maximinus, a virulent anti-Christian, and ruled the East alone until war again broke out between him and Constantine in 316. They agreed to an uneasy peace in the following year, but by about 320 their relations began to worsen, and reached open war in 324. Constantine finally penned Licinius up in Nicomedia and accepted his surrender, but soon put him to death. He now became sole ruler of an undivided empire, forty years after Diocletian had attained the same position.

The early career of Constantine is known only from sources written after his conversion in 312. Whether written by pagans or Christians, they are inevitably colored by the author's own beliefs and situation, and it is difficult to measure how far his later Christianity goes back to his birth and upbringing. It is unlikely that his father, Constantius, who so far as is known was of obscure origin and parentage, had any contact with abstract speculation, though as a career officer he must have been familiar with the widespread cult of the sun-god that was favored by the military. Perhaps taking his cue from Constantine, his biographer Eusebius claims that Constantius "knew one God alone (ruling) over all, and condemned the polytheism of the godless. . . . Together with his children and wife and the slaves in his service, he consecrated his house to the one all-ruling God, so that the crowd assembled inside the very palace seemed in no way less than a church of God, and had in its number also ministers of God, who performed unceasing prayers for the emperor." Without indulging in philosophic speculation, Constantius may have shared the pagan monotheism of his day, and have felt that the Christians had done little or nothing to justify their persecution: already in the early second century the Younger Pliny had shown a similar attitude. In the third century, pagan emperors such as Caracalla and Severus Alexander had Christians in their personal staffs, selecting them for their official skills, not for their religion.[3]

Some have inferred Constantius's Christian leanings, or his actual adoption of Christianity, from the name of one of his daughters, Anastasia, derived from the Greek word *anastasis,* "resurrection," since the name is otherwise only found among Jews and Christians. But the first mention of her name "Anastasia" occurs late in the fourth century, and she could have had some other name, now unknown, and taken a "Christian" one at the time of her baptism. The practice of taking a new or an additional name at baptism is already attested in the third century and continues to this day.[4]

A surviving series of twelve Latin panegyrics includes one addressed to Constantius in 297 or 298, and five honoring Constantine over a span of time between 307 and 321. Though they give an immediate window on the circumstances of their day, they must be treated as what they are—specimens of the eloquence for which Gaul had long been famous, and not bulletins on the emperor's spiritual progress.[5]

The only one of these panegyrics addressed to Constantius is spoken by an anonymous orator from Augustodunum (Autun), and gives no sign that the Caesar has relinquished traditional beliefs or forms. The orator speaks of the "Augustus" Maximian and the "Caesar" Constantius as having conferred "almost more benefits upon the earth than the gods," and these same gods have collaborated to grant him victory over his enemies. The first of the panegyrics to Constantine, spoken in 307 when the emperor had married Fausta, the daughter of Maximian, uses similar language. Constantius is now "transferred to the council of the gods," that is, consecrated in the traditional way of Roman emperors. The orator addresses the late emperor, imagined as listening to his speech from beyond the skies, as "you whom the Sun himself picked up to carry to heaven, as he returned to the neighboring regions at his setting."[6]

The second panegyric of Constantine was spoken at a delicate juncture in 310, when he had brought about the death of his father-in-law, Maximian, and was seeking legitimacy as the rightful Augustus of the West. On his way to confront a barbarian attack, the emperor left the main road to visit a celebrated temple of a Celtic god, Grannus, who was widely worshiped in northwestern Europe and was identified with the Greek and Roman Apollo: this shrine was probably at the modern Grand in southern Burgundy. Here he had a vision that has been seen as a precursor of the more famous one of 312, or indeed as the emperor's only authentic vision. "You saw, I believe, Constantine, Apollo accompanied by Victory and offering you laurel crowns, each of which promise you an omen of thirty years; for this is the number of human generations which are certainly due to you beyond the old age of Nestor. Indeed, why do I say 'I believe'? You saw, and in his form you recognized yourself, to whom divine poems have

PLATE 1
Coin of 316/317 showing Constantine and Sol (the sun-god), Ticinum, Italy. © The Trustees of the British Museum

foretold rule over the whole world as your due." A sober reading of this passage, on which so much has been piled, is that the supposed vision of Apollo is either a hallucination of the emperor, or some kind of flattering demonstration arranged by the priests of the temple. The crowns, in some way taking the shape of the Roman numeral thirty (XXX), promised him a further life beyond even the proverbially aged Nestor, while the "divine poems" are probably works of the poet Vergil, whose text by this time had begun to assume a prophetic aura. In this same year, Constantine starts to exhibit the god Sol (Sun) on his coinage (plate 1), and since Apollo was often identified with the sun-god, the emperor may have begun to see himself as Apollo's representative or reincarnation upon earth. Later, the frequent assimilation of the sun to the Christian God made it a convenient vehicle for bridging the gap between pagan and Christian, both in the emperor's own mind and in the minds of his subjects. While the experience of 310 deserves a special place in any narrative of Constantine's conversion to Christianity, it is not a turning point equivalent to that of 312.[7]

In the third panegyric of Constantine, dated to 313, the anonymous speaker appears to know something about the emperor's recent conversion, but continues to talk the language of educated paganism. He speaks of a supreme though not sole divinity, a "divine mind" which "delegates the care of us to the lesser gods and deigns to show itself to you alone." The Senate, he claims, had conferred "the statue of a god" on Constantine after his defeat of Maxentius, since "an image is and often will be due to divinity" (the text and the identity of the god are disputed). He ends with a prayer to a vaguely defined God, whether he is "divine mind and power" infused throughout the universe, or "some power above the whole sky who looks down upon this creation of Yours from the lofty citadel of nature." This kind of hesitation is a trope of ancient prayer, but in this case the language suggests that the speaker was seeking to find language that would allow for different interpretations, much as the Senate two years later speaks of "the prompting of divinity" on the Arch of Constantine in Rome.[8]

Of the five panegyrics addressed to Constantine, the latest, dated to 321, is the only one spoken in Rome rather in Gaul and the only one with a named author, Nazarius. Speaking of Constantine's march from Gaul into Italy to confront Maxentius, the orator relates how a heavenly army led by the deified Constantius descended from above. "Their flashing shields glowed with a kind of awesomeness *(verendum quiddam),* and their celestial armor burned with a tremendous light": mortals could hear them saying, "We seek Constantine, we have come to help Constantine." The speaker evokes the intervention of Castor and Pollux at the Battle of Lake Regillus in the early years of the republic, but this miracle surpassed that: then only two youths were seen, not whole armies, and that occurred in a distant past, while this was attested by living witnesses. Nazarius may have known about Constantine's vision of 312, whether in the comparatively sober version of it given by Lactantius or the highly elaborate one communicated by the emperor to Eusebius, but like the orator of 313, he gives no sign of being a Christian, though he may have been converted later.[9]

None of the three speakers who composed panegyrics after Constantine's conversion say outright that he had adopted a religion that only a few years before was under fierce persecution. A partial explanation comes from the rules of panegyric, which required praise of a ruler's military and moral qualities, but not of his religious views or measures. All three orators appear to know Constantine's belief that he had received aid from heaven in defeating Maxentius, but that fitted easily with the traditional idea that heavenly powers could become manifest and bring aid in time of need, especially in battle, and not only in imaginative literature but in real life. As yet, a pagan could fit a Christian emperor into a frame of pagan thought.[10]

The Roman Senate, overwhelmingly pagan in membership and strongly attached to Rome's official cults, was faced with the same problem as the orator of 313 when it decided to honor the new emperor with a triumphal arch in 315, his tenth year of rule. The resulting monument, the famous Arch of Constantine southeast of the Palatine Hill, incorporated reliefs and statues taken from monuments of great emperors of the past, Trajan, Hadrian, and Marcus Aurelius, and added new reliefs illustrating Constantine's victory over Maxentius and the subsequent celebrations, while the inscription above the principal arch mentions the "prompting of the divine, the greatness of mind" *(instinctu diuinitatis, mentis magnitudine)* which had enabled the emperor to triumph over the tyrant Maxentius. This phrasing glides over the space between paganism and Christianity by using much the same studied vagueness as the orator of 313 when he talked of the "divine mind" that communicated with Constantine.[11]

Almost from the moment of his conversion, Constantine was faced with division within the Church he had so recently joined, as were many of his successors in the course of time: "schism" and "heresy" were always more pressing problems than paganism. This first schism had been festering in the African Church for about a decade, and pitted rigorists led by the preacher Donatus against clergy whom the "Donatists" accused of being too compliant in the time of Diocletian's Great Persecution. The problem of dealing with the Donatists was to vex the African clergy, above all Augustine, well into the fifth century, and such divisions enabled pagans to claim that Christians were no more unified than themselves.[12]

As soon as he had defeated Licinius and become ruler of the whole empire, Constantine had to confront a new controversy, raised by the teachings of a deacon of the church in Alexandria, Arius. This time the issue concerned the nature of Christ, and foreshadowed the graver and more intense divisions of the next century. Arius preached that God the Son was part of God's creation, "made not begotten," and that "there was a time when He was not." In 325, Constantine convened the first worldwide ("ecumenical") council in an unsuccessful attempt to impose unity on the Church, but the dispute over Arius's views was to divide Christianity for a long time to come. Internally, Arianism was embraced by several of Constantine's immediate successors, notably his eldest surviving son, Constantius, and the last emperor of the next dynasty, Valens. Only when the "Trinitarian" Theodosius I had succeeded to power in 379 and had convened a second ecumenical council at Constantinople in 381 was Arianism officially condemned. Through the activity of an Arian missionary, Ulfilas, the Goths and other German federations had begun to adopt it already in the reign of Constantine, and in this way a Christian "heresy" had the effect of reinforcing political and military divisions, with severe consequences for the whole empire. As a separate confession Arianism survived, especially among Germans, well into the sixth century.[13] At the same time, even the Goths, the federation most closely associated with Rome, were far from being universally Christian, and there are well-documented Christian martyrdoms in "Gothia" from the fourth century and later.[14]

When Constantine became sole emperor in 324, his realm was still largely pagan and had passed through widely different vicissitudes in the East and in the West. By Eusebius's account, he took vigorous measures to suppress paganism in the East, but here his activity may have been more intense than in the West, and was certainly more visible to Eusebius. "In one law and ordinance after another [Constantine] gave orders not to sacrifice to idols, make inquiry from oracles, cause cult-statues to be set up, perform secret rites, or pollute the cities with the carnage of gladiators"; yet all three practices continued long after Constantine. Eusebius also mentions pagan sanctuaries that the emperor destroyed or closed in the East, but they are few in number, and for almost all there were particular reasons. When he destroyed a temple of Aphrodite built on the site of the Holy Sepulcher, it was the location of the shrine that was decisive. The famous temple of the god Asclepius in Aegeae of Cilicia caused offense because, as a healing god, Asclepius might seem a rival to the true Savior, Christ. Eusebius asserts that Constantine destroyed the shrine so thoroughly that no stone was left standing, but in fact the cult continued in weakened form, despite Julian's attempt to reinvigorate it. At Heliopolis (Baalbek), the emperor ended ritual prostitution and appointed a bishop, but even Eusebius admits that he did not impose Christianity, and only "urged [nonbelievers] toward knowledge of the divine"; Heliopolis remained a center of pagan cult until the late sixth century. In his public pronouncements, Constantine professed an attitude of toleration: "I wish [God's] people to be at peace and to remain undivided for the general benefit of the world and all mankind. Let those in error happily receive an enjoyment of peace and quiet similar to those who believe; for this delight shared in common will serve to correct them too, and to lead them into the straight path."[15]

Constantine continued to show favor to pagans, especially those educated "Hellenes" who formed the intellectual aristocracy of the eastern empire. An Athenian named Nicagoras belonged to the aristocratic clan of the Eumolpidae and had the office of *dadouchos,* "torchbearer," in the mysteries of Eleusis. In 326, he visited the "Syringes" or tombs of the Egyptian kings in Thebes, and there wrote in a graffito: "(coming) from Athens many years after the inspired Plato, I marveled and paid thanks to the gods and to the most pious emperor Constantine who enabled me to do so." The implication is probably that the emperor had made the imperial transport-system available to this convinced pagan. An author named Praxagoras, perhaps connected with the same priestly clan, wrote a biography of Constantine that culminated with his foundation of Constantinople in 324, though the work no doubt appeared some years later. The Byzantine scholar Photios observes of him that "though a Hellene in religion, he says that the emperor Constantine surpassed all previous emperors in complete virtue, excellence, and every success."[16]

As the reign progressed, the emperor may have moved further away from his earlier policy of indulgence toward educated Hellenes. In his letters to the eastern provincials after the defeat of Licinius, there are hints that he expected all his subjects, whatever their beliefs, to feel gratitude that he had ended civil war and brought about peace in which those not yet convinced of the Christian truth might see their error. When this did not happen, he may have felt that he had gone far enough, and his favor toward Hellenes may also have waned under the influence of his increasingly Christian court. Such a change perhaps lies behind the tendentious account given by the pagan Eunapius of Sopater, a pupil of the Neoplatonist Iamblichus. According to him, Sopater's teaching had such influence on Constantine that he made him his intimate counselor, and the emperor (or "the court": the Greek *basileia* is ambiguous) began to "learn a new philosophy." This provoked the jealousy of the praetorian prefect Ablabius, a Christian, who engineered Sopater's fall and death by alleging that he had magically fettered the winds when the grain ships failed to arrive in Constantinople. It is not likely that Constantine was returning to paganism under Sopater's influence, but whatever intrigue actually lies behind this account, the philosopher could well have succumbed to a charge of magic, which was often used against political suspects and readily clung to Neoplatonists.[17]

Yet Constantine continued to act much in the style of a pagan emperor. Like his predecessors since Augustus, he served as guardian of the state religions in the position of Highest Priest *(Pontifex Maximus),* as did all his successors down to Gratian in the 380s. In the last years of his reign, the city of Hispellum in Umbria (Spello) applied to him for permission to build a temple in honor of his family, the "Flavian House" *(domus Flavia).* Hitherto Hispellum and Umbria had taken turns in supplying priests of the Flavian House for the region, but had held their celebrations, consisting of stage shows and gladiatorial combats, only in Volsinii (Bolsena). Constantine grants the request, adding that "we wish a temple of the Flavian, that is, Our House to be completed in conspicuous style, with this express reservation that being dedicated to our name it not be polluted with the deceits of any infectious superstition." He thus permits the temple and also the gladiatorial games traditionally associated with worship of the emperors, but at the same time forbids the pollution of "superstition." The emperor may have used this term with deliberate ambiguity, but it must refer to practices that smacked too evidently of paganism, above all sacrifice or prayer to one of the pagan gods. This combination of conservatism and innovation has caused much debate about Constantine's true beliefs and attitudes. Did he not know that a priesthood of the imperial house was strictly irreconcilable with Christianity, even if the priest offered no sacrifice? Or that gladiatorial shows could be regarded as the gratuitous taking of human life? (In due course, the emperors were to discourage both belief in their own divinity and gladiatorial combat.) If, on the other hand, such "pagan" practices came only slowly to be seen as incompatible with the new faith, Constantine's apparent inconsistency becomes a projection on a larger screen of a situation that was to endure for decades and even centuries to come.[18]

As events were to show, numerically the most powerful force for conversion came not from inner struggle, of the kind exemplified above all in St. Augustine, but from public example, when the conversion of rulers was followed by the conversion of their subjects. The process could take decades or centuries, and could go into reverse, as happened in Britain after the death of Augustine of Canterbury.[19] Constantine's adoption of Christianity has its analogue in contemporary royal conversions that similarly led to national ones. Though Eusebius and other Christian thinkers considered it a dispensation of Providence that Christianity had been born and had matured within the boundaries of the Roman Empire, Jesus's command had been to preach the word to "all nations," and a tradition soon formed that the first apostles had duly conveyed the new faith to lands outside the empire. Thomas was said to have gone to Parthia and from there to India, Matthew to Ethiopia or Persia, Bartholomew to India. Though there may well have been Christians—captives, traders, or other settlers—in these regions earlier, actual missionary work appears to have begun only in the later third century. Significantly, the first certain instance of a national conversion involves territory newly wrested from the Persian Empire. In 298, the Caesar Galerius defeated Narses, the Parthian king, and by the subsequent treaty the reigning king of Armenia was deposed in favor of a new king summoned from Cappadocia, Trdat "the Great," and Armenia became a Roman protectorate. Armenian tradition records that a certain Gregory, later known as the "Illuminator," came to Armenia at the same time as the new king. Parthian by origin, Gregory had been brought up as a Christian in Cappadocian Caesarea. The new king was still a militant pagan, and as well as martyring a large number of Christian virgins imprisoned Gregory for fifteen years. On his release, which must have occurred about 314, he returned to Caesarea, where he was consecrated bishop, and on returning to Armenia succeeded in converting Trdat. Whatever the truth behind this tradition, it is clear that this conversion, like Constantine's conversion about the same time, began a religious transformation of the whole kingdom. The later tradition presents Gregory very much as the typical Christian bishop, destroying pagan temples and converting the people. Yet at the same time he founded a line of hereditary bishops who held the primacy of Armenia until 359, when the reigning king deposed the last Gregorid, Narses, in favor of a new line. In this way Gregory's bishopric resembled the dynastic houses that had long been an indigenous feature of Armenian society. As often, Christianity changed its contours according to time and place.[20]

A similar process occurred about the middle of the fourth century in Armenia's northern neighbor, Georgia, known in antiquity as "Iberia." Rufinus of Aquileia writing soon after 400 is the first to narrate the history of this conversion, which he ascribes to a woman captive, later worshiped as St. Nino. By her miraculous healings performed in the name of Christ, she came to the notice of the queen, whom she cured of a lingering disease. The queen brought her to the attention of the king, who remained unconvinced until one day he was overcome by a great darkness while hunting in a forest. He called upon Christ for help, the darkness dispersed, and he became a Christian and "the apostle of his nation." Again the details are clearly much embroidered, but the process—Christianity brought by a captive, confirmed by seemingly miraculous cures, and mediated to the ruler through his wife—conforms to known conversions elsewhere.[21]

Another royal conversion is that of Ezana (Aezanas), king of Ethiopia, which occurred approximately in the second quarter of the fourth century. Again, Rufinus gives a much-embroidered account, calling the region "India" as was customary in antiquity. A philosopher called Meropius, returning from Further India (the Indian subcontinent) with two young pupils, Frumentius and Aedesius, puts in at an unnamed port (presumably Adulis, the port of the capital Aksum), where the natives kill all on board except the two boys. The king appoints Frumentius as his accountant and secretary; after the king's death, the queen begs the two brothers to "share with her the responsibility of ruling the kingdom until her son should grow up," and makes Frumentius her chief minister. In this position, he receives a divine impulse to contact Roman merchants trading in the kingdom and to encourage them to build churches. When the young king reaches maturity, Frumentius returns to Alexandria, and there reports his activity to the bishop, unnamed but apparently to be identified as the great Athanasius, and urges him to send a bishop in order to continue the mission, whereupon the bishop consecrates Frumentius himself for the position and sends him back to Ethiopia. "When he had reached India as a bishop," says Rufinus, "it is said that such a grace of miracles was given him by God that the miracles of the apostles were performed by him and a countless number of barbarians was converted to the faith. From that time on there came into existence a Christian people and churches in India, and the priesthood began."[22]

Rufinus's "young king" can be identified from a series of extraordinary inscriptions from the Ethiopian capital of Axum. These reveal his name as Ezana, in its Greek form "Aezanas," and show the evolution of his religious beliefs, at least in the form he wished his subjects to know them. In two inscriptions written in Greek, he announces his victory over a people called the Bougaites, and here, besides styling himself "Aezanas, king of Aksumites, Himyarites [inhabitants of the southwest Arabian peninsula]" and several other peoples, he is also "King of Kings, a son of the invincible god

Ares." Both Greek versions are carved together with versions in the national language, Ge'ez, where "Ares" appears as "Mahrem," and in Sabaic versions of Ge'ez. At this stage, Ezana broadcasts his views in the international language of the Mediterranean, and has no scruple about announcing his devotion to a national war-god. At what appears to be a second stage, only known from an inscription in Ge'ez, Ezana records a campaign against different peoples, the Noba and the "Kasu" or Meroites to the north of his kingdom. Here he invokes "the Lord of heaven and earth, who is victorious over all," and "the lord of heaven, who made me *negus* (king)." He no longer names his god, nor claims him as his divine father, and he introduces a new theme, absent from his earlier records of conquest: "As He now has conquered for me and vanquished my enemies for me, so will I rule in justice and righteousness, in that I do no wrong to the peoples." At a third stage, Ezana emerges as a Trinitarian Christian. The text begins: "By faith in God and by power of the Father, Son, and Holy Spirit, (I thank) Him who has preserved my kingdom by faith in his son Jesus Christ, Him who has helped me and always helps me. . . . He has made me the guide of all my kingdom because of my faith in Christ."[23]

This gradual change does not agree with Rufinus's implication that the king was a Christian at his accession, though it does show his closeness to Athanasian theology. Ezana's gradual progress from belief in a local, "pagan" god to belief in the Christian Trinity resembles the way in which Constantine continues to place the traditional gods on his coinage for several years after his conversion in 312. Just as Constantine claims the patronage of the Invincible Sun, so Ezana asserts the "invincible god Ares"; the reference to "the prompting of divinity" on the Arch of Constantine recalls Ezana's invocation of "the Lord of heaven and earth" before his final declaration of faith in the Trinity.

The fact that two of these royal conversions, in Armenia and Iberia, occurred on the borders of the Persian Empire is relevant to the conversion of Constantine. In the previous century, the first two Sassanian kings of Persia, Ardashir and Shapur I, had united a torpid and fractured state and turned it into a formidable eastern power. Shapur thrice invaded the Roman Empire, penetrating even into Asia Minor, and in 260 captured the emperor Valerian. His inscriptions show him acting with the aid of the supreme god Ahura-Mazda, while the chief priest of the state religion, Kerdir, sets up fire altars even within lands conquered from the Romans. The

Roman Empire, by contrast, lacked a unifying cult. The national god of war, Mars, was only one of several in the pantheon, and never takes the role of supreme patron of a military campaign. The cult of the Roman emperors came close to being a statewide religion, but was not suited to inspiring an army in battle, and the civil wars of the third century had robbed it of such psychological power as it ever had. In the Christian God, especially in the form of the God of Israel who had given his chosen people victory over their enemies, Constantine found a god strong to aid, and inscribed his device on the shields of his soldiers before the Battle of the Milvian Bridge. Part of the impulse for the emperor's conversion to Christianity may have come from the supreme God of the Persians.[24]

CHAPTER THREE

After Constantine: Indifference and Intolerance

CONSTANTINE'S ATTITUDE toward his pagan subjects exhibits a mixture of toleration and intolerance, severity and indifference. From this disconcerting variation, some have inferred that he was a political animal using religion merely as a tool, others that he was a convinced Christian from the moment of his conversion who seized every opportunity to stamp out paganism. But Constantine had more immediate business than to make his subjects follow the example of his own conversion, even had such a project been possible when the majority was still pagan. As a Christian, he took immediate steps to secure peace within the Church, first within the western part of the empire that he controlled, after 324 mainly in the East. As an emperor, religious harmony was only one of his concerns, and it is a distortion of perspective to imagine that the persistence of paganism was high among them.[1]

All of Constantine's successors were Christian, with the notable exception of the last of the Constantinian line, Julian the "Apostate," who ruled for a mere eighteen months from 361 to 363. In his attempts to restore paganism to its position of supremacy and to create a pagan church patterned after the Christian one, Julian was more fanatical than most of the Christian emperors, with the possible exceptions of Theodosius I and Justinian. He was raised as a Christian, as a youth fell under the spell of Neoplatonism, and while on his march to overthrow his cousin Constantius early in 361 threw off the mask of Christianity and attempted to reform paganism as a quasi-religion. Some pagans, especially his favorites such as the Neoplatonist Maximus of Ephesus, accepted his rule wholeheartedly. Others were not so sure. In Antioch the public teacher of oratory ("sophist") Libanius was a convinced pagan, and after the emperor's death claimed to have felt unmixed pleasure in his rule: "I laughed and leapt for joy; with pleasure I wrote and I delivered speeches, for the altars again received their offerings of blood, smoke carried fumes to heaven, the gods were honored with festivals, even though only a few people were left who understood them; prophecy stepped forward to freedom, oratory to honor, Romans to confidence." Yet the speeches that Libanius delivered in Julian's lifetime show that his feelings had been tempered by other considerations, among them his concern for Antioch. The philosopher Themistius, who had prospered under Constantius, and as an Aristotelian was neglected by the Platonist Julian, returned to favor after his death and obliquely criticized his memory.[2]

The reign of Julian has drawn enormous attention both in contemporary sources and in later literature, and has contributed to the notion of a struggle between "dying" paganism and "triumphant" Christianity. Yet in many ways the reign is an interlude, of greater importance in historiography than in history. It may have made the immediately succeeding emperors more cautious in their treatment of pagans, but in the end it did not slow the gradual process of Christianization from above that began with Constantine, and continued at an uneven pace for the next two centuries.[3]

One index of this process is imperial legislation against pagan practices, but it is an index requiring cautious treatment. The main bodies of such legislation, the *Theodosian Code* of Theodosius II completed in 438, and the legal compilations of the reign of Justinian, above all his *Code* of 534, present problems of interpretation. Many of their texts have been abbreviated, corrupted in transmission, or otherwise distorted, and even at the time legislation did not always lead to enforcement: as a western bishop ruefully observed in the early fifth century, "good emperors promulgate laws in behalf of religion, but their agents do not enforce them properly" *(principes quidem boni leges pro religione promulgant, sed eas executores non exerunt competenter)*. Bribery or other forms of evasion were always at hand, and hence laws often threaten sanctions against administrators who fail to execute them. Nonetheless, the comparative rarity of laws specifically directed against pagans when viewed against the whole body of imperial legislation is a sign that paganism was not uppermost in the mind of most imperial legislators.[4]

The legal codes contain no law of Constantine directed against paganism, though several that reinforce Christianity. The first emperor to legislate against pagans is his youngest son Constans, who ordered in 341 "that superstition cease and the madness of sacrifices be abolished," but his praetorian prefect Catullinus, a pagan, seems to have persuaded him one year later to limit this ruling to sanctuaries within the walls of Rome, on the ground that the people ought still to have their ancient entertainments *(uoluptates)*. Paganism was objectionable not so much for disbelief in the Christian truth, since that was always potentially remediable, as for its traditional attractions, especially the feasting that accompanied animal sacrifice and the provision of gladiatorial games, one of the commonest forms of "entertainment," by magistrates and other benefactors. Yet these same attractions made old practices hard to stamp out, and in later centuries church authorities looked for ways of attracting and keeping converts by preserving as many of the traditional enjoyments as were compatible with the new faith.[5]

Constantius II, who became Augustus in the East in 337 and extended his rule to the whole empire in 353, continued his father's practice of employing pagans in positions of high trust, for example, the philosopher Eustathius in negotiations with Persia, and the orator and philosopher Themistius in the recruitment of a new senate in Constantinople. But toward the end of his reign he issued a law ordering that all temples be closed and access to them forbidden, "for we want all to refrain from sacrifice." This law is the first to threaten provincial governors who failed to behead convicted offenders. Constantius's policies encouraged George of Cappadocia, bishop of Alexandria, to propose that the emperor confiscate the public buildings of the city for the imperial treasury; "how long," he asked as he passed a certain temple, "shall we allow this sepulcher to stand?" Yet as a convinced Arian Constantius was not acceptable to all of his Christian subjects, and his persecution of the Trinitarian Athanasius made him especially unpopular in Alexandria. When Julian came to power and the citizens took the opportunity to lynch George, the new emperor failed to issue any punishment, and allowed Athanasius to return from exile.[6]

Julian's immediate successors lacked the religious fervor of their Constantinian predecessors, and avoided religious confrontation. The immediate and transitory successor to Julian was the career officer Jovian, who had no strong position in the theological struggles of the day; while reiterating previous legislation in favor of Christianity, he also issued a law of religious toleration that permitted sacrifice, but banned the magic and divination that were often associated with it. His successor, Valentinian, announced a policy of general toleration at the beginning of his reign, and even permitted divination so long as it was not practiced by night, when it was next door to magic. Valentinian's brother Valens likewise tolerated paganism, and even retained some of Julian's associates in positions of trust; one of these was Themistius, who welcomed and served the new regime. Yet when a widespread conspiracy came to light in Antioch in 371, Valens conducted a severe inquisition against magical practices in which several pagans were implicated.[7]

The reign of Valens ended with his disastrous defeat at Adrianople in 378, and reconstruction began when his son Gratian, now senior emperor, appointed the Spaniard Theodosius to be his coemperor in the following year. The ascendancy of Theodosius marks a turning point in the legislative history of Christianity, and a visible hardening of imperial attitudes toward paganism. In 381, he convened a new "ecumenical" council in Constantinople, and in the same year he and his corulers, Gratian and his younger brother Valentinian II, issued a law forbidding anyone to become "consulters of the uncertain" *(incertorum consultorem)* by means of sacrifice, or to enter a temple for such a purpose: though overtly directed against divinatory sacrifice, this law tended to outlaw sacrifice even in private. Four years later, in a ruling issued to Cynegius, the praetorian prefect of the East, Theodosius repeated the ban on divination, and Cynegius now began a campaign of destruction against rural shrines and against temples located in cities. Provoked either by Cynegius or by a later prefect, Libanius wrote his most eloquent defense of paganism, the speech *For the Temples*. In 391, Theodosius went beyond Constantius in severity: "Let no-one pollute himself with sacrifices, let no-one slaughter an innocent victim, let no-one approach shrines, visit temples, or revere images made by human hand, lest he become liable to divine and human sanctions." The emperor also trod new ground by forbidding administrators at all levels from entering any temple for the purpose of worship. He quickly followed this ruling with two others, addressing the second to all people of whatever rank, officeholders both active and retired, and those "powerful by the chance of birth or born in humble circumstances."[8]

Despite his stern orthodoxy, Theodosius sometimes checked the zeal of his Christian subjects. Near the beginning of his reign he ordered the governor of Osrhoene in Mesopotamia to protect a temple in a city of the province. The building was to remain open, and the statues within it were to be left undisturbed so long as they were esteemed "more for the value of their art than for their divine nature" *(artis pretio quam diuinitate metienda)*. No "fraudulently obtained decision" should impede this measure, and the governor was to see to its execution; but "let no-one suppose that under the cover of such freedom of access it is permitted to perform forbidden sacrifices." Like his predecessors, Theodosius used the talents of educated pagans such as Themistius, to whom he entrusted the care of his elder son Arcadius, the future emperor. He appointed Libanius to an honorary praetorian prefecture, and granted his long-held wish to make his illegitimate son his heir.[9]

The policies of Theodosius's successors toward paganism in the following decades, insofar as they can be followed though the law-codes and the few explicit references in nonlegal texts, show a consistent but selective movement toward restriction. It was not until 435 that the eastern emperors forbade animal sacrifice, and ordered that all religious buildings used for this purpose be destroyed and "be purified by the sign of the Christian religion." Yet even in the East, temples in cities, towns and villages continued to evade this ban.[10]

Though they restricted sacrifice and confiscated revenues that had previously gone toward the upkeep of pagan cults, the emperors did not as yet engage in witch hunts or compel conversion. A law of 416 issued by the boy-emperor Theodosius II to the praetorian prefect of the East, a firm Christian, laid down that "those who are polluted by the error or crime of profane practice, that is, pagans, shall not be admitted to the imperial service nor dignified with the honorable rank of judge *(iudex)*." Strictly applied, this law would have banned pagans from the civil service altogether, since the term *iudex* covered all officials with judicial functions such as provincial governors: yet even here the keyword is practice *(ritus)*, not belief, and pagans are still found holding high office throughout the fifth century. In 423, the emperors in one and the same ordinance suppose that there are no longer any pagans, and decree that pagans and Jews are to remain unmolested so long as they live quietly and break no law.[11]

The law of 435 is the last in the *Theodosian Code* concerning pagans. When Justinian issued the final version of his own *Code* in 534, his chapter on heretics retained Constantius's law of 346 and several of the later laws from the *Theodosian Code,* including those that protected the decorations *(ornamenta)* of the closed temples, permitted traditional festivals so long as they did not involve sacrifice, and ordered Jews and pagans to be left in peace. The new *Code* contains three additions between the reign of Theodosius II and Justinian himself. In a law of 451, the emperor Marcian reaffirms the ban on sacrifice: "let it not happen in our age that the previous honors be offered to unspeakable and execrable statues, the impious doorposts of temples be hung with garlands, fires lit on profane altars, incense burned on the same, victims slaughtered, wine poured from dishes and sacrilege believed to replace religion." If convicted, the guilty and their accomplices will suffer confiscation of all their property and capital punishment. Similarly Leo I in 472 rules that anyone committing an act of pagan superstition that has been previously banned is guilty of a public crime. If they do so on the property or in the house of another, even without that person's knowledge, the owner will lose his position in the public service *(strateia)* or his rank *(axiôma)* and his property will be confiscated: those of lower rank shall be tortured and then condemned to the mines. Though the law is directed against actions and not beliefs, the express extension of it to private homes is a further restriction on the freedom of pagans, though the wording also shows that activity continued. A third measure, which has often been attributed to Justinian, is now known to have been issued by Anastasius, probably in 502, when the emperor was reacting to disturbances that had arisen over the celebration of a festival of pagan origin called Brytae. In this constitution, he restricted the gifts that could be made to uphold "the iniquity of paganism," and reaffirmed the antipagan measures of his predecessors.[12]

With Justinian's accession in 527 begins a new phase in the legal treatment of heretics, made all the more severe by being enshrined in the emperor's new *Code*. Soon after his accession, he issued a law directed primarily against heretics, defined as all who did not share the emperor's orthodoxy, including "the Hellenes, who try to introduce polytheism, and in addition Jews and Samaritans." No member of these groups may hold any civil rank *(axiôma)* or military office, civil or military, nor may he plead as a lawyer, "since we wish all such positions to be pure, not only in this glorious city but in every province and place." This legislation is not new, the emperor declares, but up to now has been insufficiently enforced.[13]

Two years later, Justinian took steps specifically aimed at pagans, both by legislation and by a general purge, decreeing that "those with Hellenic beliefs" should not hold any state office, while those attached to Christian heresies were to be excluded from the Roman state, after being given three months to embrace orthodoxy. This measure is known both from literary texts and from the *Code*. Some baptized Christians have fallen into pagan ways by performing sacrifice and participating in festivals: these he has previously treated with leniency, but in future they will be subject to "extreme penalties." Other such deviants who have not yet been baptized must apply with their families and households to the local church and "be taught the true faith of Christians" (in other words, undergo catechism), or otherwise be stripped of all their possessions and left in poverty. As for "those diseased with the madness of the unholy Hellenes," they may not teach or receive public salaries, since they poison their students' minds. The emperor next proceeds against anyone who, "plotting against our state, is caught in the error of sacrifice or idolatry; he shall be subjected to the utmost punishment, equal to what the Manichaeans, and (what amounts to the same) the Borboritae rightly undergo, for we consider that they are similar to them." ("Borboritae," "Mud-Wallowers," was a contemptuous term for a variety of Gnostics.) For these the penalty includes the requirement that their dependents shall be baptized forthwith, if still young, but begin a course of catechism if adult. Those who have been baptized for the sake of holding office, but have allowed their families to remain "in Hellenic error," shall lose their office and their property, since they were insincere in their faith when they received baptism. Yet even now Justinian does not compel all pagans to convert to orthodox Christianity: forced conversion is the penalty for pagan sacrifice, not for pagan belief, though the charge of pagan belief had long since become a political weapon.[14]

Until Justinian, the evidence does not suggest that emperors used the laws to coerce pagans into conversion. Pagans were indeed harassed, persecuted, forced to suicide or executed for their views, but the laws restricted their freedom of action and offered inducements to convert: they were not instruments of oppression such as have been used by modern states against dissenters or those of alien religions. Where persecution occurred, it was often at the local level, the action of ordained clergy or monks or of secular authorities. Here imperial policy operated indirectly by encouraging the use of force, or at least creating an atmosphere of impunity, especially in the reigns of notably devout emperors. One such was Theodosius I, and the activity of Cynegius in Egypt and Syria is a direct reflection of the emperor's desire to impose religious orthodoxy. Similarly, Theophilus, the ruthless bishop of

Alexandria, was able to accomplish in the reign of Theodosius what George of Cappadocia had aspired to do in the reign of Constantius: aided by the governor, he destroyed the chief temple of Alexandria, the Serapeum founded by the first of the Ptolemies. A generation later Theophilus's nephew and successor, Cyril, took a large part in the notorious lynching of the Alexandrian philosopher Hypatia. Unlike his uncle, he was on bad terms with the governor, Orestes, who "hated the power of the bishops of Alexandria because they appropriated much of the power of those appointed to rule by the emperor, and particularly because Cyril wanted to oversee his decisions" (Cyril had once sent his supporters to the theater to report back to him on the governor's announcements). The feud between them grew until a rumor spread among the Christian community that Hypatia, as a friend of Orestes, was inciting him against the bishop. This led certain "hot-tempered men," headed by a minor cleric called Peter, to waylay Hypatia on her way home. In the words of the historian Socrates, "They dragged her to the church called the Caesarion, and stripping off her clothing killed her with scraps of pottery, and after tearing her limb from limb brought the limbs to the so-called Cinaron and destroyed them by fire."[15]

Monks or pious laymen were often more violent than the ordained clergy in such attacks. After the destruction of the Serapeum, says Eunapius, "they brought the so-called monks into the holy places, human beings in appearance, but swinish in their way of life . . . for everyone in those days who wore a black robe had tyrannical power." The "hot-headed men" who led the lynching of Hypatia were so-called *parabalanoi,* Christian toughs usually employed in the care of the dangerously ill. The bishop of Alexandria a century later, Peter "Mongus" (so named for his raucous voice) ordered monks to help a young band of ardent Christians in his mission to find and destroy pagan idols at nearby Menouthis. When neither secular nor religious authorities were prepared to act, they could be compelled by popular pressure: a Constantinopolitan crowd in 579 and 580 rioted when jurors in a religious trial seemed close to giving an acquittal, burned them alive, and forced the emperor to dismiss the Prefect Sebastianus, whom it suspected of trying to delay the proceedings.[16]

After Theodosius I, the emperor whose faith most clearly affected his relation with the remaining pagans of his empire was Justinian, who ruled from 527 to 565. In 529, Justinian banned the teaching of philosophy in Athens, and two years later the seven resident professors moved to Persia, though they soon returned within the Roman boundaries. Graver measures were taken in the capital. High officials were denounced as pagans and put on trial, and one, the ex-prefect Asclepiodotus, took poison. A few years later, in 545 or 546, Justinian began a new purge, using for the purpose John, the anti-Chalcedonian or "miaphysite"[17] bishop of Ephesus and an ardent hunter of pagans. Though John's own description survives only in fragments, enough remains to show that there were many alleged pagans in Constantinople, not only "patricians and nobles" but professors of literature *(grammatikoi)* and other teachers. After confessing under torture, they were compelled to undergo instruction in the faith: if the law enshrined in the *Code* was followed, they must have been accused not merely of paganism but of having engaged in magic or sacrifice. The most eminent was a patrician called Phocas, who committed suicide. He had already been questioned in 529, but after acquittal had gone on to become praetorian prefect of the East in 532 and later to hold several positions of trust. There was to be another such scandal under Justinian in 559, when, according to the historian Malalas, Hellenes were arrested and paraded through the city, and their books burned in the amphitheater. Nonetheless, pagans remained. Decades later the historian Evagrius, looking back on the Great Plague of Justinian's reign which carried off several of his children, confesses that he had wondered why pagans had not been punished as he had been: only an interview with a stylite saint restored his faith.[18]

An incident that occurred under Tiberius II about 579 is the last known of these antipagan inquisitions, and like the purges under Justinian involved highly placed suspects. Of the two historians who record the events, the Chalcedonian Evagrius and the miaphysite John of Ephesos, the first gives a comparatively short account in which he places the guilt on the central character, the high official Anatolius, and exonerates his alleged accomplice, Gregory, the duaphysite bishop of Antioch. As a miaphysite, John provides more detail and spreads the guilt more widely. The trouble began in Heliopolis, a known center of paganism, where the aristocracy was oppressing the lower-class Christians. Tiberius decided to send an official called Theophilus, who found by using torture that pagans were everywhere in the region, even in one of the centers of Christianity, Antioch. Among the guilty was the priest Rufinus, who was then visiting Anatolius in Edessa, and after following him there, Theophilus caught pagans holding a festival of Zeus in a private house. Though Rufinus committed suicide, Anatolius slipped away to the house of the local bishop, alleging that the two of them were engaged in pious conversation. Theophilus then arrested Anatolius and his secretary Theodorus and brought them to Antioch, where both of them confessed under torture, implicating not only Gregory but also Eulogius, subsequently patriarch of Alexandria; nonetheless, the whole affair was hushed up when the notary in charge of the records was murdered. Anatolius was summoned to Constantinople and tried; as already mentioned, riots forced Tiberius to dismiss the prefect of the city, Sebastianus, on the suspicion of pagan sympathies, and to replace him with a certain Julianus. The full Senate then took up the investigation, but when Julianus incurred similar suspicions the emperor entrusted the trial to a different court, which sentenced Anatolius and Theodorus to death. Investigators were now sent to Asia and Syria, and numerous trials took place involving both lay and clergy. These continued into reign of Tiberius's successor Maurice, under whom Gregory saved his episcopal throne by distributing huge bribes in the capital and buying off the people of Antioch with the promise of a new hippodrome and by importing a troop of pantomimes. The tendency of John's narrative is to impute pagan sympathies not only to those accused such as Anatolius, but indirectly to their judges in Constantinople and even to the emperor, all of whom he considered unorthodox. Even so, these investigations must have uncovered a widespread attachment to the traditional cults, particularly in Syria and Osrhoene, where cities such as Heliopolis and Carrhae were notorious for worshiping their inherited deities.[19]

The emperors' attitude toward their pagan subjects does not follow a straight line from tolerance under Constantine to persecution under Justinian. As had earlier been true of the imperial treatment of Christians by pagan emperors, some emperors acted with more severity than others, and personal beliefs and political pressure acted with different force at different times. Even in their treatment of Christians, though all emperors considered themselves orthodox and guardians of orthodoxy, their views often met with opposition, especially during and after the controversies of the fifth century; in the West, religious authority drained from the palace to the church, from emperors to popes and bishops. As secular rulers, the emperors were always more concerned with preserving Christian unity than with crushing paganism; their disfavor fell less on pagans, whose fault was a curable blindness, than on the Jews, who in the Christian view had deliberately closed their eyes to the divine revelation offered to them, and instead had killed God's own Son and Messenger. Nonetheless, just as Constantine hoped to put "those in error" on the way to the "right path," so his successors saw it as their duty to promote the Faith by measures both direct and indirect—by law, by the use of secular and ecclesiastical agents, and by the inducements of wealth and privilege. Acts of violence could be considered un-Christian: as Socrates observed of the murder of Hypatia, "murders, fights and similar things are completely alien to those whose minds are Christian." There was another strain in Christianity that held that persuasion was a better way to ensure true conversion, and this strain, which historically precedes the use of force, was to survive well into Late Antiquity.[20]

CHAPTER FOUR

God and Other Divinities

TWO OF THE principal labels pinned on pagans by Christians were "polytheists" and "idolaters." The two ideas are inseparable: since the plurality of pagan gods found its starkest expression in their visible images, and since pagans usually offered sacrifice to their gods in their imaged forms, "idolatry" in Christian eyes implied both ascribing divinity to mere matter and a repellent form of sacrifice, made worse by the accompanying rituals of slaughter. Yet despite this apparent gulf between the two sides, the Christian community enjoyed its strongest growth in the polytheistic world, which it finally displaced at least within the borders of the former Roman Empire, whereas it never supplanted the Judaism from which it largely originated.

To understand how Christians and pagans differed in their conception of the divine realm, it is necessary to go back many centuries before Late Antiquity. Christians took from Judaism a complex picture of the higher powers that not only allowed for a conception of multiple gods, even if one god alone was supreme, but also acknowledged an opposing power, Satan or "the Devil," who could even count as a god. The Psalms, regarded as inspired and authoritative texts by both Jews and Christians, several times refer to a plurality of gods. One of them is a mysterious poem in which God addresses an assembly of inferior beings: "I said, 'You are gods, sons of the Most High, all of you'; but you shall die like humans, and fall like one of the rulers." In John's gospel, Jesus quotes these words to Jews who wished to stone him for claiming to be the Son of God: "Is it not written in your Law, 'I said, "You are gods'"? If He called those people gods for whom the Word of God came into existence (and Scripture cannot be abolished), the Word that the Father hallowed and sent into the world, do you say, 'You are a blasphemer,' because I said 'I am the Son of God?' " Later this appearance of polytheism caused difficulty, and Augustine argued that Jesus meant "gods" to refer to the "people of God." The apostle Paul also speaks of "so-called gods, whether in heaven or in earth, as there are many gods and many lords," though it is disputed whether he is conceding a subordinate divinity to these supposed gods. In an even more mysterious expression, he calls the Devil "the god of this age," though he may be stretching language to make the point that the Devil is the supreme ruler of the material world.[1]

In Hebrew Scripture, the name "Satan" originally belongs not to the lord of evil, but to an agent entrusted with the task of testing mankind and bringing its errors to God's notice, a role especially clear in the book of Job, where he is one of the "sons of God" whom God allows to test Job's piety. "Satan" is thus an "accuser," which the Septuagint translators rendered by *diabolos,* "slanderer"; from this in turn comes the modern "devil" and its cognates in other languages such as *diavolo, diable, Teufel.* In the intertestamental period, the Devil became the chief of all the powers of evil, the "Enemy" *(echthros),* the "Evil One" *(ponêros);* he becomes the leader of the "sons of God" who according to Genesis had intercourse with mortal women and fathered giants, and these later became rebellious "angels," with Satan as their chief, who were cast with him out of heaven into everlasting fire.[2]

Despite believing in a single God, Christians did not call themselves "monotheists," a term that came into existence only in early modern times. Over the Jewish foundation of a single God they built a new construction in which God the Father, equated with the God of Israel, sent his only Son into the world, and after the Son's return to the Father, the divine "Breath" or "Spirit" *(pneuma),* often simply called the "Spirit," descended to earth and continued to operate among mankind. It was not until the second century that Christian thinkers devised the concept of a "triad" or "trinity" *(trias, trinitas)* to express the idea of a divine being who was simultaneously one and three, and the exact relationship between these three "persons" was to require constant redefinition and adjustment over the centuries, leading to deep divisions within Christianity. Though the Father was nameless (Christians never applied to him the sacred name or "tetragram" of Judaism, JHWH), his Son came into the world under a name identical to

"Joshua" and meaning "JHWH has saved," which Greek-speakers rendered as *Iêsous*. As God's "Anointed" *(Christos)*, the Son was usually called "Christ" after his ascension, the name "Jesus" being reserved for the narratives of his earthly life.

In the fifth century, the burning issue became that of the "nature" *(physis)* or "natures" of Christ. The Council of Ephesus, held in 431, was summoned to condemn the doctrine imputed to Nestorius, patriarch of Constantinople, that Christ after taking human form embodied two separate natures, divine and human; this represented a victory for the bishop of Alexandria, Cyril, who asserted the unity of the two natures. The dispute was still not settled, and a second council held in Ephesus in 449 inclined to the position that there was only one nature in Christ. This led to a fierce reaction and the summoning of a further council, held at Chalcedon in 451, on the other side of the Bosporos from Constantinople. Here the doctrine was proclaimed that Christ was "one person in two natures," a formula that won wide acceptance. though disputed especially in Egypt and among Christian communities in Persia. The term "monophysites" for believers in the "only" or undivided nature of Christ first appears in the late seventh century, but "miaphysite," believers in one nature, is more precise.[3]

In addition to a "triune" God, Christians recognized a class of intermediate beings, some good and some bad, the "messengers" *(angeloi, angeli)* of God or of the Devil. This idea too is a borrowing from Judaism. The Septuagint translators chose the plural form *angeloi* to render the Hebrew *mal'akim*, which derives from a root meaning "send," though the root-meaning of the Greek word is not "send" but "announce." In Jewish texts, the "messengers" serve as intermediaries between God and humanity, and can also stand over individuals as their protectors or "guardian angels." The belief in angels, sometimes imagined as watching over a person as his personal "angel," persisted in later Judaism, and this idea too entered into Christianity, though Christian angels are almost always beneficent. In the gospel accounts of Jesus's life and death, they appear in dreams or visions to Mary the mother of Jesus and to others, they minister to Jesus in the desert, and they guard his tomb after the crucifixion. They also play a part in the narrative of Acts, as when an angel miraculously frees Peter from prison.[4]

Christianity also took from Judaism a conception of numberless evil powers, often identified with the gods of the surrounding "nations," for which the Hebrew texts used several terms, principally a loanword from

Akkadian, *sidum*. The Septuagint translators replaced these several terms with a single plural form, *daimonia*, a diminutive of the noun *daimôn*, from which comes the English "demon"; hence a verse of the Psalms, translated in the Septuagint as "all the gods of the nations are demons" *(daimonia)*, becomes a favorite text of Christian writers. The first canonical writings of Christianity perpetuate the Jewish conception of pagan gods as "demons," and the Christians' initial reaffirmation of kosher rules, later relaxed as they moved away from Judaism, was reinforced by the belief that such "demons" fed on the blood of sacrificial animals. Demons could also "possess" a person and make him mad or physically ill. The "synoptic" gospels of Matthew, Mark, and Luke relate at length the miracle of the Gadarene swine, using the terms *daimones, daimonia*, and *pneumata* (spirits) interchangeably. In this story, Jesus meets a man possessed by many demons, and on asking him his name receives the answer, "My name is Legion, for we are many." Jesus then dismisses the demons or spirits into a herd of swine grazing nearby, which rush down into the nearby lake and are drowned, a story that was to be recycled many times in accounts of Christian exorcism. Another miracle narrated by the "synoptic" evangelists concerns a man possessed by a deaf demon, which Jesus expels and enables the man to talk, whereupon his Pharisaic enemies claim that he "has Beelzeboul, and casts out demons by the lord of the demons." ("Beelzeboul," often changed to "Beelzebub," "Lord of the Flies," is a biblical name for one of the powers of evil.)[5]

Complex as are Christian notions of divinity, the divine world of paganism is much more varied. Though the earliest great poets of Greek literature, Homer and Hesiod, were rightly credited with forming the Greek and later the Roman notions of the gods, the Olympian pantheon is a literary construct, and its anthropomorphism, though providing a ready target to both pagan and Christian critics, was not shared by the majority, to whom educated literature was a closed book.[6] The pagans' conventional conception shared with the Christian one the notion of a supreme god dwelling in the heaven *(ouranos)* and ruling the universe, in certain respects resembling humans (though Christians felt discomfort at the anthropomorphism of the Old Testament God, for example his walking in the Garden of Eden). For both Christians and pagans this god had assistants or messengers *(angeloi)*. Pagans diverged more strongly in their conception of evil powers, though to some extent their language was similar. They did not imagine a single lord of all evil, and there is no pagan Satan. Though the earliest Greek literature speaks of *daimôn* as a supernatural power, and later writers use the single *daimonion* and the plural *daimonia,* in general the "demonic" was a much less negative concept for pagans than it was for Christians. Many believed in an underworld ruled by infernal gods and inhabited by the souls of the dead, and like Christians they could imagine an alternative abode of light and bliss for the souls of the virtuous. As early as the fifth century BCE, there appears the idea of such souls ascending to heaven.

Such a general account is inevitably drawn from literary texts, which tend to reflect the views of an educated minority, and though it was on this literary level that the debates between pagan and Christian have survived, such debates are a kind of air battle with only a partial bearing on the ground combat below. Moreover, just as paganism itself evolved over time, with new gods, beliefs, and practices coming into existence while others faded away, so also there is immense variation over space. The cults of a Celtic god such as Endobellicus in Lusitania or of a Semitic god such as Dusares in Arabia and Syria enter scarcely or not at all into literature, but the archaeological remains show that their cults were powerful within their areas. Hence any general characterization of paganism as it was known to Christians can be valid only within limits, and with due consideration of the gap separating social levels and different times and places.[7]

The Greek and Latin words for "god," *theos* and *deus,* are similar-sounding but etymologically unrelated. Both could be applied to the divine power in general, in which sense they are equivalent to the plural "gods," or to a particular god or (in the feminine *thea, dea*) goddess. A vaguer term in Greek is *to theion,* literally "the divine," equivalent to English "godhead," while for the same concept Latin uses *numen,* a word derived from a root meaning "nod" and signifying a god's gesture of permission or refusal. Unlike the Christian God, pagan gods usually had their own names, and it was not necessary to specify that they were gods when speaking about or to them. Certain gods were anonymous or virtually anonymous, such as "the Syrian goddess" *(thea Syria, dea Syria)* or "the invincible god" *(theos anikêtos, deus inuictus).* A tendency in pagan thought that becomes stronger over time is to isolate one god as the sole divine power, or as a supreme ruler over the other gods. He is often identified with the sky-god Zeus and the Latin Jupiter, and his title of "king" *(basileus, rex)* or

"Father" (Greek *patêr;* in Latin the suffix *–piter*) expresses this supremacy. This notion of a supreme but not sole god, not unlike the God of early Judaism seated among lesser gods, is sometimes called "henotheism."[8]

The word *daimôn,* whose diminutive *daimonion* Greek-speaking Jews and Christians employed to designate the false gods of "the nations," originally had a very different sense. When it first appears in the poems of Homer, it is either equivalent to *theos,* "god," or denotes a divine entity having power to affect the course of human existence, a being who is more than an abstraction and yet not fully personal. Hesiod expands the word to make *daimones* divine beings lower than the gods, so that when the first "golden race" of humans died and was buried, they became "*daimones* by the plan of great Zeus, good, earth-bound, guardians of mortal men." In everyday usage, *daimôn* had a meaning close to "fate" or "destiny," as is shown by the compounds *eudaimôn,* "fortunate," and the rarer *dysdaimôn,* "unfortunate," "ill-fated." Fused with the idea of a *daimôn* as a supernatural entity, this concept produced the notion of *daimones* as beings attached to persons or communities and bringing good or evil fortune. Thus in Aeschylus's *Agamemnon,* the evil that has befallen the house of Atreus is the work of a "*daimôn* that falls upon the house . . . the thrice-gorged *daimôn* of this race." Another coinage, *daimonân,* "to be possessed," encapsulates the popular idea that a *daimôn* could seize hold of a person or a community. Many of these ideas—evil *daimones, daimones* possessing human beings—were to find analogues in Christianity. After the classical period, Greeks imagined *daimones* as snuffing up the fumes from the blood of sacrificial victims, thus handing Christians one of their favorite charges against pagan idolatry.[9]

Plato, whose thought was to have a decisive influence both on later philosophy and also the "new philosophy" of Christianity, entrenched a crucial modification in the conception of the *daimones.* To describe Love (*Erôs*), Diotima in the *Symposium* calls it a "mighty *daimôn,* since everything demonic (*pan to daimonion*) is between mortal and immortal." She explains that demons move between gods and humans, ferrying requests and sacrifices from below, orders and rewards from above, and are responsible for prophetic utterance, "for God does not mingle with man: the demons mediate all association and conversation of gods with men and of men with gods." Plato's pupil Xenocrates held that these intermediate beings were subject to the passions, and could exhibit both virtue and vice;

the evil deeds attributed by myth to the gods were in reality the work of bad *daimones,* who were also associated with disasters and other misfortunes of humanity. Later Platonists such as Plutarch imagined that two *daimones* attended a person in life, one evil and one good. Thus a phantom *(phasma)* visits Brutus before the battle of Philippi, and when asked, "Who are you of men or gods?," it replies, "I am your evil *daimôn.*" (Shakespeare gives Brutus's question a Christian turn, "Art thou some god, some angel, or some devil?")[10]

Concurrently with these philosophical speculations, there existed on a subliterary level a conception of "demons" as malevolent beings, sometimes identified with the souls of the dead, that could fasten on persons or families. The satirist Lucian, mocking contemporary superstition in the second century CE, imagines a group of educated men exchanging stories of the supernatural. One reports how a specialist from Palestine exorcizes demons from the possessed. "When he stands over them as they lie prostrate and asks from where they entered the body, the patient remains silent while the demon, using Greek or a barbarian language depending on his origin, answers how and from where it entered the man, and the exorcist binds it with oaths, and threatens it if it disobeys, and so drives out the demon. I saw it as it was emerging, black and smoky in color." In due course, Christians began to think of Satan and the devils as black.[11]

In the later third century, the Neoplatonist Porphyry of Tyre, one of the most formidable critics of Christianity, propounded a view of the relation between gods and *daimones* that went far beyond a simple division between superior beings dwelling in heaven and lower ones occupying the intervening air. In his work *On Philosophy to be Drawn from Oracles,* written early in his career, he distinguished a supreme god, Zeus, the creator and mind of the universe, from lesser gods who could descend to earth and communicate with mortals, of whom the chief was Apollo speaking through his oracles in Claros and Didyma. In the second and third centuries, it had become customary to question Apollo about the gods, and thus Porphyry was able to draw on a stock of "theological oracles" to expound a theosophy which gave a large place to evil demons.[12]

One oracle that Porphyry included in his collection was to please even Christians, since it seemed to show Apollo, one of the pagans' false gods, admitting that there was in reality only one god. The crucial lines ran as follows (a translation into prose is inevitably clumsy by comparison with the original): "Self-generated, not taught [that is, needing no teaching], motherless [that is, ungenerated], unshakeable, admitting of no name, many-named, dwelling in fire, this is God: but we angels [that is, messengers] are a small part of God." In the reign of Constantine, the Christian Lactantius quoted these three lines, but discreetly replaced the half line "admitting of no name, many-named" with a new version: "whose name cannot be contained by reason." This sufficed to remove the whiff of polytheism in the original, and Lactantius could go on claim triumphantly: "Who could suppose that this refers to Jupiter, who had both a mother and a name?" It had not required much tweaking to turn a text of philosophical paganism into one that Christians could welcome.[13]

Pagans had for many centuries imagined supernatural beings who acted as "messengers" *(angeloi)* of the gods. Early Greek poetry envisaged "messengers" of the gods such as Hermes, and also beings below the level of gods, as when Zeus sends "divine Dream" *(theios Oneiros)* to the sleeping Agamemnon, and Dream says to the king, "I am a messenger *(angelos)* of Zeus." Birds as the bringers of omens can also be "messengers." Later Greek thought conceived such messengers as a distinct class of being, apparently deriving this idea from a Near Eastern matrix. In Syria and Palestine of the Hellenistic period, there occur divine "messengers" *(ml'k)* in various Semitic languages, and these begin to appear in Greek as *angeloi* in the Roman period, not only in the East but in the western provinces also. In addition to the oracle exploited by Lactantius, Porphyry cited one addressed to the "ineffable father of the immortals." From this father's mind *(nous)* there issued "the generations of holy lords," below whom there were others who "perform everything by your mind and power," and below them "a third race of lords" who "carry you by day, hymning you with songs." These "lords" Porphyry equated with angels, of whom those of higher grade were "archangels," and his younger contemporary Iamblichus makes even more elaborate distinctions between gods, archangels, demons, "rulers" *(archontes),* heroes, and souls.[14]

The notion of "breath" or "spirit" *(pneuma),* so essential to Jewish and Christian concepts of godhead, only slowly acquires such associations in paganism. Already in the fifth century BCE, the philosopher Democritus talks of poets writing "with holy breath" *(meth' hierou pneumatos),* and in the next century Plato similarly calls those who speak without knowing what they are talking about, such as poets and politicians, "inspired *(epipnooi)* [literally, "breathed upon"] and possessed by the god," language that perhaps comes from the idea that gods possess their prophets and "inspire" them to deliver oracles. But *pneuma* does not evoke a kind of demonic being until the imperial period. Plutarch comes close to such a notion when telling how a Delphic priestess, forced to prophesy against her will, showed "by the harshness of her voice" that she was "full of an inarticulate and evil spirit," but even here he is thinking not of a "spirit" but of a harmful exhalation from the earth. Later in the second century, the anti-Christian Celsus alleged that mendicant soothsayers in Phoenicia and Palestine commonly claimed, "I am God, or a son of God, or a divine spirit *(theion pneuma)*." This has been thought an exaggeration or a parody, but it could rather reflect the transfer of traditions, Jewish, Christian, and others, in the culture of the eastern Mediterranean. Porphyry credits the Egyptian Serapis with the power to protect his worshipers from demons who would otherwise fill them with evil "spirit" *(pneuma)*. For his pupil Iamblichus, "demonic and heroic spirits" are the bodies that such demons and heroes assume when coming into contact with matter.[15]

The notion of souls ascending after death into an upper realm comes into Greek thought only gradually, and again the first intimations of it are in the fifth century. In the earliest references, the destination of the souls is "ether" *(aithêr)*, the region of the planets and the stars above the air *(aêr)* that surrounds the earth. In time this resting place becomes heaven (*ouranos*), whether the dead is imagined as transformed into a star, as in a famous epigram ascribed to Plato, or carried off by a divinity such as the Muses. In the imperial period, this idea has become almost banal, but how far it was a learned or literary idea, and how far shared by the majority of pagans, is difficult to determine.[16]

Thus in many ways pagan and Christian beliefs resembled one another. The effect of this resemblance was like a magnet, creating both positive and negative force, both attraction and repulsion. Positively, it gave analogies of belief and practice to Christians trying to explain their faith to pagans and possibly to convert them. This is the procedure that Acts ascribes to Paul when he maintains that the "unknown god" worshiped by the Athenians is the same as the God he has come to announce, a claim he reinforces by quoting a scrap of Greek poetry, "For of him we are descended." In the second century, the Athenian Christian Athenagoras addresses an open letter to the emperors, and argues that the beliefs of Christians are not radically different from those of enlightened, "philosophic" pagans. Euripides, for example, knew that names such as Zeus applied to nonexistent referents, whereas the true god could be apprehended through the intellect, and Sophocles said, "In truth there is one God, who made the heaven and the wide earth."[17]

Given this proximity of thought, it is no surprise that even under Christian emperors pagans could safely refer to a single Being, unnamed and superior to the named gods. Late in the reign of Constantine, the senator Firmicus Maternus wrote an eight-book treatise on astrology entitled *Mathesis (Instruction)*. The first book ends with a eulogy of the emperor in which the author urges the sun, moon, and planets, which he calls by their pagan names Saturn, Mars, Mercury, and Venus, to "follow the judgment of the Highest God" *(Dei Summi obsecuti iudicio)* and to assure the eternal rule of Constantine and his descendants. At this stage, Firmicus was still a pagan, but later he was converted to Christianity and wrote a second treatise, *On the Error of Profane Religions,* calling on Constantine's successors to eradicate paganism.[18]

The same proximity also encouraged cults to spring up that combined elements of Christianity and paganism. One such is that of the Carpocratians, followers of a certain Carpocrates, who lived in the first half of the second century. There are two basic accounts, one by Irenaeus of Lyon in the later second century and the other by his contemporary, Clement of Alexandria. According to Irenaeus, the Carpocratians maintained that the world was created not by God but by angels; Jesus was a fully mortal man whose soul nevertheless retained the knowledge it had gained before coming to earth. Endowed by god with exceptional "power" *(dynamis),* his soul was able to escape the "makers of the world," and after passing through them it had ascended to heaven, and the souls of his followers could do the same. Jesus had imparted these doctrines secretly to his disciples, with the order to transmit them to worthy hearers. Among the rites of the Carpocratians was the practice of placing crowns on images: "They possess images, some painted, others made of other material, saying that Pilate had had a portrait of Christ made while Jesus was among men. They crown these and set them out together with images of the philosophers of this world, that is, with the portraits of Pythagoras, Plato, Aristotle, and others, and they pay other worship to them in the same way as the gentiles." Unlike Irenaeus, Clement concentrates on a single aspect of the

Carpocratians' teaching—their view of "justice" as set forth by the founder's son Epiphanes, which involved a strict community of goods and complete sexual freedom. Whereas Irenaeus mentioned the worship paid by the sect to Plato and others, Clement asserts that Epiphanes died at the age of seventeen and "is honored as a god on Cephallenia, where he has a sanctuary dedicated to him, built of quarried stones, together with altars, shrines, and a Temple of the Muses."[19]

As Clement observed, some of these views derive from Plato, for example, the sexual sharing of his *Republic* and the notion of a divine element embodied in those who follow justice, as expounded in the *Timaeus*. At the same time, there is a complete rejection of essential Christian doctrines such as the divine origin of the distinction between good and evil, the spiritual birth of Christ, and his superiority to ordinary humans. If a celebrated letter attributed to Clement is genuine, the Carpocratians tampered with the Gospel of Mark, so that the text described Jesus as spending a night with a near-naked youth and "teaching him the mystery of the kingdom of God." Carpocratianism is an early attempt to fuse elements of Christianity, Judaism, and Greek philosophy in a strange hybrid that could not survive the withering blast of Christian opposition. It seems to have left no material trace, and perhaps never enjoyed a large following.[20]

Similar convergences of belief, leading to the formation of new sects or (in Christian eyes) heresies, occurred around the concept of the "Almighty," literally "Ruler of all" *(Pantokratôr)*, or the "Highest God" *(Theos Hypsistos)*. The notion that God or the gods rule all has a long history in Greek thought, and many pagan divinities are called *Pantokratôr*. The "Highest God" is a designation taken by Christianity from Judaism, where it was a favored circumlocution for the unnamable YHWH: yet Genesis mentions Melchizedek, king of Salem, as "priest of the Highest God" *(El-Elyon)* in the time of Abraham, even though this "Highest God" is not the God of Israel. The same designation is frequent in inscriptions of the imperial period, sometimes with the simple epithet "Hypsistos," at other times with the epithet attached to a particular name such as Zeus. There is no single "Highest God" to which all or most of the inscriptions refer, and it is not always easy to tell which of these texts are Jewish, Christian, or pagan, and which represent a fusion of one or more beliefs.[21]

An instance of fusion is the group known as *Hypsistarioi* or *Hypsistianoi*, attested only in the fourth century. Gregory of Nazianzus's father was a "Hypsistarian," and his son gives the fullest account of their beliefs. They were "a mixture of two entire opposites, Hellenic error and legal absurdity [that is, Judaism, seen by Christians as attached to outmoded legalism]. They reject the idols and sacrifices of the former, and honor lamp-lighting and lights, while of the latter they observe the Sabbath and the fussiness over certain foods, and dishonor circumcision." Gregory's contemporary, Gregory of Nyssa, says only that "Hypsistians" resemble Jews in that they acknowledge "some god, whom they call 'Highest' or 'Almighty,' but do not accept that he is a father," that is, they do not recognize him as the father of Jesus Christ.[22]

In alleging that the Hypsistians called their god the "Almighty," Gregory of Nyssa suggests a connection with another group, the so-called Messalians, a name derived from a Syriac word meaning "pray," whence their Greek name *Euphêmitai*, "Praisers." Epiphanius, a bishop of Salamis in Cyprus contemporary with the two Gregories, divides them into two successive waves, of which only the first is at all comparable with the Hypsistians, while the second is a Christian heresy that began in Mesopotamia, spread widely over eastern Christianity and into Persia well into the sixth century, and involved a belief in the special power of the Holy Spirit; the charge of "Messalianism" continued to be made throughout the Middle Ages long after the original heresy had disappeared. According to Epiphanius, who is the only authority for the earlier Messalians, they "came out of the Hellenes, neither adhering to Judaism nor being Christian, nor from the Samaritans, but being merely Hellenes, and asserted that there are gods, but worshiped none of them, paid worship to one alone and called him 'Almighty.' They built for themselves houses or wide spaces that they called 'oratories' *(proseuchai)*. In these they assembled at evening and at dawn with much lamp-lighting and many lights, and for a long time offered 'praises' to their gods through their true believers *(spoudaioi)*." Gregory reports that one of their "oratories" in Phoenicia was destroyed by lightning. Certain zealous governors, including a Lupicinus known to have been active in the 360s, persecuted them for "counterfeiting the truth and imitating the form of a church." Hence these Messalians made martyrs of their dead and got the further name of "Martyrians."[23]

The first Messalians thus shared with the Hypsistians a belief in a single god, called Highest or Almighty, and both denied that Jesus was his son. The Hypsistians are explicitly said to have borrowed doctrines from Judaism, whereas the Messalians are "merely Hellenes," though they referred to their meeting places by the term *proseuchê*, which more often meant "synagogue." It is less conclusive that both sects made much use of lamps and lighting, since this is a very widespread feature of religion in the imperial period and later. In the present state of knowledge, it is probably best to keep them apart, and to consider both as late fusions of paganism with Judaism and Christianity. Many of their followers were perhaps coaxed or coerced into conversion, and neither survived the fourth century.[24]

Like most religions, Christianity was inherently fissile from the start, liable to divisions temporary or permanent. A distinction grew up between disagreements not involving doctrine, "schisms," and more fundamental divisions, "heresies," a word originally meaning "choice" that had come to mean "school." In the landscape of the early Church, where the Devil was "the god of this world," it was easy to imagine that such deviations came from a contamination of Christian beliefs with pagan ones. Those sects that emphasized the separation of the three persons in the Trinity were guilty of "tritheism," next door to polytheism. Gregory of Nyssa, an orthodox Trinitarian, devotes a treatise on the notion of plurality to "Hellenes" to show that "when we say there are three persons in divinity we do not speak of three gods"; to do otherwise would be to fall into the impiety of polytheism. Writing to his friend Ablabius on the same subject, he explains that an easy answer to the question why Christian scripture does not talk of three gods is to avoid any resemblance to Hellenic polytheism, though an inquiring mind demands a more sophisticated answer. The distinction between one god and plural gods was more than a boundary between Christianity and paganism: it was a mine buried beside Christianity's onward path.[25]

CHAPTER FIVE

Idolatry

POLYTHEISM WAS ONE of the principal charges made by Christians against pagans, but it was inseparable from the charge of "idolatry," and as with disputes about the nature of godhead it is necessary to go far back to understand the issues. Both subjects led to grave internal divisions among Christians, and thus sharpened their debates with "those outside." The abhorrence of "idols" is a recurrent theme of the Hebrew Scriptures, which most early Christians knew in the Greek version of the Septuagint. The crucial text was the First Commandment read in conjunction with the Second: "You shall have no other gods than me. You shall not make an idol *(eidôlon)* for yourself, or an image of anything, among all things in heaven above, in the earth below, or in the water below the earth; you shall not adore *(prokynêseis)* or worship them *(latreuseis)*." Later texts expanded on this primary injunction. A much-quoted verse of the Psalms, which Christians regarded as prophetic and authoritative, runs: "The idols of the nations are silver and gold, the work of human hands." A passage of *Isaiah* satirizes the making of idols: "All who mold and sculpt are fools, doing what pleases them but brings no profit, and they shall be put to shame. . . . (The craftsman) cuts from the grove wood which the Lord planted and the rain made to grow tall for humans to use as firewood; he took some of it and was warmed, and burning it they baked bread on it, and the rest they made into gods, whom they worship." The Wisdom of Solomon, surviving only in Greek, purports to be a pronouncement of the tenth-century king of Israel, though its actual date is about the beginning of the Christian era. It contains a remarkable attack on the divinization of humans that was ubiquitous in the author's world: "The idea of making idols is the beginning of fornication *(porneia),* and the invention of them is the corruption of life, for they did not exist from the beginning, nor will they exist for ever. By the folly of men they entered the world, and therefore they are doomed to a swift end. A father, consumed by premature mourning, made an image *(eikôn)* of the child quickly taken away from him, and thereafter honored a dead human being as a god, and handed on to his dependents secret rites *(mystêria)* and initiations. Then in time the impious custom got stronger and was observed as a law, and at the behests of tyrants carved objects *(glupta)* received worship."[1]

For the Jewish people the worship of "idols," material objects that had no real power, was the distinguishing mark of the surrounding "nations." But idolatry was also a temptation for the Jews themselves. The story of the Golden Calf, set up with Aaron's blessing at the very time that Moses was receiving the Ten Commandments, symbolized the tenuousness of the barrier that separated Jew from gentile and obedience from disobedience. As Christians began to think of their movement as a new, purer Judaism, the "nations" became the world of the Roman Empire, with its ubiquitous worship of images and the concomitant practice of sacrifice, especially sacrifice involving the slaughter of living creatures. "Idolatry" could also be construed more broadly as the worship of material goods, and the story of the Golden Calf could be read as a warning against the worship of gold.

The author of Acts describes a meeting in Jerusalem of the first Christian leaders, the first of all Christian councils. The historicity of Acts, here and elsewhere, is debated; there is the additional problem that the text comes down in several versions, reflecting various doctrinal and disciplinary concerns. The writer alleges that the Council drew up four negative rules for the admission of gentiles into the community. Acts lists these three times, not always in the same order or wording: "the pollution of idolatry," also called "things sacrificed to idols" (*eidôlothuta*), fornication (literally "whoring," *porneia*), "what is strangled," and "blood"; it is sometimes thought that the last two cohere, and refer to avoidance of meat not ritually slaughtered.[2]

Though Paul in his own writings describes the meeting in Jerusalem in a way that is hard to reconcile with Acts, he reaffirms the rule against eating sacrificial food, since "you cannot drink the cup of the Lord and the cup of demons: you cannot share in the table of the Lord and the table of demons"; yet when in pagan society a Christian should not refuse what is put before him unless he is told that it is "sacrificed to idols." A passage of Paul's letter to the Christian community of Rome was to become a central text in discussions of idolatry. Pagans "have exchanged the glory of imperishable God for a semblance of the image of a perishable human, of birds, quadrupeds, and reptiles. . . . They have exchanged God's truth for falsehood, and have revered and worshiped the creation, not the creator." Elsewhere Paul expands the notion of idolatry in a way that could be turned on Christians themselves, by denouncing avarice and greed as another way of worshiping creation: "Be sure of this, that every lecherous, unclean or person greedy for wealth, in other words an idolater, has no inheritance in the kingdom of Christ and God."[3]

The Christian abhorrence of idols was partly rooted in a tendency common to Christians and pagans alike, to regard images, especially those in the round, as having some of the qualities of the person or the being that they represented. "Belief in the magic power of images," it has been said, "was never far from the surface in the Greek world." Pagan literature, including histories, had many examples of animated statues. Lucian in the second century presents a group of philosophers exchanging stories of statues that stepped down from their pedestals and punished thieves who stole their offerings. In real life, statues could be fed, as in the Roman ritual of the *lectisternium,* washed, dressed, and even punished or chained. The architect Apollodorus criticized Hadrian's plan for his temple of Venus and Roma, saying, "If the goddesses wish to get up and go out, they will not be able to do so." Late Antique philosophers claimed by means of theurgy to make images of the gods laugh and smile.[4]

Paul's attack on idolatry in the Epistle to the Romans is the first of a series of denunciations that extends through the Christian apologists such as Justin in the second century and Tertullian in the early third down to Cyril of Alexandria and Theodoret of Cyrrhus in the fifth. In these attacks, they could cite opinions expressed by reflective pagans: the supposed gods were deified human beings, man-made images were inadequate to convey the nature of godhead, and were on the contrary subject to decay and degradation, liable to be gnawed by vermin or melted down into chamberpots. In reply, pagans argued that Christians had their own form of idolatry in adoration of the cross, a charge that defenders of Christianity were obliged to answer from the second century until at least the fifth. As it did with the cult of images, Christian sensitivity to the charge of "staurolatry" declined as paganism weakened, and from the fourth century on the cross becomes ever more frequent in art, especially after a belief grew up that Constantine's mother Helena had discovered the True Cross in Palestine.[5]

Yet the cross was more a symbol than an image, and Christians soon began to feel the need for imaginative depictions of their history. The Christian catacombs of Rome, of which the earliest are of the first or second century, show pictures of Christ and the apostles. The excavations of Europos on the Euphrates have revealed a house, converted into a church in the 240s, that contains paintings showing the Good Shepherd and several scenes drawn from the gospels. The Jewish congregation of Dura had an even more lavishly decorated synagogue, built earlier than the church and furnished with paintings of higher quality. Neither the Jews nor the Christians of Dura considered painted imagery to be equivalent to "idols," and neither feared being accused of idolatry by the rival community or by their pagan neighbors.[6]

Though the Dura church is so far unique both in its date and in its decorative scheme, it cannot have been unique in its time. A general council of Spanish bishops held early in the fourth century at Iliberris near modern Granada issued a series of rulings ("canons") for church discipline. Some of these are specifically directed against idolatry, but one condemns wall paintings: "It was decreed that there shall be no pictures in a church, lest that which receives adoration and worship be depicted on walls." The meaning and the intention of this canon are disputed, not least because the question of images as objects of cult continues to divide different streams of modern Christianity. Since this canon is not included among those concerning idolatry, the Spanish bishops were probably more worried about worshiping created objects than about idolatry in itself: pictures of Christ's miracles like those in the baptistery of Dura perhaps seemed likely to attract misguided forms of devotion such as kissing or genuflection.[7]

One of the bishops present at Elvira, Ossius of Corduba, was to have great influence over Constantine later, and along with others he may have dissuaded the emperor from depicting sacred personages or scenes on his coins or buildings. The statues of the Good Shepherd and of Daniel in the lions' den that Constantine set up on fountains of Constantinople do not constitute an exception, since standing in public space they were not likely to give rise to idolatry. The collection of papal biographies called the *Liber Pontificalis* alleges that Constantine used two seated images of Christ as a "gable" *(fastigium)* for his Lateran basilica, whether this word indicates objects on the roof or within the church, but this tradition is highly suspect: later sources tended to credit Constantine with building projects that are in fact subsequent to his reign. Under Constantine or soon after, Eugenius, bishop of "Burnt Laodicea" in Lycaonia, adorned his church with "pictures and mosaics," while by a curious contrast another Eugenius of the same city is buried in a tomb decorated with aniconic motifs: he was a priest of the "church of the Pure" *(katharoi),* which was opposed to images.[8]

After Constantine's adoption of Christianity, Christian statuary becomes rare, to the extent that some have suspected a written or unwritten prohibition.[9] A statuette of the seated Christ, just over two feet tall and dated to the middle of the fourth century, shows him as a long-haired youth, seated and holding a book roll in his left hand, with his right hand (now broken off) perhaps in the gesture of one expounding or teaching; its size suggests that it is for private devotion, not for church use (plate 2). There appears to have been less scruple about objects in relief. Scenes from the life of Christ are frequent on sarcophagi of the fourth and fifth centuries, even when placed in churches. A famous example is the sarcophagus of Junius Bassus, who died in the year 359; decorated on the sides with scenes from the Old and New Testament, at each end this had scenes of the four seasons, showing *putti* in each season's activities. Sacred imagery in relief is also found on objects such as church doors and reliquary caskets.[10]

Sometimes images of Christ are combined with motifs borrowed from the pagan repertory. A mosaic from Hinton St. Mary in Dorset, England, shows an image either of Christ or (less probably) Constantine imposed on the Christian chi-rho monogram, while in an adjacent panel it shows Bellerophon spearing the Chimaera, an image perhaps meant to evoke the triumph of good over evil: several surrounding lunettes have the secular motif of hunting dogs chasing animals (plate 3). Pagan and Christian motifs can seem so close that it is difficult to decide between direct influence and independent creativity, as when images of goddesses suckling infants *(kourotrophoi)* closely resemble those of Mary and the Christ-child. In a mosaic panel from New Paphos on Cyprus, Apollo orders Marsyas to be flayed while the personified Error *(Planê)* looks on, raising her hand in a

PLATE 2

Statuette of Christ teaching, Rome, mid-fourth century.

Scala/Ministero per i Beni e le Attività culturali. Art Resource, New York

PLATE 3
Mosaic from Hinton St. Mary, Dorset, UK, showing head of Christ, fourth century. © The Trustees of the British Museum

gesture of dismay or abhorrence. Though "error" is a favorite term in Christian literature, here she probably represents the "error" of Marsyas in challenging the god of music.[11]

Had a strict opposition to all forms of sacred imagery remained the policy of official Christianity, it might have opened an unbridgeable gulf between pagan and Christian. Yet as Christianity became the official religion of the empire, the desire for representation became stronger, perhaps more among pious laypersons than among the hierarchy. A letter of Constantine's half sister Constantia is only known from its quotation at the Second Council of Nicaea in 787, which ended the first and most serious phase of the iconoclastic dispute. Constantia had asked Eusebius to send her an image of Christ, apparently not one already existing but a new one made under his supervision and with his approval. It is not known for what purpose she wanted the object, whether for private devotion or for placing in a church, and whether it was to be a portrait or a statue, but in any case she received a sharp rebuke. In what form could Christ be represented, the bishop replied, his eternal and unalterable one, or the one he took after the Incarnation? Even the second would not do justice to the divinity inherent in his earthly form, and the first, showing him in his ineffable glory, was beyond human capacity. It was a pagan habit to make images of their supposed gods or heroes, though they had no prototype to copy; for Christians such things were universally forbidden. A woman had brought him two images, perhaps of philosophers, whom she said were Paul and the Savior, but he had taken them away in case such practices spread, and "we might seem to be carrying around an image of our God, like the idolaters."[12]

An even more emphatic enemy of iconic representation than Eusebius is Epiphanius, bishop of Salamis in the late fourth century, called the "Hammer of the Pagans" because of his colossal *Panarion* or *Medicine Chest,* a description of eighty heresies. A letter from Epiphanius to John the bishop of Jerusalem now survives in full in a translation made by Jerome, while an extract from the original is quoted by Nicephorus, a ninth-century patriarch of Constantinople and an ardent defender of images. Epiphanius tells how, when passing a village on his way from Jerusalem to Bethel, he saw a church with "a dyed cloth *(bêlon)* on the door, and containing a human image like an idol, which they perhaps said was a portrait *(ektupôma)* of Christ or one of the saints (I don't remember what I saw). Knowing that it was pollution for such things to be seen in a church, I tore it and advised (the clergy) to use it for wrapping the corpse of a pauper." Epiphanius agreed to send a replacement, but asked John "to lay down that such things not be displayed in the churches." He also wrote several works directed explicitly against representation, now known only from later quotations. These include a letter to Theodosius I in which he complains that he has often urged his fellow clergy that images should be removed, but without success. The authenticity of these lost writings has been debated from the iconoclastic period onward, but they accord with the letter to John of Jerusalem, and with the archaeological fact that images of Christ and the saints become ever more frequent in the fourth and later centuries.[13]

In the first half of the fifth century, a high official called Olympiodorus communicated his plans for decorating a martyr-church *(martyrion)* to Nilus of Ancyra, an influential monk and spiritual adviser, and this exchange illustrates the tension between the desire for representation and the countercurrent that was to lead to iconoclasm two centuries later. Olympiodorus intended to decorate the walls of the sanctuary with pictures of hunting and fishing, and with similar images in stucco, while in the main church he planned to depict ten thousand crosses (this may only mean a large number), as well as pictures *(historiai)* of birds, animals, reptiles, and plants. Nilus poured cold water on this plan, much as Eusebius had done with Constantia's desire for an image of Christ. Instead, Olympiodorus should "affix" *(pêxasthai)* a cross in the easternmost point of the church, "since by the one, saving cross, the whole race of mankind is saved from servitude" (he appears to mean a mosaic cross in the apse). He should employ an excellent artist to decorate the walls of the main church with narratives from the Old and New Testaments, "so that those who are illiterate and do not know how to read the divine Scriptures may be reminded of the achievements of those who have valiantly served the true god." In the side chapels he should depict a single cross.[14]

Olympiodorus may have intended that his scenes of ordinary life, with hunting, fishing, animals and the like, could be read in more than one way. They would recall sights and activities familiar to the laity, and would also remind the wealthier members of the decoration that they had in their own homes, for such subjects are a well-known part of the mosaic repertoire. At the same time, such scenes could be seen as representing the abundance of God's creation. Nilus not only advises a more austere decorative scheme, but by eliminating the proposed stucco work he appears to reflect a concern about three- as opposed to two-dimensional imagery. His insistence on the prominence of the cross both reflects the growing cult of this symbol since the discovery of the True Cross by Helena, and anticipates the anti-iconic movement of the eighth and ninth centuries, which allowed the image of the cross while forbidding the representation of animate beings, whether divine or terrestrial.[15]

Just as Nilus wished to eliminate secular scenes from Olympiodorus's church while permitting sacred imagery for the benefit of the faithful, so also Hypatios, the influential bishop of Ephesos between 519 and 540, reassures one of his subordinate bishops, Julian of Adramyttion. Julian had written to his superior, recalling the biblical texts that forbade the making of images, and he had decried the folly of pagans thinking that they could represent what they had never seen. In reply, Hypatios admits that while he takes no personal pleasure in such representation, "simpler" people may be helped by them as a vehicle for approaching the divine. Similarly, he argues, the divine voice speaking though the Septuagint names stars and constellations such as the Pleiades by their Greek names, not because it approves the pagan myths about them, but rather so that humans may recognize which stars are meant.[16]

The pagan belief that images had power to move, to speak, to protect, or to cure reasserted itself just as paganism weakened. Eusebius claims to have seen in Caesarea Philippi a statue group representing the woman with an issue of blood who had prayed to Jesus for healing (the same scene appears at Dura and on Christian sarcophagi). Local informants told him that pagans had set the statue up in gratitude to Christ as a benefactor, and that a strange herb growing around his statue could cure every kind of illness. Eusebius's interest seems to have been stirred by the thought that these were contemporary images of Christ, but believing them to be the work of pagans, he raises no theological objection. In the next century, the historian Philostorgius reports a story about this same image. It had become nearly covered with earth, but the locals dug it up and found an inscription telling how the woman had set it up in gratitude for her cure. They then moved the statue to the deanery *(diakonikon)* of a church, "not revering or adoring it, for it was forbidden to adore bronze or any other matter . . . but displaying their love of the prototype." The shift from Eusebius's sober account to the fanciful one of Philostorgius is a measure of the power that had begun to emanate from holy images, even though the fear of idolatry remained. In later centuries, in a further similarity with paganism, Christian icons began to talk, to weep, and to bleed.[17]

Though pagan temples and statues continued to be destroyed in both East and West well into the sixth century, in the more urbanized regions there was a contrary tendency to protect such objects as works of art, once they had been purged of their religious associations. Here again Constantine had shown the way by carrying off pagan artworks to his new capital on the Bosporus, such as the bronze snake from Delphi still to be seen in the Hippodrome; later emperors removed masterpieces like Pheidias's Athena Promachos from Athens and his Zeus from Olympia. Despite Theodosius's measures against pagan practices, nowhere in his extant legislation does he order the destruction of idols, and in a law of 382, restated by his son Honorius in 399, he expressly commands that they be preserved, though only in the secularized form of public decorations. In the West, inscriptions from Africa and Italy show that statues were removed from "sordid" or "hidden" places to be put on view in public baths or other buildings.

Such removals seem to have started about the middle of the fourth century and continued well into the fifth, and excavation has revealed these assemblages in Caesarea in Mauretania and Bulla Regia in Africa Proconsularis. By contrast, humbler monuments were no doubt swept away as monstrosities, especially when they promoted paganism among rural conservatives. In 399, the same year in which his brother ordered pagan statuary preserved for decoration, Arcadius ordered the destruction of country temples, "for when these are demolished and removed, all material for superstition will be consumed."[18]

Christian liking for pagan themes in art, so long as they were safely immunized against demonic forces, allowed benefactors to adorn public spaces much as they had in the days of paganism. At Rhodes a certain Anastasios, a provincial governor or a local benefactor in the fourth or fifth century, set up a statue of Heracles on a hexagonal base, with a depiction of the hero's labors nearby. An epigram on the statue base runs: "Heracles, descended from Zeus, you were not born in years past as the sole averter of evil: our generation too has brought forth a Heracles, the virtuous Anastasios, the renowned founder of Rhodes, who here set you up with your famous labors." An Anastasios who is probably the same person set up a relief image of the mythical Maron, a hero associated with wine, and below the relief inscribed an epigram preceded by a cross in the first line. On the base of the statue, some later Christian has carved the words "Lord, help us" *(Kyrie boêthi)* and a crudely incised cross, and someone, perhaps the same Christian, has chiseled out the relief of Maron altogether. Both monuments reflect an evolution in the Christian attitude to pagan imagery, from acceptance to anxiety.[19]

As Christianity grew stronger and tightened its measures against paganism, idols became not merely symbols of spiritual blindness but proof of religious deviance. Just as the early Christians had avoided notice by worshiping in "house-churches" such as that of Dura Europos, so now convinced pagans, unable to worship in public, moved their cults indoors, sometimes concealing their idols behind walls or disguising them as holy icons. Late in the fifth century, a pagan turned informer revealed to the authorities in Alexandria that idolatrous worship was afoot in a suburb called Menouthis. When the civilian governor hesitated to act (it was alleged that a member of his staff was a pagan), the bishop arranged for a party of monks and Christian activists to go and investigate. The sequel is related many years later by a writer who had been one of the activists. "After praying as we ought, we left for Menouthis and came to a house that was covered with all sorts of pagan inscriptions [that is, hieroglyphics]. In one of its corners there had been built a double wall, behind which idols were hidden. A narrow entrance shaped like a window led to it, and the priest entered through it to perform the sacrifices. The pagans, wanting our search to come to nothing, and helped by the priestess who was living in the house (since they were informed of the outbreak that had occurred in the city) had blocked the entrance with stones and plaster. Moreover, in order that one could not see the newness of the masonry and so discover their trick and their disguise, they had put in front of this place a chest filled with frankincense and *popana* [sacrificial cakes], and above it they had hung a lamp that was lit even though it was in the middle of the day." The author goes on to describe how the original informer, Paralios, was at first dismayed but then realized the deception. He called on the monks to bring axes and demolish the wall, behind which they found a whole collection of idols. "We threw into the flames, right there in Menouthis, those of the idols which because of their great age had already largely deteriorated. The pagans who lived in the village, influenced by the demons who possessed them, thought it impossible to escape with one's life after inflicting any injury on the idols, and believed that we would die on the spot. So we wanted to show them by the facts that all the power of the pagan gods and of the demons was broken and annulled after the coming and the incarnation of the Messiah, the Word of God, who by His own will suffered the Cross for us in order to destroy all hostile power . . . and it was for this reason that we delivered some of the idols to the flames."[20]

The concealment of statues described by Zacharias has its analogue in the archaeological record. In 1963, a cache of twenty-three pagan objects, statues, and votive reliefs were found in a ditch at Tomis on the Black Sea (the modern Constantza): one is a gigantic cult statue of the snake-god Glycon, a deity invented in the second century by the "prophet" Alexander of Abonuteichos. The ditch was sealed behind a wall approximately in the fifth or sixth century, exactly as the statues at Menouthis were concealed. Several such caches have been found in Athens, Antioch, and even London: in Athens, the "Varvakeion Athena," a perfectly preserved copy of the Athena Parthenos, was found protected by a brick vault.[21] Yet the motive for such concealment was not only the fear of Christian iconoclasts. At least in major cities, Christian authorities may have wished to save precious works of art from being destroyed or carried off by barbarians. The despoliation of Rome by Germans such as Alaric and Ricimer in the fifth century almost certainly explains the concealment and preservation of precious works of art in Rome.[22]

Backsliding into paganism was not the only way in which a Christian could fall into idolatry. In Exodus, the worship of the Golden Calf expressed the Israelites' turning from the true God to false ones: for the Christian, the worship of money was another form of idolatry, more insidious since it involved no visible idol. This extension of idolatry is already present in the saying of Jesus that no man can serve both God and Mammon (from Aramaic *mâmûn,* "riches"): it is made explicit by Paul's warning against covetousness in the Letter to the Ephesians. An eastern theologian of the early sixth century, Jacob of Serug, develops it in his sermon *On the Fall of Idols.* With the destruction of idols Satan has been driven to new expedients, and joins with Error (a favorite concept of Christianity) in looking for a replacement.

> Come, Error, let us find some way to console ourselves, and let us lay some trap for the world which will smother it. Let us proceed carefully; let us introduce the love of money, and it will avenge all the gods that have been broken. The love of gold will replace all the deities. Come, let us get to work, and may the world feel this love and die of it! As for bringing back idols on earth, we must not think of it, since the Son of God who banished them lives in the world. The earth has seen Him and will no longer agree to adore empty idols as its masters. Since idolatry has been destroyed on earth, may the love of money take its place, and it will be enough. The world would not agree to hear us if we told it to renounce its master: may it love gold instead. It will come to hate its God and its faith, which is the mistress of humankind. Let us teach humans greed: that will make apostates. . . . The idol of gold is an idol greater than that of the gods. The apostles expelled it and trampled it beneath their feet as they did the gods; may it live on alone, and if it escapes the ruin that has struck down my gods, it alone is worth all of them. It is with this love that I strangled Iscariot, Jesus' disciple: it is with this idol that I also caused Ananias and his wife to perish, for by then no idol had any influence. . . . Love of money is therefore idolatry. Blessed is he who has destroyed idolatry among the just! Blessed is he who prevents the saints [the Christian congregation] from falling in love with it![23]

For Jacob of Serug, idolatry was still present in the form of avarice, as Paul had preached, whereas the pagan idols had lost their power. Yet other churchmen found idolatry creeping back in a more insidious form. The images had gained so powerful a hold on the Christian imagination that even orthodox bishops like Hypatios of Ephesos saw no harm in them; yet they might teach the faithful to worship the created rather than the creator, the material rather than the immaterial, and might disguise rather than reveal the true nature of God. The ever-present distrust of images finally received official sanction in 726, when the emperor Leo III banned sacred representation, and removed a famous statue of Christ over the Bronze Gate of Constantinople. In defiance of the emperor, the cause of the icons was taken up by a Greek theologian, John of Damascus, a member of a noble Christian family that had served the Ummayyad caliphs for several generations. Though John had now retired to Jerusalem, he was still within the Ummayyad realm, and thus was free to attack the emperor for usurping the right to legislate for the Church, indeed for doing the Devil's work. The adoration of icons, he argues, is not like the practice of the Hellenes, who divinize their images. If anyone so treats an image of a human, animal, or reptile or any created thing, we anathematize him, "for just as our saintly fathers overturned the shrines and temples of the gods, and in their place built churches in the name of the saints, and we honor these, so they destroyed the images *(eikones)* of the demons, and in their place set up images of Christ, the Mother of God, and the saints." The destruction of pagan idols lay in the past: now there opened a division in Christianity that still waits to be bridged.[24]

CHAPTER SIX

Sacrifice, Blood, and Prayer

THE AFRICAN TERTULLIAN, who wrote approximately between 195 and 215, is the first author of Christian Latin literature. His speech *On Shows (De spectaculis)* is a denunciation of the entertainments adored by pagans—gladiatorial combat, chariot racing, the theater—in which his aim is both to denounce pagans for their addiction to such shows, and to deter Christians from the temptation of watching them. The most violent spectacle was gladiatorial combat, and Tertullian throws a brutal challenge at his Christian readers: "Do you want some blood? You have the blood of Christ."[1]

The question goes far beyond the problem of Christians watching violent entertainments, and touches on one of the most sensitive issues that divided them from pagans: Tertullian's contrast between Christ's sacrifice, superseding all further sacrifice, and the bloody sacrifice of pagans (for gladiatorial combat too was thought to originate from human sacrifice). Yet pagan sacrifice was itself extremely varied. It had many different meanings, about which Greeks and Romans debated. It could involve a vast range of sacrificial objects—animals of every kind, plants, incense, honey, wine, or nonmaterial offerings of prayer or meditation. But the usual form of both Greek and Roman sacrifice involved the slaughter of animals, preferably oxen, and consumption of the blood and the meat. The connection between animal victims and sacrifice is underlined by language. The Greek for animal victim, already found in Bronze Age Linear B, is *hiereion,* "the holy object": the Latin word *victima* also comes from an Indo-European root meaning "holy."[2]

Sacrifice is frequent in the two great epics of Greek literature, the *Iliad* and the *Odyssey.* Odysseus in the underworld digs a trench over which he slaughters a black ram and black ewe; the ghosts crowd around in their eagerness to drink the blood, but he allows none to do so until he has questioned the ghost of the prophet Teiresias, whose advice he has come to seek. This sacrifice resembles the rite later called *enagismos,* used to propitiate the souls of the dead. Blood continued to be an essential feature of sacrifice for the Greeks, though less so for the Romans.[3]

For pagans contemporary with the first Christians, the most conspicuous form of sacrifice involved the ritual slaughter of an animal, preferably a bull, with the blood ceremonially spilled on the ground or caught in a bowl by the priest. Sacrifice took place in the open air within a sacred space *(hieron, fanum),* with the god's image *(agalma, imago)* nearby and visible and representing his or her presence. The animal was flayed, the less edible parts were burned, and the human sacrificers consumed the rest, either in a communal meal held in the god's sanctuary or at home. When not all the meat of a sacrifice was used up in this way, it was sold on the market, so that after Pliny had begun to suppress Christianity in his province, he found that "the traditional rites are being revived after long neglect, and the meat of sacrificial victims is everywhere on sale, after having had very few buyers before." Sacrifice could also take a token form, as in the offering of incense and wine *(ture ac uino)* often employed at Rome. Such limited offerings were suited to enclosed spaces where animal sacrifice would have been messy and smoky. One such space was the Senate house in Rome, where by an order of Augustus meetings of the Senate were required to begin with an offering of incense and wine.[4]

Greeks and Romans valued sacrifice not only because it was thought a traditional and powerful form of communication with the gods but also, as Pliny's remark implies, because it was closely connected with feasting, so much so that the Greek word for "sacrifice," *thysia,* had the secondary meaning of "banquet." The most elaborate form of sacrifice in the Greek city was the responsibility either of the magistrates or of wealthy individuals acting as priests, who distributed the meat of the victim, and other foods such as bread and wine, to some or all of the population. Women were almost always excluded, even on those rare occasions when slaves and freedmen were not. At about the beginning of the Christian era, Cleanax a benefactor of Cyme in Aeolis (northwestern Turkey) is praised in a decree showing the limits of his liberalities. The citizens, resident Romans, and the resident and visiting foreigners are the principal recipients of his banquets, while to the population at large he gives more modest food—breakfast *(ariston)*, sweet wine *(glykismos)*, a kind of porridge *(chondrogala)*. The distributions of meat thus go to the more honorable guests, not to the majority of the population. Even the restricted type of public banquet exemplified by Cleanax had largely vanished in the course of the pinched third century, and a pagan contemplating conversion is not likely to have been restrained by the prospect of a meatless diet.[5]

Despite the fundamental role that animal sacrifice played in ancient life, it faced a strain of philosophical opposition that began early in Greek thought. Pythagoras in the sixth century was sometimes held to have been one such opponent: after discovering his famous geometrical theorem, he allegedly sacrificed an ox made out of pastry in gratitude to Apollo. A few generations later, Empedocles of Aragas (Agrigento) imagined a past golden age in which humans had not worshiped Zeus, Ares, and the male gods, but only the goddess of love. In those days they had sacrificed with images of animals, not with real ones, and with incense: "The altar was not splashed with pure gore *(phonoi)* of bulls: mankind held it as a great pollution to tear out life to devour noble limbs." Empedocles's words "to tear out life" adumbrate an idea made explicit by Plato's pupil Theophrastus—that blood sacrifice robs the innocent of life and is akin to murder. The views of Empedocles, Theophrastus, and others have survived largely because of Porphyry, the bête noire of devout Christians because of his attack on their faith. Unlike other Neoplatonists, Porphyry rejected eating anything that that once been "ensouled" *(empsycha)*, and his treatise *On Abstinence from Ensouled Creatures*, because it was close to the views of many Christians, has survived when his multivolume attack on Christianity has perished.[6]

Porphyry's opposition to animal sacrifice was not shared by an emperor who was close to many of the Greek philosophers of his day, Julian. In the course of his brief reign, he attempted to resurrect traditional religion in a new form that would supplant Christianity, a project that included a reversion to blood sacrifice, the most flamboyant rite of paganism, on a massive scale. Another of Julian's motives was to reverse the policies of his despised cousin Constantius, with which he had been associated as the emperor's junior partner, and his love of popularity may have added a further motive, since animal sacrifice allowed him to treat pagans to the rare enjoyment of meat.

Looking back on Julian's reign, Libanius blames the gods for their ingratitude in allowing the emperor's death: they should have protected him in return for "the many victims, the many prayers, the endless incense, the blood that flowed plentifully by night and day." Ammianus Marcellinus, a native of Antioch writing some thirty years after Julian's death, gives a cooler appraisal. When in Antioch preparing his Persian campaign, the emperor "with excessive frequency drenched altars with streams of blood." His soldiers, stuffed with sacrificial meat and saturated with wine, were carried senseless through the streets. Among the taunts that the Antiochenes aimed at Julian was that of "sacrificial butcher" *(uictimarius)* rather than "priest" *(sacricola)*. In his obituary of Julian, Ammianus returns to the theme. "He was superstitious rather than a proper observer of religion, slaughtering countless cattle without regard to expense, so that it was predicted that, if he returned from the Parthians, there would be no more oxen" (this was doubtless another joke of the Antiochenes).[7]

Though Greek philosophers such as Porphyry condemned animal sacrifice, others had the opposite opinion, including Julian's close friend Salutius, who considered it an essential channel of communication between creator and created: "Prayers without sacrifice are mere words, whereas, if sacrifice is added, the words gain life, the word giving power to the life and the life animating the word." This was the strain of Neoplatonism that fitted and justified Julian's policy.[8]

Part of Julian's anti-Christian campaign was his plan to rebuild the Temple of Jerusalem, since by so doing he would falsify Jesus's prediction that the Temple would never be rebuilt, and he would revive the animal sacrifice that had ceased in 70. In his denunciation of Christianity entitled *Against the Galilaeans,* he claims always to have revered the god of Abraham, Isaac, and Jacob, but the Christians' claim to worship this same god was false: "they do not imitate Abraham by building altars or offering sacrifice. . . . For Abraham used to sacrifice just as we do, always and continually." If a letter addressed by Julian to the Jewish community is authentic, he intended on his return from Persia not only to resettle the Jews in Jerusalem, from which they had been banished for more than two centuries, but to join them in "giving glory to the Almighty." This must mean "offer sacrifice," since Gentiles had been allowed to sacrifice in the Temple before its destruction.[9]

Paradoxically, the Christian opposition to blood sacrifice stemmed from Christianity's Jewish origins, even though such sacrifice was an essential part of Jewish tradition and of Temple ritual. After receiving the Commandments and the Laws from God on Sinai, Moses ordered "young men of the people of Israel" to sacrifice "peace offerings of oxen to the Lord." He then "took half of the blood and put it in bowls, and half of the blood he poured out against the altar. Next, taking the book of the covenant, he read it in the hearing of the people; and they said, 'All that the Lord has said we will do, and we will listen.' And Moses took the blood and scattered it on the people, and said, 'Look, the blood of the covenant that the Lord has made with you according to all these words.'" Jesus's own last journey to Jerusalem was to celebrate the Passover sacrifice with his disciples. Temple sacrifice, which required the priests to throw blood against the altar as Moses had done, lasted down to the destruction of the Second Temple in the year 70; even during the Roman siege, the Temple service continued until the Romans breached the walls three weeks before the final capture of the city. Yet certain of the Prophets, from Amos in the eighth century down to Jeremiah in the seventh, had proclaimed God's disapproval of sacrifice when unaccompanied by true piety, and such prophetic utterances later provide textual justification for Christians to reject all material sacrifice.[10]

The reasons for the Christian opposition to blood sacrifice, despite its rootedness in Jewish ritual, are several, but the central one is Jesus's own founding or (to use the theological term) "institution" of the central rite of Christianity, the Eucharist (*eucharistia,* literally "thanksgiving"), now also called Holy Communion. The three synoptic gospels are unanimous in stating that Jesus himself had "instituted" the Eucharist at his Last Supper. Mark's account is the simplest and earliest: "While they were eating, having taken bread and blessing it, he said, 'Take; this is my body.' And taking a cup, after giving thanks he gave it to them, and they all drank out of it. And he said to them, 'This is my blood of the covenant, (the blood) that is poured out for many.'" The phrase "my blood of the covenant" shows that Jesus intended this as a renewal of the original Sacrifice of the Covenant as performed by Moses. Paul's version of the Institution, which in writing to the Corinthians he claims to have "received from the Lord," is similar, but he adds words that were crucial for later developments of the rite, turning it from a single act, specific to the occasion of Jesus's impending death, to one implying sacramental repetition: "Do this in commemoration of me." In Paul's view, participation in the Eucharist is both participation in the body and blood of Christ and at the same time an affirmation of Christian unity: "Because there is one bread, we who are many are one body, for we all share in the one bread." Since Paul was writing before the destruction of the Temple in 70, the theory that this event, by ending Jewish sacrifice, also led Christians to reject it, is untenable.[11]

John's gospel is later than Paul's letter to the Corinthians and the three synoptic gospels, and does not describe the Institution, but alludes to it when describing Jesus as he preached in a synagogue at the time of the Passover. When his listeners say to him, "Our ancestors ate manna in the desert," he replies: "Your fathers ate the manna in the desert, and they died. This is the bread that comes down from heaven, so that one may eat of it and not die. I am the living bread that came down from heaven. Whoever eats of this bread will live for ever, and the bread which I shall give for the life of the world is my flesh. . . . For my flesh is true food indeed, and my blood is true drink. He who feeds on my flesh and drinks my blood remains in me and I in him." Hostile pagans thought this idea disgusting, unworthy of someone with a liberal education.[12]

Writing to the Ephesians, Paul speaks of Christ's crucifixion as "as an offering and a sacrifice whose fragrance is pleasing to God," and other Christians of the first and second generations also interpreted the event as a kind of sacrifice, though not always in the same way. For the unknown author of the Epistle to the Hebrews, Christ is both sacrificer and sacrificed: he is the victim, but he is also the high priest whose blood once shed permits his followers to pass the veil into the inner sanctum, and who offers atonement for mankind. John, perhaps writing later than the author of Hebrews, represents Christ as the Lamb of God, and symbolically as the Passover Lamb slaughtered and consumed on the fourteenth of the month Nisan, the day before the beginning of Passover Week. In accord with this interpretation, John puts the Crucifixion on that day, whereas the three synoptic evangelists put it on the fifteenth, the first day of the Passover festival. For the author of Apocalypse, martyrs who bear witness to Christ's name have "washed their clothes in the blood of the Lamb." In time the blood of the martyrs was to acquire a power of its own, even if less than the power of the blood of Christ.[13]

From commemorating the sacrifice of Christ, the central rite of Christianity, the Eucharist itself came to be thought of as a sacrifice. The early manual of discipline called the *Teaching of the Apostles,* dating perhaps from the first century, orders that the community meet on Sundays "to break bread and to give thanks, after having confessed your faults so that your sacrifice *(thysia)* may be pure." The metaphysical question of how this transformation occurred does not seem to have arisen until much later, or if it did, it was discussed in the spiritual hierarchy of the community, and imparted only to initiates.[14] Yet the Eucharist was in outward form a reenactment of Christ's words and deeds at the Last Supper: for Christians it resembled traditional sacrifice only insofar as it was an offering *(prosphora, oblatio)* to God of what was already his own. According to an eastern liturgical formula, often repeated in inscriptions, "We offer you yours from what is yours." Christian prayers and hymns could also be characterized as the "sacrifice of praise."[15]

A further motive for the Christian abhorrence of pagan sacrifice derives from Judaism, but was strengthened by considerations that are peculiar to the Christian community. As with idolatry, the paramount injunction was expressed in the First Commandment and the Laws of the Covenant. Writing to the Corinthians, Paul begins his discussion of eating food offered to pagan gods by citing *Deuteronomy:* "There is no other god but one." Though some Corinthian Christians ate such food in the confident knowledge that the pagan gods did not exist, Paul advises that by so doing they will only trip the "brothers" up: "and so if food causes my brother to stumble, I will never eat meat. . . . What do I imply then—that food offered to idols is anything, or that an idol is anything? No, I imply that what pagans sacrifice they offer to demons and not to God. I do not want you to be partners with demons. You cannot drink the cup of the Lord and the cup of demons. You cannot share in the table of the Lord and the table of demons."[16]

The Christians' distaste for pagan sacrifice was strengthened by their own modification of the Jewish dietary laws. The book of Acts describes how the first generation of Christian leaders in Jerusalem drew up a set of rules, the so-called "Apostolic Decrees," that were to be binding on gentile converts; as gentile Christians became the majority, and Christianity separated from the parent religion, these rules became binding on the whole community. The second and third of them forbade the consumption of "blood" and of "what has been strangled" *(pnikton)* (in some versions of the text, the third rule is omitted). In his *Speech of Defense (Apologeticum),* written later than *On Shows,* Tertullian proclaimed: "We do not even include animal blood in the food we consume, and therefore we abstain from strangled animals and ones that die a natural death to avoid being polluted by blood, even if it is buried in our entrails. When you are testing Christians, you offer them sausages bursting with blood, knowing full well that it is forbidden among those whom you are trying to lead into error." The *Apostolic Canons,* a collection of eighty-five ecclesiastical regulations dating from the fourth or fifth century, and later regarded as the earliest set of "canon" laws, laid down that no Christian should eat meat containing "the blood of its life," or meat from an animal that had been killed by another animal or had died a natural death; an ecclesiastic of any rank who broke the rule suffered deposition, a layperson excommunication. Yet the same canons required ecclesiastics to eat meat and drink wine on holy days on pain of deposition.[17]

Jesus's sacrificial death on the cross made him the prototype of those Christians who sacrificed their life as "witnesses" *(martyres)* for the faith; such martyrs often died by burning, but more often by being exposed to wild beasts for the public's amusement. A few years after Tertullian's *On the Shows* occurred one of the best-known of Christian martyrdoms, that of Perpetua and her companions, in which blood is a significant motif; their "passion," the account of their trial and death, became a widely read text, still extant in the Greek and Latin versions, and Tertullian has often been thought to be the unnamed author of the Latin. When one of the martyrs, Saturus, is bitten by a leopard, "he was covered in so much blood that the crowd as he turned away (?) shouted its affirmation of his second baptism: 'A fine bath, a fine bath.' " A soldier sympathetic to Christianity was overseeing the execution, and Saturus asked him for his ring, dipped it in his own blood, and gave it to him "as a memorial and a token of his blood." The pagan audience cruelly likens the "blood-bath" to an ordinary bath in a public bathhouse, where it was customary to wish good luck to those entering and leaving, not least because such places were believed a favorite haunt of evil forces. For a Christian observer of the same scene, the flow of blood recalled the blood of Christ and the water of their own symbolic bath, baptism. The last words of Saturus and the cry of the pagan audience encapsulate the antinomies in the pagan and the Christian attitude to blood.[18]

Behind the exchange between Saturus and the soldier there also lies a development in Christianity first attested in the late second century. The blood, bones, and other physical remains of martyrs had begun to acquire a supernatural power, and from the fourth century onward such "relics" received their own cult, a source of offense to convinced pagans such as Julian. In a famous sentence, sometimes misquoted, Tertullian observed, "We become more numerous whenever you mow us down: the blood of Christians is seed" *(plures efficimur quotiens a uobis metimur: semen est sanguis Christianorum)*. This idea was to be refined by Ambrose, bishop of Milan, when arguing for the suppression of pagan sacrifice in the late fourth century: "We began long ago, and now they (pagans) are less than those they excluded. We glory in blood, they worry about loss of money. They never contributed more to us than when they ordered Christians to be beaten, proscribed, and slaughtered."[19]

A further motive for Christian opposition to pagan sacrifice, already hinted at in Tertullian's reference to blood sausages, was its use as a means of identifying Christians in circumstances of persecution. Reporting back to Trajan about Christianity in his province, Pliny says that he tested those accused of being Christians by making them offer incense and wine to the emperor's portrait. In 249, the emperor Decius ordered an empire-wide sacrifice in which all Roman citizens were to participate, men, women, and children, slave and free, though Jews were exempted. It is unclear whether the primary motive of this act was to uncover Christians, but that was certainly one of its effects. The detail of these effects shows up in the correspondence of the African bishop Cyprian and in the martyr account of Pionius of Smyrna, and more than forty certificates of compliance have survived, issued to those who had sacrificed to the gods.[20]

Sacrifice was also the fuse that lit the "Great Persecution" of Diocletian and Galerius, which its historian, Eusebius, characterized as "the struggle over sacrifice." It allegedly began about 300, when Christians in the imperial service made the sign of the cross as the emperor was sacrificing, thus causing the demons to flee and the sacrifice to fail. The chief diviner announced that profane persons were present: in Roman ritual, "profane" denoted a state of temporary or permanent unacceptability to the gods, and sacrifice always began with the dismissal of the "profane." Diocletian, "mad with anger, ordered everyone to sacrifice, not only those whose function it was, but all those who were in the Palace." This order he followed by a command that all the soldiers in the army should sacrifice, and that those who refused should be dismissed from military service. He next widened his orders until all Christians within his domain were obliged either to sacrifice or to face the consequences: many of those who refused were thrown, as Perpetua had been, to animals in the arena. According to Eusebius, certain of the local magistrates who presided over the process, exhausted by the shedding of blood and no longer wishing the cities to be polluted by citizens' blood, turned to other forms of punishment, and gouged out the eyes and maimed a leg of recalcitrant Christians.[21]

Thus by the fourth century, when Christianity became the religion of the emperors, Christians had many motives for their rejection of pagan sacrifice, and especially the bloody sacrifice of living creatures that was central to both Greek and Roman forms of religion. It is characteristic of Constantine that he moved only gradually and carefully against the practice. Despite Eusebius's claim that he issued many laws against sacrifice to idols, the only legal restriction known from his reign concerns sacrifices in the home, where the participants tried to read the future from the entrails of the victim (haruspicy). This was a traditional form of prediction that the Romans had borrowed from Etruria and incorporated into their public religion, and Constantine's ban on the private practice of it belongs in a series reaching back several centuries. Roman emperors had always been concerned about private attempts to foretell the future, regarding them as next door to conspiracy and treason.[22]

After Constantine, the legal campaign against sacrifice closely tracks the campaign against idolatry, with which it was closely connected. Either in 356, the year in which the emperor Constantius visited Rome, or in 357, he and the subordinate Caesar, Julian, ordered that all temples be closed and that "all should abstain from sacrifice." In this same connection, Constantius ordered a change in the procedure of the Roman Senate. Augustus had set up a statue and an Altar of Victory in the Senate house, and ordered that all meetings should begin with a modest sacrifice of incense and wine. This altar Constantius now ordered removed and the sacrifices terminated, an action reversed soon afterward by Julian. Thus began a religious and political struggle that was to end only in the reign of Theodosius.[23]

After Julian's death, the senior emperor in the West, Valentinian I, in accordance with his policy of calming the religious controversies of the recent past, allowed the altar to remain in the Senate house, but his elder son, Gratian, who succeeded him in 375, reversed his policy of compromise, especially after he had proclaimed the Spanish general Theodosius eastern emperor in 380. He refused to wear the robe of chief priest *(pontifex maximus)* that all emperors had hitherto worn, including his Christian predecessors, forbade state funds to be spent on subsidizing the college of Vestal Virgins, and ordered the removal of the Altar of Victory. On his death in 383, Gratian was succeeded as senior emperor in the West by his brother Valentinian II, then only eight years old. The way was now open for the pagan senators of Rome, led by the eloquent Symmachus, and the bishop of Milan, Ambrose, to begin a struggle for the ear of the boy-emperor that has come to epitomize the last confrontation of "triumphant" Christianity and "dying" paganism. These two major figures of Late Antique Latin literature addressed Valentinian in works that make explicit many of the underlying issues between pagans and Christians: the nature and meaning of sacrifice, the means by which humans approach the divine, the actions that bring them into contamination or pollution. And yet, when the two protagonists debated these questions in their addresses to Valentinian, the Altar of Victory was the most visible issue, but not the essential one. The larger part of both Symmachus's famous *Third Report* and of Ambrose's two letters in reply is devoted not to the altar, but to Gratian's withdrawal of subsidies to the traditional cults.[24]

For Ambrose, pagan religion was inseparable from animal sacrifice. Using an argument that had already been used by Greek philosophers, he tacitly equates blood sacrifice with murder, and makes the personified Rome complain: "Why do you bloody me every day with the useless blood of innocent cattle?" *(quid me casso cottidie gregis innoxii sanguine cruentatis).* When he alleges, "The manner of your sacrifices is to be spattered with the blood of animals" *(sacrificium uestrum ritus est bestiarum cruore respergi),* he deliberately generalizes from the rites of one cult in particular, Mithraism, in which the initiate was drenched in bulls' blood. The charge reveals the underlying religious issue, that of contamination by participation. To be touched by blood, especially innocent blood, could never be a true sacrifice, but could only please evil demons, and Ambrose cites the familiar verse from Psalm 95, "The gods of the gentiles are demons."

Participation is also central to the narrower issue of the Altar of Victory. Twice the bishop argues that to compel Christians to be present when offerings are made in the enclosed space of the Senate house is to force them to undergo pollution. "Is it tolerable that a pagan should sacrifice and a Christian be present? They say, 'Let them imbibe smoke in their eyes, music in their ears, ash in their throats, incense in their nostrils; let dust blown from our altars spatter the faces of those who stand opposed.'" As for the

Vestal Virgins, Ambrose caustically observed that Christian women did not need to be paid to preserve their virginity. The bishop carried the day until the usurper Eugenius came to power in 392, when a new delegation, again led by Symmachus, persuaded him to restore state funds to public cults, with Ambrose again in opposition. It is uncertain whether Eugenius also allowed the altar to be reinstalled, but if so it cannot have survived his death in 394.[25]

In 391, Theodosius, who was now the senior Augustus, issued the first law that explicitly banned pagan activity of every kind. The first clause laid down that "no-one may pollute himself with sacrifices, no-one may slay an innocent victim": Ambrose had previously used the phrase "innocent cattle" in his reply to Symmachus. Theodosius soon followed this law with others that extended its effects to the eastern empire. Nonetheless, the issue of sacrifice was not dead, and early in the next century Prudentius, the first major poet of Christian Latin, returned to it in his two-volume work, *Against Symmachus*. Though sacrifice is only one of the themes handled in this sprawling poem, Prudentius raises it in connection with a form of entertainment that Tertullian had denounced two centuries before—gladiatorial shows. Well read in Roman antiquarian literature, Tertullian knew that such entertainments were an importation from Etruria, and that they had once been funerary games intended to appease the spirits of the dead. They had long since lost this function, and become spectacles closely attached to the worship of the emperors, but it was easy to represent them as a form of sacrifice to the spirits of the dead or to the ruler of the underworld. Prudentius takes up the same argument. "Look at the criminal rites of fearful Dis, for whom the gladiator falls, sprawled on the ill-omened sand, alas, a hellish victim for Rome that is not purified." The poet imagines Theodosius urging Rome to reject her pagan past, and in fact his son and successor in the West, Honorius, may have been the first emperor to outlaw gladiatorial shows. In the next generation Cyril, bishop of Alexandria, talks of them as a thing of the past, again in the context of sacrifice. "When pagan *(Hellenikê)* superstition still prevailed, gladiatorial contests took place among the Romans at fixed times; a certain Cronos was hiding below the ground, gaping beneath perforated stones so as to be polluted with the gore of the fallen." As with blood sacrifice, educated Christians borrowed many of their arguments from pagan writers, some of whom had expressed similar abhorrence of gladiatorial spectacles.[26]

As always, the laws had only a limited effect. In the 420s Theodoret of Cyrrhus devotes a whole section of his *Cure of Pagan Maladies* to the question of sacrifice. He confronts the fact that sacrifice was part of Mosaic Law by arguing that when the Israelites were wandering in the wilderness, God began to wean them from this debased practice by permitting a limited form of sacrifice. David in certain of the Psalms, and after him the Prophets, having a superior knowledge of the divine plan, knew that God did not want material sacrifice but rather "the sacrifice of praise." "Be persuaded to do likewise yourselves, not by the laws of the emperors or the fear of punishment, but by the strength of truth." Not all listened, and pagans continued to sacrifice in secret well into the sixth century, even in the major cities of the empire.[27]

Where central control was weak or nonexistent, sacrifice persisted even longer. In a letter of 595, Gregory the Great writes to Constantina, the wife of the emperor Maurice, drawing her attention to a scandal in Sardinia: "Because I have heard that there were many heathen *(gentiles)* in the island of Sardinia, and that they still by the depraved custom of heathendom make sacrifices to idols, and that the priests of that island were lazy in preaching our Redeemer, I sent one of the bishops from Italy, who has brought many of the heathen to faith, by God's help. But he has told me about an impious affair *(rem sacrilegam):* those who sacrifice to idols there pay a sum to the governor *(iudex)* so that they may be permitted to do so."[28]

Christian authorities, both secular and ecclesiastical, had long since recognized that they could abolish pagan sacrifice, but could not abolish the desire of ordinary people to vary their normal routine by holidays and an accompanying change in diet. This task fell more and more to the Church in the person of its representatives, the bishops and (with the spread of monasticism) the abbots. The anonymous biographer of Saint Nicholas, abbot of the monastery of Sion in Lycia, recounts how the saint, prompted by the Holy Spirit, went around to the local churches and made a sacrificial offering *(hagiasma thysias)* of oxen, at the same time distributing bread and wine. Nicholas had recently been accused of forbidding local farmers to visit the largest city of the region, Myra. Whatever his motive, this had caused his enemies to complain to the local bishop, and this extravagant campaign of public feasting was perhaps meant to allay rural discontent. So also Gregory the Great, concerned that too radical a change might endanger the conversion of the Angles of Britain, and knowing that they had a tradition of sacrificing cattle to their gods, proposed that they should slaughter their cattle on Christian holy days, for instance at the inauguration of a church.[29]

Sacrifice is attested in different forms and in many cultures, and since the early modern period it has been a subject of scholarly investigation. From the late nineteenth century on, it has attracted the attention of sociologists and ethnologists. Some have tried to uncover the essential meaning of sacrifice as a whole, or its original significance in particular cultures such as that of early Greece. Though both pagans and Christians regarded sacrifice *(thysia, sacrificium)* as a central part of religion, their conceptions of it varied so widely that bridging it might have seemed an impossible task. While Christian opposition to idolatry could be mediated by means of religious imagery, there could be no compromise with animal sacrifice. Christ's sacrifice was the final one, and while Christians could regard the Eucharist, or even their own prayers and offerings as a form of sacrifice, nevertheless on this issue the break with both Judaism and paganism was complete.

Prayer resembles sacrifice in being a widespread and perhaps universal form of communication with the divine. Christian prayer resembles Christian sacrifice in having many external similarities to its pagan counterpart, while at the same time it becomes profoundly different through the words and practice of Jesus and his early followers.

Greek and Roman literature preserves some discussions of prayer, but these rarely venture into metaphysical territory, and instead discuss prayer as it reflects everyday morality. The *Second Alcibiades* attributed to Plato is agreed to be a Hellenistic work, devoted to two questions—the danger of praying for something that only seems good when in fact it is bad, and the error of supposing that the gods are more interested in material goods than in human souls. Persius's second satire condemns the wickedness of certain prayers, for example, for the death of a relative, and the folly of trying to bribe the gods, who need nothing. Juvenal in his famous tenth satire resembles pseudo-Plato in portraying the "vanity of human wishes"—the error of praying for supposed goods rather than for a sound mind in a sound body. Many of these ideas have a long history in Greek thought, and have analogues in Jewish and Christian literature, but do not require supposing cultural transference.[30]

Again as with sacrifice, Christian prayer developed out of Jewish, though given a new direction by Jesus and his first followers. Set liturgical prayers already appear in the Pentateuch. Paul's injunction that men should pray on behalf of all humanity, "in any place, raising holy hands without anger or disputes," while women should listen quietly, and not dress in their finery, appears to reflect the arrangement of the first-century synagogue. The novelty of Christian prayer started from the teaching and practice of Jesus, especially as they are recorded in the New Testament. What Christians call the "Lord's Prayer" goes back to a passage of Matthew's gospel, while a shorter form is transmitted by Luke. In Matthew, Jesus first gives instructions about the manner and the mental attitude with which his followers should pray. They should not pray like the hypocrites, who pray standing in the synagogue or on street corners. Instead, they should go into a room, shut the door, and pray in secret, and "Your father who sees in secret will reward you." Similarly, they should not "waffle" or "babble" like the gentiles (Matthew here uses a rare Greek word of uncertain meaning), since God knows what we want without being told. The text of the "Lord's Prayer" as reported by Matthew contained ideas that might have appeared strange to a potential convert, but less bizarre than partaking of Jesus's flesh and blood in the Eucharist. For the educated, the idea that god was the "father" of mankind went back to Homer, though in him the sense is more that of supreme authority than of paternity. In Hellenistic thought, as expressed by Aratus in the passage quoted by Paul on the Areopagus, fatherhood had expanded to mean kinship and not only a position of supremacy, but did not express a personal intimacy. In any case, these are ideas of the educated minority, and give little guidance to the feelings of the ordinary convert. He might more readily have understood the notion of receiving "daily bread" (though the word usually translated "daily," *epiousios*, is another word of uncertain meaning) and of being saved from "testing" *(peirasmos)*.[31]

The notion that a particular group should pray using a fixed formula is foreign to Greek religion, though not to Roman. The Elder Cato dictates the prayer with which the farmer should prayer to Jupiter of Feasts *(Jupiter Dapalis)*: "when it is time to make the offering, you will do thus" (and Cato gives the precise formula). Next, "Wash your hands, then take the wine" (there follows a second formula). Similarly, the Arval Brothers, an ancient fraternity brought by Augustus under imperial control, used set

PLATE 4

Fresco of praying woman from Catacomb of Priscilla, Rome, third or fourth century. Scala/Ministero per i Beni e le Attività culturali. Art Resource, New York

hymns and prayers. But such private and public prayers are due to the quasi-legal nature of Roman religion, which required precise words and actions in order for prayers and sacrifices to be effective. They are different from the moral injunctions of the Lord's Prayer, or from Paul's wish that the Christian should pray for all humanity.[32]

The early Christians were also anxious about the externalities of prayer. In describing Jesus as he prayed in the garden of Gethsemane, the three synoptics showed a curious divergence; in Matthew he fell "on his face," in Mark he fell "on the ground," and in Luke he knelt. Should the Christian stand, sit, or kneel? Paul had said that men should raise "holy hands," but what gesture had he meant? Did his remarks about women concern all or only some? Tertullian's treatise on prayer *(De oratione)* attempts to answer all these questions. Hands should be not only raised, but spread out in imitation of the Passion; the person praying should not sit, since that is what pagans do; some may stand if their own traditions require it, but it is better to kneel; all women without exception should be veiled. Christian representations of persons praying ("orants") usually show them with their arms spread out and slightly bent at the elbows, and women are veiled, as in a fourth-century painting from the Catacomb of Priscilla in Rome, sometimes called the *Donna velata* (plate 4).[33]

Christian prayer was easier to accept for a potential convert than abstention from pagan forms of sacrifice, and it did not lead to religious disputes such as that between Symmachus and Ambrose over the Altar of Victory. Yet both sacrifice and prayer embodied a notion of the divine that, while having its roots in Judaism, marked a new departure.

CHAPTER SEVEN

Debate

THE CHRISTIAN New Testament embodies several forms of debate both within the Christian community and with outsiders, whether Jew or pagan. Paul's speech before the Athenian Areopagus is preceded by his discussions with several such groups: "He conversed in the synagogue with the Jews and the worshipers, and also in the agora every day with anyone there. Some of the Epicurean and Stoic philosophers argued with him, and some said, 'What can this babbler *(spermatologos)* mean?' " The book of Acts itself has been seen as a contribution to a debate, though there is no agreement as to the parties involved—the views of Peter against those of Paul, of the nascent Christian community against its parent Judaism, or of Christianity in general against paganism.[1]

Literary works taking the form of disputes or debates multiply in the following centuries. Some are direct attacks on pagan beliefs, such as the *Apology* of Tatian, or *To the Gentiles (Ad nationes)* of Tertullian. They can comprise a dialogue between a Christian and an interested gentile, who is then converted, or a dispute between a Christian and a Jew, who is attended by fellow believers and remains unconvinced, as in Justin's *Dialog with the Jew Trypho*. In the second century, Justin, Aristides, and Athenagoras write addresses to the emperors, in which the hoped-for readership is probably not the apparent addressee but pagans capable of reading Greek. The *Octavius* of Minucius Felix, written in the first half of the third century, takes the form of a dispute between a convinced pagan and a Christian in which another Christian is arbitrator and the pagan is finally converted. As in Acts, narrative can also serve a persuasive or "apologetic" function by embedding direct speech, and describing the reactions of the audience.

On the pagan side, literary attacks on Christianity became more sophisticated as their authors went deeper into the claims of the new faith, and handled their own arguments more skillfully. The philosopher Celsus in the second century relied largely on hearsay and had read few Christian texts, so that Origen was able to crush him in his massive reply. A more formidable critic arose in the late third century, the Neoplatonist Porphyry. His fifteen-book work *Against the Christians* is known only from quotations, and its precise date and form, even its existence as a single work, are in dispute. Porphyry was able to prove that the book of Daniel is a work of the second century BCE rather than of the sixth, and questioned the culture and the honesty of the evangelists. Despite Constantine's attempt to suppress it, his work supplied material to later opponents of Christianity, and forced its defenders to answer with argument, not merely with silence or abuse.[2]

A passage that may derive from Porphyry's preface blames the Christians for deserting the traditional gods and practices: "How could people not be totally impious and godless if they desert the ancestral customs on which every nation and every city are based?" Given the uncertainty of the date at which he wrote (opinions vary between about 270 and the early fourth century), it cannot be known if Porphyry blamed Christian "impiety" for the present state of the Roman Empire, but this was an argument that other defenders of Christianity were forced to confront by the rise of new powers such as the Sassanid Persians. Arnobius of Sicca, writing in the late third or early fourth century, confronts this argument before treating any other in the seven books of his *Against the Gentiles,* and it was to gain new urgency after Alaric's sack of Rome in 410.[3]

Though the reign of Theodosius I was crucial in the history of Christian antipaganism, a series of "apologetic" works stretching into the fifth and sixth centuries show that Christian writers still felt the need to combat pagan arguments. Paganism continued to be a threat, not only because some pagans refused to be converted, but because Christians could be led astray by their reading of secular works, or by events that suggested that their opponents were in the right.[4]

One such work is usually known as the *Apocriticos (Discourse in Reply)* of Macarios of Magnesia, who may be a bishop of this same name attested in 404. The text was lost until a mutilated manuscript turned up in Athens in 1867, only to disappear soon afterward. Of the original five books, the manuscript contained the latter part of the second, the whole of the third, and the first part of the fourth. The work takes the form of a dialogue occurring over five days between the implied author ("I") and an unnamed pagan. Like certain of the Platonic dialogues, it is set in the frame of an account given by the author to a friend named Theosthenes ("Strong in God"), even though Theosthenes is supposed to have been present on the occasion. Despite the Platonic antecedents, there is no real interplay between the two speakers. The pagan makes certain objections, to which the narrator responds at much greater length, and not always to the point made by his adversary. Though the narrator complains about the adversary's rhetoric, he is much the more rhetorical of the two, and is the only speaker to use the device of imaginary interlocutors *(prosopopoea)* who advance arguments or objections of their own.[5]

When the pagan first appears in book 2, he seems to have the advantage. "Sneering, and looking at me very fiercely in a rather impressive way, he said with a shake of his head . . ."; "when this man who boastfully supported pagan belief had poured out his rhetoric in these words, we, (though?) not at all dismayed in spirit by the noise of his words, quaked: but after calling on the substantial Word (of the Trinity) as usual we spoke as divine grace aided us." The beginning of books 3 and 4 show the dramatic setting to be a "quiet place" in which the pagan had gathered a "distinguished audience," though the narrator seems to have had his own supporters, including Theosthenes. As the debate proceeds, the pagan becomes less assured, the narrator more so, and their last exchange runs: "The Hellene, after injecting so great a display of cunning into his questions, seemed to shake us and to have thrown us into the alarm of disarray. But we, secretly imploring Him who reveals the depth out of darkness and clearly teaches mankind the most evident truth, encountered each of his observations appropriately."[6]

The stiffness of the dramaturgy suggests that earlier anti-Christian literature lies behind most of the pagan's arguments, and Porphyry is often supposed to have been Macarios's principal source. Macarios allows his pagan to attack the tenets of Christianity with surprising vehemence. The gospel accounts are "stale and discordant." Jesus's statement "Unless you chew my flesh and drink my blood, you do not have Life in you" is so repulsive that even Matthew, Mark, and Luke could not accept it, let alone anyone possessed of a decent education, and it is fit only for the most ferocious savages. Though the work bears some resemblance to the question-

and-answer literature used for the instruction of catechumens, it far exceeds them in the virulence of the language. It is now impossible to judge how much the scene presupposed by the work—a Christian and pagan, both well-armed with argument, debating before an audience of supporters on both sides—corresponds with confrontations still occurring in the eastern empire in the late fourth century. Later works that combat the objections of pagans are either more expository, such as Cyril of Alexandria's *Against Julian,* or describe debates conducted at a lower temperature and with the conversion or at least the acknowledged defeat of the pagan, such as Zacharias of Mitylene's *On the Creation of the World* (though it is possible that Macarios's pagan interlocutor was converted at the end of the work, like the pagan Caecilius in Minucius Felix).[7]

Cyril of Alexandria is now remembered mainly for his part in the murder of Hypatia in 415, and for condemning the views of Nestorius at the Council of Ephesos in 431. Among the huge number of his surviving works is a ten-book refutation of the diatribe *Against the Galileans* that the emperor Julian had written some eighty years before: ten more books now survive only in quotation.[8] Dedicating the whole work to Theodosius II, Cyril speaks as if there were still pagans who are "evidently in error and who impose upon the world innumerable gods, demons, and souls of heroes." He has been incited to refute them by reading Julian's attack (though as the work proceeds he devotes much space also to Porphyry). After the first book, which is wholly expository, Cyril's method is to quote Julian verbatim and then to answer his charges at length, a procedure by which he inadvertently became the principal source for modern knowledge of the original. Despite the bishop's famously fiery temperament, he conducts the discussion with restraint and with few references to pagan practices of his own time. Gladiatorial games, frequent when "Hellenic superstition" was at its height, are now a thing of the past. In a recent scandal, a virtuous woman was seduced and violated by priests of Cronos in the god's own temple. Pagans concede that Greeks long ago sacrificed human beings, but claim that they did not sacrifice to real gods, but rather to demons. Cyril replies that, if this is true, "where then shall we place Cronos, Zeus, Ares, the sister of Apollo and proud 'arrow-shooter' Artemis, and Semele's son, the crazy Dionysus, who are still worshiped even now, and perhaps have the chief place among the gods. . . . If, my good friend, the ancients offered blood-sacrifice not to gods but to wicked and detestable demons, sacrifices not just of men but also of brute beasts, to whom did you build temples in every country and city, and set up the altars in them?" Later Cyril uses a similar argument, and almost the same words, in reply to Julian's charge that Christians imitate the "fury" of the ancient Jews in overturning temples and altars, whereas Jesus and Paul had never given them authority to do so. To this he gives the specious answer that, since the pagans themselves say that only one god deserves worship, they cannot object to seeing the temples and altars of plural gods overthrown. In general Cyril restricts the debate to texts and their interpretation, since his main concern is not with the paganism of the streets and the countryside, but with the intellectual paganism of "Hellenic" authors such as Porphyry and Julian, whose influence must still have been strong.[9]

A literary genre much closer to observable actuality than dialogue is that of epistolography. The author of an ancient letter often wrote with the intention of being read by several audiences. The letters of Paul are an early example, followed by Cyprian, bishop of Carthage, in the mid-third century. A remarkable series of Augustine's letters concern the spiritual health of the pagan aristocrat Volusianus, several of whose relatives were already Christian. Volusianus's mother had entrusted Augustine with the task of saving her son's soul, and Augustine urged him during his governorship of Africa to read sacred literature, particularly the works of the apostles, and to write back with any problems that this reading caused him. Volusianus replied, ostensibly reporting the conversation he had recently had with a group of pagan friends. One of these had wondered how "the lord and governor of the world" had impregnated a virgin, and how after nine months' pregnancy she had remained a virgin. And how could the resulting son have lived an earthly life without manifesting any signs of divinity except for a few miracles which, "if you think of other people, are not much for a god"? Augustine's friend Marcellinus, who shared the task of caring for Volusianus's soul, followed this letter with one of his own to Augustine, containing a number of other problems with which the governor had not wished to bother the bishop. For example, how could the Christian God, assuming that he was identical with the God of the Old Testament, be so changeable as to desire a novel form of sacrifice from his worshipers? Augustine sent a long response answering all Volusianus's questions in detail, but the Roman remained a pagan to his last hours, and there is surely an ironical undertone in his inquiries.[10]

Isidore, a monk at Pelusium on the eastern branch of the Nile, a contemporary of Augustine and a correspondent of Cyril of Alexandria, has left a collection of about two thousand letters. It is not known if he was born a Christian, but he had received a full education in pagan literature, and to judge by his classical Greek and his wide knowledge of pagan literature, he had been a teacher of rhetoric *(sophistês)* before entering the monastery. His correspondents range from the emperor down to goldsmiths, farmers, and merchant seamen. A substantial subgroup consists of men in the educated middle class—philosophers *(philosophoi),* men trained in rhetoric and law *(scholastikoi),* teachers of rhetoric *(sophistai),* and teachers of literature *(grammatikoi),* of whom the last-named might be mere schoolteachers, but might also be professors of literature, especially poetry, an important calling in an age when both Christians and pagans interpreted and wrote poetry in the service of their beliefs. Some of these must have been self-employed, others salaried by their cities, while *scholastikoi* often served in civil and ecclesiastical administration. Most of Isidore's correspondents are Christian, but some are pagan, and many have no clear religious position. Philosophers are perhaps the most obdurate. Isidore rebukes a "pagan philosopher," Maximus, for treating "sources of wickedness" as divinities. Olympiodorus, probably also a philosopher, is told that those who attack Christianity are refuted by their own arguments. A *scholastikos,* Harpocras, receives a long letter denouncing divination, which usually involved sacrifice to idols, and carried the additional risk of being thought subversive. Other pagans were at least prepared to argue, and were not always unsympathetic. The *scholastikos* Antiochus questioned the doctrine of turning the other cheek, so foreign to ancient sensibilities (the same problem had bothered Volusianus). To another *scholastikos,* Ammonius, Isidore sends a copy of both the Old and the New Testament, telling him to see if they provide a better account of divine creation than the divine-birth stories of Homer and Hesiod. Ammonius later asked Isidore why Jesus rebuked the women of Jerusalem for weeping for him, and was told that those who undergo suffering deserve congratulation rather than grief. The *scholastikos* Casius praises a dictum of Demosthenes, "Money is necessary, and without it nothing that is necessary can be done." Isidore explains that Demosthenes was talking about public policy, not private conduct, and with much citation of ancient authors he justifies the Christian view that money is a source of evil, to which Casius returns a polite reply.[11]

The inquiries of these three *scholastikoi* show that the practical requirements of Christianity—nonretaliation, glorification of suffering and of poverty—were obstacles even for those well-disposed to Christianity. Another such was the rule of chastity. Nilus, a pagan *grammatikos,* receives several letters from Isidore, one of which discusses the temptation caused by looking at a beautiful woman. It is one thing to see, the monk explains, another to be stricken: that is the meaning of the "divine oracle," "Everyone who looks at a woman lustfully has already committed adultery with her in his heart." Another of his correspondents, Andromachus, receives a long letter warning him against the same temptation, with appeal to the same "oracle." Since Andromachus "admires all that is Greek," and so is either a pagan or lukewarm Christian, Isidore regales him with a story from Xenophon's *Education of Cyrus.*[12]

Certain of Isidore's pagan correspondents were in the imperial service. He addresses the *comes* Domitius (*comes* was a rank held by a variety of civil and military officeholders) as "very wise" *(sophôtatos),* and as a devotee of Plato. One letter shows that he had argued against Isidore that death as a Christian martyr was a form of defeat. His sons appear to have been divided, at least one of them being a Christian who had abandoned the family, and in a letter addressed to the pagan members Isidore predicts that "your brother by blood but ours in faith" will return, and perhaps lead them to accept the true religion. A certain Diogenes is a *magistrianus,* an official on the staff of one of the highest imperial ministers, the master of the offices *(magister officiorum),* perhaps with philosophical leanings, since Isidore addresses him as "wise" *(sophos).* Diogenes uses the Old Testament to argue against Christianity on the ground that despite Christian claims it gave no support to their doctrines.[13]

Nilus, a monk of Ancyra, is a close contemporary of Isidore about whom very little is known. He has left many fewer letters than Isidore, and though they have suffered from later tampering, they depict a similar world. The largest number of his pagan correspondents are from the educated middle class. The philosopher Aeneas continues to sacrifice sheep and calves. The *scholastikos* Hephaestus will not abandon his gods in spite of their immorality, and the sophist Chryseros continues to praise the gods in his speeches. The teacher of rhetoric *(rhêtôr)* Apollodorus maintains that the disasters befalling the empire have occurred because the gods are no longer receiving sacrifice. On the contrary, replies Nilus, God is displeased by the existence of impious demon-worshipers. (Apollodorus's argument echoes those which, about the same time, Augustine was combating in the *City of God* and Orosius in his *History against the Pagans.*) Comasius, once a *rhêtôr* and now a monk, has scandalously smuggled works of pagan literature into his cell, and Alexander, a *grammatikos* likewise turned monk, cannot give up his love of poetry.[14]

Like Isidore, Nilus has imperial officials among his correspondents. Menander, a *domestikos* (assistant-in-chief), declares, "I do not wish to leave my ancestral Hellenism." Taurianus, if his title is correctly preserved, is an ex-prefect (presumably praetorian prefect, responsible for the administration of the entire eastern empire). It appears that a group of estates managers *(phrontistai)* had taken refuge in the church of St. Plato, the patron saint of Ancyra, and with the help of a lawyer for the treasury, Laurentius, Taurianus had driven or dragged them out. When the news of this reaches the emperor's ears, so Nilus warns him, he may have to take asylum in this very church, and when that happens he will have only "Zeus' father Cronos" to pity him. This affair shows that a pagan could still hold high office in the fifth century, but could be in danger if suspected of pagan sympathies.[15]

Theodoret of Cyrrhus, one of the most important figures of fifth-century Christianity, became bishop in 423 and held office until he was deposed in the Christological turbulence of the late 440s, after which he retired to a monastery near Syrian Apamea. He is the author of the last formal refutation of paganism, the *Cure of Pagan Afflictions,* and of some 250 extant letters, as well as many doctrinal and historical works. The *Cure* is thought to be a work from early in his tenure, and its elaborate argumentation, extended over twelve separate books, shows that intellectual paganism was still very much alive. Theodoret labors to rebut many of the traditional charges such as that Christians rely on blind faith *(pistis)* without submitting their claims to logic, that they really worship three gods, not one, that they worship angels as well as their supposed gods, that their cult of martyrs' remains is revolting, and the self-denial of monks absurd. Though Theodoret is in part replying to arguments made long before by Porphyry, Julian, and others, his letters show that he prided himself on his replies to "Hellenes and Jews," and much of what he says reflects the more aggressive policies of Theodosius I and his successors. Idolatry, claims Theodoret, no longer exists, and the temples of demons have been destroyed and their altars overthrown. Pagans used to worship Asclepius openly, and if they still do so, they do so in secret. They offer libations to their dead, but at night and against the laws: in fact, "the practices of the Hellenes" *(ta Hellênôn)* are extinct. The prophet Isaiah predicted that idolaters would conceal their idols, and this has now come true. Theodoret unfolds his meaning in his *Commentary on Isaiah*. Where the prophet had said: "They shall conceal all their man-made things, carrying them into caves," he comments: "We have seen the truth of this prophecy. Very many that were in thrall to error, observing the power of piety, hid the gods they worship in grottoes and caves, but were detected; they reaped disgrace, and the children of piety handed their idols over to the flames."[16]

Theodoret's correspondents are on a higher social plane than those of Isidore and Nilus, as befits his status as a bishop and an influential theologian, and this social difference no doubt explains the rarity of pagans among his addressees. Writing to a count of the East, he expresses the wish that he would crown his other virtues with piety *(eusebeia),* but this probably means orthodoxy; in this age of intense Christological ferment, when Theodoret's own views caused his orthodoxy to be questioned, he freely brands those he considers heterodox as "impious" *(dussebeis, asebeis)*. Writing to a governor of Cyprus, he hopes to "see [his] soul illumined by the light of knowledge," but again this may mean either a conversion to orthodoxy or an acceptance of baptism. Only two of his correspondents are identifiably pagan. Consoling the philosopher Palladius, who is embroiled in a lawsuit, Theodoret cites moral maxims from Demosthenes and Thucydides as suitable for his friend, whereas he himself is "nourished on the writings of fishermen." A much grander figure is Isocasius, a sophist based in Constantinople, to whom he recommends certain local students, and sends a skilled wood carver to decorate his house. Because of his great abilities, Isocasius held a series of official posts up to that of imperial treasurer *(quaestor sacri palatii)*. In 467, after Theodoret's death, he was tried on the suspicion of being a pagan, but popular support led to his acquittal, though he was relieved of his office and obliged to receive baptism.[17]

Though Theodoret's *Cure* is the last extant work in a line that goes back several centuries, eastern Christians still felt a need to reply to the arguments of pagan intellectuals. In the late fifth century, the sophist Aeneas of

Gaza composed a dialogue entitled *Theophrastus.* This is set in Alexandria, and has two principal characters, Euxitheos, a Syrian who plans to study philosophy in Athens even though philosophy is now in decline there, and Theophrastus, an Athenian Platonist and pagan, who is visiting Alexandria, while a third character, Egyptus, provides mildly comic relief. In the first part of the dialogue, Theophrastus takes the lead, expounding a Platonic view of the soul as inhabiting many bodies in the quest for perfection. Gradually Euxitheos takes over, expounding the Christian view that the soul is created by God and inhabits only one body, in which it exists for eternity after the resurrection. Although he uses Christian terms such as the Trinity *(Trias),* the Word *(Logos),* the Spirit *(Pneuma),* Aeneas artfully contrives the whole discourse so as to maintain a philosophic, nonpartisan atmosphere, with no mention of Jesus as Christ, of the Virgin or the saints, and no allusion to the sacred texts of Christianity.[18]

A much more aggressively Christian work is the dialogue *On Creation* by Zacharias of Mytilene, a miaphysite much better known for his biography of Severus, bishop of Antioch. Like Aeneas's *Theophrastus,* this takes the form of a Platonic dialogue, with the chief speaker, evidently Zacharias himself, conversing with a friend who has recently arrived in Berytus (Beirut) to study law after a period of study with the leading Neoplatonic philosopher of Alexandria, Ammonius; he in turn was a pupil of the Neoplatonist Proclus, here characterized as "unphilosophical and unwise" *(aphilosophos kai asophos).* To counteract the effect of Alexandria on his young friend, the main speaker describes his own debates there with Ammonius and one of the most famous physicians of the day, Gessius. The dramatic date of composition is in Zacharias's own youth, since Gessius flourished in the late fifth century, and the reference to Eustathius as the bishop of Beirut also points to a date in the 480s.[19]

At the beginning, the friend confesses that, though a Christian, he has been swayed by the arguments of Ammonius concerning the creation of the world. This was one of the most vexed questions in the debate between pagan philosophers of Late Antiquity and philosophically minded Christians. The starting point was Plato's account of creation in the *Timaeus,* already subject to divergent interpretations among his followers. Whereas followers of Plato and Aristotle held that the material universe was coexistent and coeternal with God, since the "Artificer" *(Dêmiourgos)* had not created matter out of nothing but only given it intelligible form, Christians held both that it was created and, as a necessary corollary, that it must also be perishable.

To rescue him from the dangerous influence of Ammonius, the main speaker leads his friend into the magnificent church recently built by Eustathius, and there recounts his own debates with Ammonius and Gessius. The first took place in high summer in Ammonius's lecture hall, with the west wind blowing softly and the Nile flowing in spate, while the teacher, "like an oracle-interpreter, described and expounded the wisdom of Aristotle and the beginning of existing things, sitting very sophistically and solemnly on a high platform *(bêma)*." The first day's subjects were the beauty of the world and the question whether God could have made such a beautiful creation only to let it perish. At first, Ammonius presses the narrator, and seems to have the advantage, but the narrator gradually starts to prevail, so that by the end of the first day many of those who before believed Plato and Aristotle now accept the Christian view (though Ammonius remains unconvinced). On the second day, Gessius, "who now claims the wisdom of Hippocrates of Cos and of Galen of Pergamon, and is enthroned beside the Nile as the teacher of philosophers interested in medicine," takes up the cause. He leads the narrator by the hand to the Shrine of the Muses, and they turn to the subject of the Artificer *(Dêmiourgos)* and his role in Creation. As on the first day, the narrator steadily gains the upper hand, and Gessius ends by assenting to his argument, though he is not said to have become a convert to Christianity. The third day's discussion again pits the narrator against Ammonius, and the subject is the eternity of the world. Just as on the second day and in the same words, Ammonius assents to the other's argument, though he too is not said to be converted. The two then turn to the subject of the Trinity, and, surprisingly, Ammonius acknowledges the author's own view that God exists in three persons *(hypostases)* but one nature *(physis)*. At this "the assembly of listeners gave a great shout of praise, with a certain pleasure and gratitude . . . but he (Ammonius) gave a bitter smile with a slight blush, fell silent, and began on another subject." The work ends with the narrator and his friend again in conversation. The friend is not yet satisfied, but wants more clarification on points that occurred in the central narrative, and when these have been settled, the two pray to the Maker and Artificer of the Universe.[20]

It is unclear how far this work is historical, especially since it represents an apparently young Zacharias as he defeats one of the leading Neoplatonists of the day in argument and persuades him to accept his own beliefs. The schoolrooms of Late Antique philosophers were lively, and students could bombard their teachers with questions and objections, as a pupil of Plutarch of Athens is said to have "filled the teacher's lessons with problems, and prevented the argument from proceeding because of the interruption." Even if the work does not report actual encounters in Ammonius's schoolroom, it shows how pagan thinkers continued to resist the doctrines of Christianity, and how Christian writers still felt the need to counteract the influence of such unbelievers on their Christian listeners.[21]

An unidentified author took the mask of Dionysius, the member of the Athenian Areopagus who had lent a sympathetic ear to Paul's preaching, and in this guise he wrote a series of works that bridged Neoplatonism and Christianity. The real author has been suspected to be none other than Zacharias of Mitylene's friend, Severus of Antioch. Just as debate with pagan intellectuals helped to refine Christian arguments about questions such as the person of Christ, so Christians gained access to Plato and Aristotle through their pagan interpreters of Late Antiquity such as Proclus. In the West, Boethius had a similar role in bringing Plato and Aristotle into the Middle Ages, and his *Consolation of Philosophy* is famously free from any overt trace of Christianity. Though the debate between pagans and Christians ended with the victory of the Christians, it was a victory by absorption rather than by conquest.[22]

CHAPTER EIGHT

Conversion

It was a fundamental duty of Christians to bring outsiders, both Jew and gentile, into the "way" of the community. According to Mark, Jesus's last injunction to his disciples was: "Go forth to every part of the world, and proclaim the Good News [*euangelion*] to the whole creation. Those who believe it and receive baptism will find salvation; those who do not believe will be condemned." Similarly Matthew, except that in his account Jesus orders the disciples to baptize "in the name of the Father and the Son and the Holy Spirit." Acts shows Peter, Paul, and other disciples carrying out this mission, traveling, persuading, baptizing, and creating many "believers" *(pepisteukotes)* or "learners" *(mathêtai)*. The author of Acts describes this spiritual change as a "turning" *(epistrephô, epistrophê)*: "a large number that had believed turned to the Lord," "those of the gentiles who had turned to God," "the turning of the gentiles." Paul similarly claims that Jesus ordered him "to open the eyes of the gentiles and turn them from darkness to light." From these expressions, rendered in Latin by *converto, conversio*, comes the modern term "conversion."[1]

As already the first Christian writings indicate, conversion could take many forms, including both verbal persuasion and what is commonly translated as "miracle," though the texts more often use the expression "sign" *(sêmeion)* or "(act of) power" *(dynamis)*. Yet even in this heroic age of early Christianity, outsiders can express interest without committing themselves to full belief. So it is with Paul in Athens. After inviting him to explain his doctrine, some of his audience "scoffed," some promised to hear more later, "but some joined him and became believers." When Paul has made his defense before the tetrarch Agrippa, Agrippa tells him, probably speaking in irony, "In a short time you are persuading me to play the Christian."[2]

Between the first century and the age of Constantine, the Christian community devised a series of steps to ensure that those who received the essential sign of full admission, baptism, were properly prepared by instruction or "catechism" *(catêchismos)*. In the so-called *Second Epistle of Clement,* actually a very early Christian sermon, the preacher says: "Let us then repent with our whole heart. For if we have orders also to do this, to tear (people) away from idols and instruct them *(katêchein),* how much more must a soul that already knows God not perish?" "Catechism" was not necessary only for pagans, but was an essential step for all Christians, though baptism without catechism was permitted for children in danger of death and adults approaching death while still catechumens. Some such as Constantine delayed baptism until late in life in order to die in a state of grace. By the late fourth century, the rules for "instruction" and for the ritual of baptism had become very elaborate, and late baptisms had fallen into disfavor.[3]

The *Confessions* of Augustine, bishop of Hippo, written in the last decade of the same century, give a rich account of the conversion of a highly educated and reflective thinker, and also of the conversion of his father and of others whom he knew personally or by repute. Augustine's father, Patricius, was firmly pagan and his mother, Monica, a devoutly orthodox Christian who was to prove decisive in her son's final return to Christianity. While still a boy, he fell dangerously ill, so that Monica, expecting his early death, arranged for him to receive instruction and baptism, but he recovered and the "cleansing" was delayed. In a famous passage, he describes how his reading of Cicero's *Hortensius* at the age of eighteen fired him with a desire to study the Scriptures critically, but this enthusiasm led him away from the seeming deficiencies of Christianity, and he underwent a first conversion to Manichaeism. Devised a century earlier by the Mesopotamian Mani, this was a mixture of stark dualism and Christianity, and at first it seemed to satisfy Augustine's needs, until after some ten years his confidence in it began to wane. This was in part due to his Christian education, always powerfully seconded by Monica's prayers and example, but also to his own intellectual restlessness, which led him first to Neoplatonic and then to Christian literature, and eventually to the preaching of Ambrose, the eloquent bishop of Milan. This finally broke his faith in Manichaeism, and he decided "to become a catechumen in the Catholic church which my parents had recommended to me, until something certain should appear to which I could direct my course." He did not give up his worldly career as a teacher of rhetoric until one summer when, after the end of the teaching term, he and his friend Alypius went to Cassiciacum, a country estate near Milan lent them by a certain Verecundus, who was then in Rome. A famous passage of the *Confessions* describes how a mysterious voice from a neighboring garden told him to "Pick up and read" *(tolle, lege),* whereupon he opened a passage of Paul's Epistle to the Romans, his eyes were opened, and he was baptized together with Alypius and his own illegitimate son Adeodatus. His "conversion" was now complete.[4]

Though not a convert from paganism, Augustine illustrates a form of conversion that resembles modern ones such as that of John Henry Newman—an intellectual quest which leads the seeker through various systems before he finally reaches a safe haven. Such intellectual conversions are claimed by Christian apologists of the second century such as Justin Martyr, and Augustine describes a similar conversion of the scholar Marius Victorinus in the reign of Constantius. This "most learned old man, most familiar with all liberal studies, who had read and weighed so many writings of the philosophers, the teacher of so many noble senators," had remained until his old age "a worshiper of idols, a participant in sacrilegious rites, by which at that time almost all the Roman nobility was puffed up." After reading through "all the writings of the Christians," he told his friend Simplicianus, later to be Ambrose's successor as bishop of Milan, that he was now a Christian. Simplicianus replied that he would not consider him as such until he saw him in the Church of Christ. Afraid of the reaction of his pagan friends, the old man replied ironically, "Do then walls make Christians?" Nonetheless, he finally agreed to receive "the first sacraments of instruction" (that is, a preliminary course of Christian knowledge, imparted to catechumens before baptism) and then gave in his name for baptism. Though the priests offered to let him make his declaration of faith privately, he did so before the whole congregation. This conversion Augustine in some ways took as a model for his own.[5]

Nonetheless, Augustine's was not the only or indeed the usual form of conversion. Throughout the *Confessions,* he emphasizes the influence of his mother, Monica, who from the very beginning had watched over his religious development. Such family influences probably led as much or more to individual conversions than the internal voyages of intellectuals like Victorinus and Augustine. Augustine's father, Patricius, who had been a staunch pagan as well as an unfaithful husband, finally became a catechumen, and Monica "won" him *(lucrata est)* for God, presumably by his baptism, "at the very end of his temporal life" *(in extrema uita temporali)*. Augustine records a similar late conversion in his friend Verecundus, who had lent him the use of his country house near Milan. Like Augustine's parents, he was a pagan married to a Christian, and received baptism only after falling mortally ill.[6]

A comparable instance at a loftier social level is the death-bed conversion of the Roman aristocrat Volusianus. As a high official of the western court, he came to Constantinople in 436 to arrange a marriage between the eastern princess Eudoxia and the young western emperor Valentinian III. He was a pagan *(Hellên)*, and on hearing of his mission, his Christian niece Melania left her retreat in Jerusalem to meet him. In the capital she found her uncle dangerously ill, and begged him to "approach the bath of immortality [baptism], so that just as you enjoyed temporal goods you may win the eternal ones also." As a great Christian benefactress, Melania was able to induce the patriarch Proclus to add his persuasion, and after talking with him, Volusianus declared, "If Rome had three men such as Proclus, there would be no pagans there." Sometime later came the news that Volusianus was in danger of dying while still a catechumen, whereupon Melania, though suffering from an illness caused by the Devil, went to the palace, where she found that he had now been "illuminated," or baptized. Miraculously cured of her own affliction, she was able to converse with her uncle and induce him to take communion before he died the next day.[7]

Pagans often characterized Christianity as a religion for women and children, and though women often appear as vectors of Christianity into their families, men sometimes take this role. Again, Augustine gives the example of his close friend Nebridius, long inclined to a heretical Christianity which held that the visible Christ was only an apparition *(phantasma)*. Soon after Augustine's baptism, he too turned orthodox, returned to Africa, and there converted his entire household before his early death. Augustine's tribute to him is one of the most moving passages of the *Confessions*.[8]

Describing the effect on him of Ambrose's preaching, Augustine says that he had come merely to hear the words, and was gradually drawn to pay attention to the sense, so that he was inspired to enroll as a catechumen.

Conversion by "the word" had been one of the commands laid on the disciples by the risen Jesus, and the Acts gives many examples, for instance, the Ethiopian eunuch converted by Philip's exposition of Scripture and immediately baptized. A prime example of such conversion is given by Gregory of Nyssa's *Life of Gregory the Miracle-Worker* ("Thaumaturge"), bishop of Neocaesarea in eastern Pontus in the mid-third century. The senior bishop of the region, Phaedimos of Amasia, appointed Gregory bishop of Neocaesarea, which then counted only seventeen Christians within its borders. As he approached his see, he found that "the whole region was subject to the deceptions of demons, a true church of God had nowhere been built, and the city and the surrounding countryside were full of altars, shrines and idols, since the whole province had only this concern—to beautify the sanctuaries and shrines of idols, and to maintain the general idolatry, fortifying it with processions, rites and abominable sacrifice." Among these temples was one in which "the demons who were worshiped there used to appear and approach the priests and the temple-wardens." In the first of his miracles, Gregory proved his power to command these demons, whereupon the chief priest was converted to Christianity, left all his relatives and possessions, and became Gregory's faithful assistant. On the new bishop's very first day in the city, "so many came to meet him that the number of believers were sufficient for a congregation." On the next day, "many came with their wives and children, and also the elderly, and all who because of outrages committed by demons or for some other cause had some physical injury; and standing in their midst he distributed for each of those who had gathered a remedy in accordance with the Holy Spirit, preaching, disputing, admonishing, teaching, curing." The biographer goes on to praise the extraordinary effect of Gregory's preaching: "he won over to himself so many with the collaboration of the Spirit that they longed to build a church, everyone seconding their zeal with their money and their bodies." The construction was so solid that when an earthquake struck a century later it was the only building left standing. When Gregory was near his end, he made a tour of the surrounding region to learn if there were still any unbelievers, and found only seventeen, the same number as there had been Christians when he first entered on his mission.[9]

This account of Gregory illustrates a form of conversion that was probably far more usual than the slow and painful conversion of an Augustine—the performance of medical cures that, given the state of medical knowledge in antiquity, could readily seem like miracles. Curative miracles are frequent in the accounts of Jesus and the apostles, and even Augustine's conversion was aided by the miraculous cure of a bad toothache. About the middle of the fourth century, a monk named Hilarion converted a family of a certain Alaphion, which two generations later was to produce the church historian Sozomen. "When this Alaphion had been possessed by a demon, for a long time Hellenes and Jews had no success using certain spells and enchantments, but (Hilarion), merely by shouting the name of Christ, drove away the demon, and (the families) went over to the Christian religion." Jerome wrote a novelistic life of this same Hilarion, in which he records a similar cure. When the three children of the high official Helpidios, a Christian, fell ill with malaria, Hilarion cured them merely by invoking the name of Jesus. "When this became known, and the news of it spread further and further, there was an eager rush to him from Egypt into Syria, so that many believed in Christ, and professed themselves monks."[10]

In the West, Martin of Tours is another churchman with powers of healing. Though Sulpicius Severus's classic hagiography contains minor faults of chronology, it still gives a vivid picture of rural life in what is now northwestern Gaul of the later fourth century. Of the several cures that Sulpicius mentions, only one brings about a conversion. "A certain proconsular" named Taetradius had a slave possessed by a demon, and invites Martin home in order to perform an exorcism. Martin declares that he cannot enter a pagan house, but Taetradius promises that he will become Christian if the bishop cures the slave. He does so, Taetradius "believes in the Lord Christ," immediately becomes a catechumen, and is baptized not long after.[11]

In Augustine's account of the conversion of Victorinus, his friend Simplicianus told him that he would not consider him a Christian until he saw him within a church. Attendance at church was the visible affirmation of the Christian's faith, since it was strengthened there by ritual, instruction, and prayer. The peasants converted by Gregory the Miracle-Worker and Martin of Tours might be momentarily dazzled by an apparent near-miss or a seemingly miraculous cure, but organization was needed to keep the flock together and to prevent straying. Hence the emphasis laid by hagiographers on the construction of churches, such as that of Neocaesarea which even a strong earthquake could not bring down.

The counterpart and the concomitant of this constructive activity is the demolition or deconsecration of pagan buildings, sometimes accompanied by their "conversion" into Christian ones, and several texts show that such acts were considered essential for effecting a spiritual conversion of pagans. Constantine had led the way with the destruction of a temple built on the site of the Holy Sepulcher.[12] According to his biographer, Martin was elected bishop of Tours by an enthusiastic populace, and immediately began to exhibit his "virtues" *(uirtutes),* a term that signifies both moral virtues and miraculous powers given by God. In obedience to the biblical injunction, "Destroy their altars, smash their statues, and cut down their groves," he demolished a "very ancient" village shrine and set about cutting down a sacred pine tree growing nearby. One of the bolder peasants challenged him to show the power of his God by standing near the tree while the peasants undertook to cut it down. When the tree miraculously missed the bishop, "there was scarcely anyone in this huge crowd of pagans who did not request the laying on of hands and believe in the Lord Jesus, abandoning their impious error. Truly before that time there had been very few, indeed almost none, in those regions who had accepted the Name of Christ. This indeed grew so strong through his miracles *(uirtutes)* and example that there is now nowhere there that is not full of very crowded churches or monasteries. For where he had destroyed shrines, there he immediately built either churches or monasteries." When Martin began to destroy a "very rich temple" in a village named Levrosum (Levroux), he was driven off with violence. After three days of prayer, he had a vision of two angels who promised to help him in his work. He returned to the village, "and while the crowds of pagans watched him without moving, he reduced all the altars and images to ashes. Seeing this, almost all the peasants . . . believed in the Lord Jesus, shouting aloud and confessing that the God of Martin was to be worshiped, but their idols were to be neglected, since they could not help them." "In general," concludes the biographer, "when the peasants fought to prevent his destroying their shrines, he so softened their pagan minds with his holy preaching that they destroyed their temples with their own hands, once they had been shown the light of truth."[13]

Marcellus, bishop of Syrian Apamea under Theodosius, was not so lucky. "Considering that there was no way of easily converting (pagans) from their previous worship, he overturned the temples in the city and villages. Learning however that there was a very large temple in Aulon (this is a region in the territory of Apamea), he went there taking some soldiers and gladiators. After getting near, he stayed out of range, since he was gouty and could neither fight, pursue or run away. While the soldiers and the gladiators were busy seizing the temple, certain of the pagans, learning that he had been left alone, made a sally from the only part of the place where there was no fighting. Catching him unawares and seizing him, they killed him by throwing him on a bonfire."[14]

Greater success was enjoyed by Theophilus, the bishop of Alexandria, when he destroyed the city's chief temple, the Serapeum, in 391. This event came to be regarded as a turning point both by pagans and by Christians. Eunapius compared it to the victories of the giants in myth, while Christians saw it as marking the "destruction of demonic shrines everywhere on land and sea." The account closest in time and fullest in detail is by Rufinus of Aquileia, who was in Jerusalem when the riots took place. The Arian Constantius had given a basilica to the bishop for worship, and Theophilus, presumably taking advantage of Theodosius's recent measures against pagans and Arians, claimed the building for the orthodox church. With the backing of the prefect Evagrius and the count Romanus, Theophilus was able to uncover "certain hidden caves dug in the ground, more suited to banditry and crime than to ritual" (this may have been a temple of Mithras, who was usually worshiped in spaces constructed underground). The discovery led to rioting between Christians and pagans, in the course of which the pagans barricaded themselves inside the Serapeum. Early in the disturbances, the authorities had obtained a ruling from the emperor Theodosius which, though outwardly conciliatory, favored the Christian side, and the public reading of this became the signal for the authorities to act. The pagans were driven out, and the Christians entered the abandoned temple. The sequel is memorably recounted by Gibbon, who closely follows Rufinus:

> An intrepid soldier, animated by zeal, and armed with a weighty battle-axe, ascended the ladder; and even the Christian multitude expected, with some anxiety, the event of the combat. He aimed a vigorous stroke against the cheek of Serapis; the cheek fell to the ground; the thunder was still silent, and both the heavens and the earth continued to preserve their accustomed order and tranquillity. The victorious soldier repeated his blows: the huge idol was overthrown, and broken in pieces; and the limbs of Serapis were ignominiously dragged through the streets of Alexandria. His mangled carcase was burnt in the Amphitheatre, amidst the shouts of the populace; and many persons attributed their conversion to this discovery of the impotence of their tutelar deity.[15]

The destruction of Serapis's statue was followed by a number of other measures designed not only to abolish the cult but to Christianize everything associated with it. Within the temple enclosure, the main temple was demolished, while on the west, Theophilus built a martyr's shrine *(martyrion)* in honor of John the Baptist and a church beside it named for the emperor Arcadius. Within the city, many of the houses had been decorated with what were called "Serapis's breastplates" in the form of the hieroglyphic *ankh,* which Egyptian priests converted to Christianity explained as meaning "life" (the *ankh* subsequently evolved into what is now the "Coptic Cross"). In consequence, according to Rufinus, "those who had been priests or ministers of temples were even more converted to the faith than those who had taken pleasure in the tricks of error and the engines of deception." Similarly, the Nilometer or "cubit" *(pêchys)* that had been stored in the temple of Serapis was transferred to "the Lord of Waters" and became the property of the Church. Just as no cosmic disaster had followed the destruction of Serapis's idol, so the Nile flooded with exceptional abundance in the following year. Theophilus next carried his campaign to Canopus, a town lying about ten miles east of Alexandria, where the chief god was again Serapis. Here "everything was laid waste and razed to the ground."[16]

After the destruction of the Alexandrian Serapeum, claims Rufinus, "all the temples of whatever demon fell down to the last column. Through all the cities of Egypt, through forts, villages, the whole countryside, the riverbanks, even in the desert, if any shrines (or rather sepulchers) could be found, they were overthrown on the authority of the appropriate bishop, and brought to the ground, so that the countryside that had been unjustly assigned to demons was once more returned to cultivation." This claim is unduly optimistic. In the following century, pagan cults flourished underground in Alexandria and in Menouthis, close to Canopus, and more openly in Upper Egypt. As often, it was in the cities that Christianity could be implanted by the action of religious and secular authorities. In these, a diminishing, mostly educated class managed to maintain its cults in private, while in the countryside a conservative peasantry either clung to its old ways or made an uneasy compromise with the new faith.[17]

These conversions of buildings had their analogue in the conversion of pagan rituals to Christian ones. Gregory of Nyssa's account of Gregory the Miracle-Worker provides an early example. Gregory "allowed his subjects to frolic a little in good cheer beneath the yoke of faith. He saw that the simple and uneducated crowd persisted in the error of idolatry because of bodily pleasures, and so, as the best way of correcting what was still their predominant inclination, he permitted them to celebrate, enjoy themselves, and relax in their commemorations of the martyrs. In this way their lives would spontaneously be changed so as to become more solemn and devout, and as their faith led them there, all their enjoyment should be converted from the pleasures of the body to the spiritual form of pleasure."[18]

These rowdy celebrations of martyrs were to cause much anxiety to later churchmen. In 395, Augustine recounts to his old friend Alypius a sermon that he had recently preached in Thagaste on the "birthday" of a previous bishop ("birthday" signified for Christians of this period the day of a person's death and his entry into heaven). He had told the congregation that, after the end of persecution, crowds of gentiles wanted to come over to the new faith, but were unwilling to give up their old habit of feasting in honor of their idols. "So our predecessors thought it good to make concession for the time being to those weaker brethren, and to let them celebrate in honor of the holy martyrs other feast-days, in place of those they were giving up, unlike them at least in profanation, though like them in excess." It was now time for Christians to "put behind them the concessions made to induce them to become Christian." A second Augustine, Pope Gregory's missionary to England, received permission to reconcile newly converted pagans to the faith by just such concessions. He was instructed to preserve their sanctuaries and even their feasts in honor of the old gods, but to transfer their allegiance to the church and its saints.[19]

These practices drew the notice of unfriendly critics. One of Augustine of Hippo's adversaries, the Manichaean bishop Faustus of Milevis, asserted: "You have turned the sacrifices of (Gentiles) into eucharistic feasts *(agapes)* and idols into martyrs, whom you worship with similar prayers. You appease the shades of the dead with wine and feasting. You celebrate the customary days of the gentiles together with them, such as the first days of the month *(kalendae)* and the solstices. You certainly have changed nothing of their way of life." By *kalendae,* Faustus means January 1, a customary pagan holiday, which Christians continued to observe with the traditional gifts of presents *(strenae),* though church officials preached against the practice. As for solstices, the Council of Nicaea, borrowing from Jewish custom, had fixed the main feast of the Christian year, Easter, on the Sunday after the full moon following the spring equinox, and in due course the feast of Christmas, hitherto unfixed, was made to coincide with the winter solstice.[20]

According to the historian Sozomen, Constantine's destruction of pagan shrines such as that of Asclepius at Aegeae had a triple effect on contemporary pagans: "Some seeing objects that were previously venerable and fearful thrown carelessly down, and filled with straw and rubbish, became contemptuous of their previous objects of worship and blamed their forebears for their error. Others envied Christians for the honor shown them by the emperor and deemed it necessary to imitate the customs of the ruler. Others applied themselves to studying doctrine and by means of signs, dreams, or contact with monks and bishops, decided that it was better to turn Christian." All three of these motives may well have operated with different weight according to time, place, and social level, though their strength relative to each other is impossible to measure. No doubt some pagans were moved by the powerlessness of Serapis to defend his idol and his shrine in Alexandria, all the more if there was a belief that the security of the universe depended on the idol's preservation. Sozomen's second motive—the social motive of complying with the ruler's religion—must have become especially powerful as Christians gradually replaced pagans in the higher ranks of administration.[21]

Christian emperors could use the promise of promotion as an inducement when dealing with communities as well as with individuals. While Gaza remained stubbornly pagan, its port of Maiouma, which before the reign of Constantine had also been "very superstitious," converted en masse to Christianity. In compensation, the emperor detached it from Gaza and raised it to the rank of a city, giving it the name of Constantia after his son Constantius. The inevitable effect was to decrease the revenues of Gaza, now deprived of harbor dues and other sources of income. Yet the city was to remain a stronghold of paganism until the end of the fourth century, and when the new bishop Porphyrius arrived there in 394, there were few believers, though in the fifth century it became an important center of the faith.[22]

A similar evolution is visible in the largely Christian community of Orcistos in Phrygia. Soon after Constantine's victory over Licinius in 324, the town petitioned Constantine to be detached from the nearby Nacoleia, of which it had hitherto been a dependency. In granting the request, the emperor noted Orcistos's natural advantages, lying at a junction of four roads, well supplied with water and public amenities, and "to all these is added as a kind of capstone that all who live there are reported to be followers of the most sacred religion." The official whom the emperor appointed to carry out these measures was Flavius Ablabius, at this time *vicarius* of the province of Asia. He was an ardent Christian, later to be consul and praetorian prefect, and one of Constantine's most influential ministers, in which position he overthrew the pagan philosopher Sopater.[23]

The letters of Gregory the Great, pope from 590 to 604, that concern Augustine's mission to Anglia provide a unique window on the mechanics of conversion. They show in various permutations the use of local rulers to promote the conversion of their subjects, the spread of the faith by means of a growing organization, and the physical conversion of pagan buildings into churches. Despite the abandonment of Britain by the Romans about 410 and its occupation by pagan Angles and Saxons, Christianity had not died out, but was much weaker than it had been in the fourth century. Gregory appears to have conceived the plan of reconverting the kingdom about 596. He was disturbed that "the nation of the Angles, situated in a corner of the world, has remained up to now in thrall to tree-trunks and stones." The Angles desired Christianity, so he believed, but the "priests in the vicinity" (meaning Ireland) ignored them. He therefore decided to send Augustine, at that time a monk in Rome, to carry out the mission. To secure his passage through the various kingdoms into which Francia was now divided, he wrote to several of the local rulers, including the powerful queen Brunigild. After setting out in 597, Augustine at first turned back in dismay, but eventually arrived at his destination. By July 598, the pope was able to tell his colleague, the patriarch of Alexandria, that at the previous Christmas more than ten thousand Angles had accepted baptism. As later letters show, Gregory placed his hopes on the Anglian queen Berta, a Christian and a Frank, whose husband, Aethelbert king of Kent, was still pagan. As late as 601, Gregory had to prompt her to make Aethelbert support Augustine's efforts, promising that she would be a new Helena, who similarly influenced her husband, Constantine. To Aethelbert himself he writes urging him to bring his subjects to the faith, to persecute idolatry, and destroy pagan idols; he for his part will be a new Constantine, and if that consideration were not enough, he should reflect that the end of the world was near. Apparently afraid that Augustine's methods might be too drastic, Gregory asks a trusted intermediary, the abbot Mellitus, to tell him not to destroy the shrines, but only their idols. As pagans, the Angles were used to sacrificing cattle to their gods; now they should slaughter their cattle to celebrate the dedication of a church or the "birthday" in heaven of a saint, and hold their feasts in temporary sanctuaries built with branches.[24]

Though missionaries had gone beyond the borders of the empire for centuries, as Frumentius to Ethiopia, or Christian captives or slaves had spread "the word," as Nino had in Georgia and Patrick in Ireland, the mission of Augustine represents a new situation in the West. The church could exercise its temporal influence to extend Christianity into new regions, which were more receptive than Persia, soon about to fall to the Arabs, and certainly more receptive than the Arabs, once they began to carry their own new faith into the empire ruled from Constantinople. Paganism was far from extinct. Druidism survived in Ireland, for instance, until the eighth century. But a Christian Europe, "Christendom," was beginning to take shape in the old Roman West, while what had once been the Roman East began to shrink as it was absorbed into an empire ruled from Damascus, Baghdad, and finally Constantinople, now with the new name of Istanbul.[25]

The mass conversion of unlettered Anglian peasants contrasts sharply with the philosophic conversions of an Augustine or a Nebridius, and prompts the question of the psychological change that conversion meant, at least for the vast majority who have left no record, or none beyond a simple epitaph. These converts can hardly have delved deep into theological debates, such as whether the universe was eternal or whether Christ had one or two natures or one or two wills. In cities where Christianity was deeply rooted and eloquent theologians preached, there may perhaps have been a high level of religious knowledge, or at least of doctrinal partisanship. Toward the end of his reign, the emperor Anastasius added the phrase "Who was crucified for us" to the *trishagion,* the liturgical invocation "Holy god, Holy and Strong, Holy and Immortal." This innovation caused a riot so violent that the emperor was forced to offer his resignation to the people. Yet preachers addressing rustic congregations, such as Maximus of Turin and Caesarius of Arles, are concerned with the everyday morals of their flock and not with abstract speculation.[26]

There must still have been marked psychological adjustments, even if they took place over time. Perhaps the most profound, and most easily comprehensible for the newly converted, was the notion of sin, and its related notions of "redemption," "salvation," and "forgiveness of sins," with their implications for the fate of the soul after death. Sin had no precise analogue in pagan thought, even though in Greek the same word, *hamartia,* and in Latin *peccatum,* is used by pagans and Christians in similar ways. Greeks and Romans believed that the gods were just, and punished infringements of a generally understood moral law, but could be placated when the transgressor or others acting on his behalf righted the wrong. In the first book of the *Iliad*, Agamemnon reluctantly agrees to appease the wrath of Apollo by returning the captive Briseis to her father and offering the god sacrifice; entrusting her to his followers to return her, he tells them to wash in seawater after completing their mission and then to sacrifice. Washing was necessary to avoid the sacrilege of approaching a god in a state of pollution *(miasma),* which could occur with or without conscious intent. Apollo forgives Agamemnon by revoking the punishment, and yet forgiveness is not gratuitous, but requires prior appeasement.[27]

A similar nexus of ideas is visible in certain inscriptions from western Anatolia that extend in date from the mid-second to the mid-third century, the formative period of Christianity. They have been called "confession-inscriptions" *(Beichtinschriften),* and their language has many points of contact with the Greek of contemporary Christians, though they show no influence of the new religion.[28] In these, the writer declares, often in cryptic language, that he, she, or someone else has committed a moral infraction, using the same group of words *(hamartanô, hamartia, hamartêma)* used by Christians for "sin." Though there are many variations, the usual pattern is that the "confessor" describes the "sin" and the punishment (often by a disease of the eyes), declares that he has "confessed" by "writing the inscription" *(stêlographein)*, and blesses the god or gods. One example runs: "Great is Meix [a form of the name of the moon-god Mên] Aziottênos ruling in Tarsis. Since a scepter [a symbol of the god's status as judge, and so in effect a warning against infractions] had been set up if anyone stole anything from the bath-house, and an item of clothing was stolen, the god punished the thief and made him bring back the item after a time to the god, and he confessed. The god then ordered by a messenger *(angelos)* that the item be sold and that his powers be recorded on a stele." The confession is made by the guilty party, but not by the persons setting up the inscription, who are perhaps the priests of the sanctuary acting on the advice of a dream-messenger. There is no implication that the thief's confession absolves him: on the contrary, several of the inscriptions state that the god "did away with" *(apetelesato)* the transgressor, or brought illness or death on him or an innocent party. The announced purpose of setting up the inscription is not to announce the writer's repentance, but to manifest the god's powers and to give him thanks.[29]

Christianity, by contrast, introduced the idea that God had an "only-begotten" Son, whom he sent to "take away the sins of the world," allowing him to suffer the indignity of dying like a common criminal—what Paul called "the offense *(skandalon)* of the cross." During His time on earth, the Son appointed his disciple Peter as the "rock" *(petra)* on which he would found his community *(ecclêsia)*, telling him: "What you bind on earth shall be bound in the heavens, and what you set free on earth shall be set free in the heavens." The idea that God himself wished to "save" humanity from sin, and that an institution set up on earth by God's own son could forgive sin, was a radical departure from the idea that a human could escape divine wrath only by sacrifice and other means of appeasement.[30]

The chief mechanism whereby the penitent achieved such release from sin, in fact a rebirth into Christian life, resembled pagan rites of purification in that it involved washing with water, but in Christianity this became a very elaborate ritual that normally required years of instruction ("catechism"). At the end of this process, the catechumen did not merely wash himself, but was "bathed" *(baptizesthai)* by an official of the Church. Baptism was a *rite de passage* of crucial importance in the Christian life. Its origin lay in the Jewish *mikveh*, the bath of clean water making the subject ritually clean. John the "Baptist" used the waters of the Jordan for this purpose, and Jesus's baptism, when God the Father and the Spirit became manifest in the first appearance of the Trinity, was regarded as exemplary for all Christians, so that some held that by this act Jesus had consecrated all the waters of the earth. The surviving baptisteries of Late Antique Christianity vary in design, and while some of them are no more than large tubs, others have ten steps or more leading down into the purifying water. It is not surprising that the ceremony could be thought of as having a quasi-magical effect, and that some delayed it until the last moment in order to die with their sins washed away (plate 5).[31]

No less radical a psychological change was necessary for a pagan to grasp the new meaning of death that conversion opened for him. Educated

PLATE 5
Baptismal font, Dura-Europos, Syria, mid-third century.
Yale University Art Gallery, Dura-Europos Collection

Greeks and Romans were used to the idea that the soul survived death and underwent judgment by the gods of the underworld, though such conceptions were far from universal. The pagan dead could return as ghosts, haunt houses, rattle their chains, but they returned as phantoms, not as flesh and blood (some Christians such as Augustine's friend Nebridius also held that the crucified Christ was a phantom). A sophisticate such as Philostratus of Athens in his biography of Apollonius of Tyana could play with the Pythagorean notion of metempsychosis, whereby one person's soul entered another's body and retained the memory of its former life. The same author depicts the Trojan hero Protesilaos befriending a vine grower who cultivates the soil around the hero's tomb. Such extensions of ordinary life could be called "revivification" *(anabiôsis),* but fell short of "resurrection" *(anastasis),* whereby the dead retained their identity in their transformed body. This idea, taken over by Christianity from one school of contemporary Judaism, continued to baffle pagan observers. The many thousands of simple tombstones that survive with such texts as "May you sleep in peace" *(requiescas in pace, en eirêne hê koimêsis sou)* represent something wholly new, a transformed notion of the meaning of life and death.[32]

CHAPTER NINE

The West

IN ITALY, the heart of the old Roman Empire, the later history of paganism runs very differently from its history in the East, where the New Rome survived until 1453. In the East, Hellenism continued to draw its strength from Greek literature, art, and philosophy, and from religious traditions that were still vigorous in urban centers such as Athens, Heliopolis, and Carrhae. In the West, Rome was the repository of the national religion, though Etruria maintained some of its ancient power as a source of ritual, particularly in matters of divination. Yet Rome had long since become a cauldron of the many cults brought by immigrants, including Christians: one of Paul's most important letters is directed to the Christian community there, and the western church in Rome as in other centers such as Lugdunum (Lyon) remained largely Greek-speaking well into the second century. By the fourth century, traditional Roman religion was centered on the senatorial class of Rome, though certain great senators such as Praetextatus included in their worship imported gods such as the eastern Mithras. Though this aristocracy became Christianized in the course of the fifth century, at a lower social level, and especially in what had been the provinces, local cults persisted into the Middle Ages.

The fourth-century orator and philosopher Themistius illustrates the contrast of East and West. Whereas his contemporary Libanius disliked the new Rome founded by Constantine on the Bosporus, Themistius spent most of his life there as a teacher, imperial servant, and senatorial ambassador. Most of his extant works are addresses to emperors, from Constantius down to Theodosius. In these, he maintains a discreet, Hellenically tinged monotheism, referring usually only to a single god either simply as "god" *(ho theos)* or as Zeus, and naming Zeus sometimes directly, at other times by means of his traditional epithets such as "Zeus of kingship" *(basileios)* and "Zeus of friendship" *(philios)*. He compares imperial tolerance of diverse beliefs to a "competition of piety" in which God presides as president and prize-giver *(athlothetês):* "Just as in the presence of the same prize-giver all the runners race, not all of them along the same course, but one runs from this direction and the other from that—so too you suppose that there is one great and true prize-giver, but that more than one path leads to him, this more crooked and that more straight, this rough and that smooth, but yet all of them leading to the same goal." Unusually for a pagan writer, Themistius cites Scripture, comparing Hesiod's saying "From Zeus come kings" with something he has heard of in "Assyrian writings," "The mind of the king is carried in God's hand," which he cites from Proverbs no fewer than three times.[1]

While on embassy from the eastern Senate to Rome in 376, Themistius delivered a speech before the Roman Senate as it awaited the arrival of the seventeen-year-old emperor Gratian, and here he speaks as an overt polytheist, in sharp contrast with his language before emperors. Curiously, this *Speech of Love (Erôtikos)* addresses the young emperor as the speaker's beloved, and toward the end, Themistius turns to the senators: "Because of you, you blessed ones, the gods have not yet left the earth, and it is you who have hitherto prevented a complete rupture between mortal and immortal nature." Even if this is not a glance at the Christian doctrine of the Incarnation, whereby the Word "took flesh and dwelt among us," still the strongly pagan tone would not have sounded well in Constantinople. Themistius urges the Senate to dress in white for the emperor's arrival, "to dance and feast, and fill the streets with the savor of sacrifice," and ends his speech with a prayer: "May you, father of the gods and father of men, Zeus the founder and guardian of Rome, and you, ancestor Athena, and Quirinus, spirit *(daimôn)* that guards the empire of Rome, grant that my lover love Rome and be loved by Rome in return."[2]

That same Senate was, in the same years, passing through a crisis in its relation with the emperors that turned precisely on the maintenance of traditional cults. The senator whose name is most closely associated with this struggle is Symmachus, by his full name Q. Aurelius Symmachus Theodosius, born about 340 and thus a generation younger than Libanius and Themistius. He has sometimes been seen as a champion of Roman paganism, the center of a pagan literary circle, and a stubborn holdout against the rapidly encroaching Christianization of the Roman aristocracy. Like Themistius, Symmachus delivered panegyrics of Christian emperors; the three that are extant survive among his *Reports (relationes),* and were spoken when he was a senatorial envoy to Valentinian I and the young Gratian in 369 and 370. They touch on religion only in incidental ways: an emperor who knows about all parts of his empire is like an all-seeing god; "what is begun by the man closest to God lasts for ever"; "the heavenly ones *(caelestes)* aided your designs" ("heavenly ones" is conveniently ambiguous, since Christians believed in a single god but a multiplicity of divine helpers).[3]

Only in one passage of these panegyrics does Symmachus speak at length of the traditional gods. Addressing Valentinian I and his son Gratian, he exclaims: "How much less expensive *(parcior)* is the worship of your divinity *(numinis uestri cultus)* than that of the gods! For each of them a separate temple is founded *(fundantur),* to each of them separately altars are erected *(locantur)*. That I think is why they preferred dissimilar rites, so that they not be forced to share, for it is forbidden to dedicate a temple *(puluinar)* to two of them together." After giving a series of examples, ending with the Julian house and the worship of Venus, the orator concludes: "The expense almost exhausted the world itself, because worship filled it. But the modesty of your cult is conjoined, its majesty separate. We your subjects consider you in a sense as one, your adversaries realize that you are two." Symmachus's use of the present tense may imply that temples and altars were still being erected to the pagan gods, but as the panegyrist of two Christian emperors, his aim is to contrast the modest devotion paid to them with the extravagance once usual in the cult of their pagan predecessors. Though Christian emperors still possessed the limited aura of divinity called *numen,* from Constantine onward they were fully human, though exceptional in being God's vicegerents.[4]

Symmachus's reputation as a paladin of paganism rests mainly on his famous third *Report,* addressed to Valentinian II in 384, two years after Gratian had withdrawn state subsidies from public cult and, reintroducing a measure of Constantius later reversed by Julian, had ordered the Altar of Victory removed from the Senate house. This *Report* takes the form of a speech in which Symmachus deploys a series of pleas for the restoration of the altar and the subsidies. His room for maneuver was limited by the

Christian faith of the thirteen-year-old emperor, at whose elbow loomed the formidable and eloquent bishop of Milan, Ambrose. Hence he bases his arguments not on the superiority of paganism to other systems of belief, but rather on the inscrutability of the divine, which necessitates a plurality of religions. His plea had a majority of the Senate in its support, including several Christians, but Ambrose persuaded Valentinian that the gods of the pagans were idols and not gods, and that Victory was not even a god, but the personification of a goal to which Christians no less than pagans aspired.[5]

Symmachus is less circumspect in his voluminous correspondence than in his public pronouncements, though even here he tempers his language to the recipient, speaking more openly to such convinced pagans as Praetextatus and the Elder Flavian, his daughter's father-in-law, than to other pagans, let alone to Christians. To Praetextatus he complains that the priestly sacrifices recently made to expiate a portent in Spoletum (Spoleto) have failed, and that "it is now a way of getting advancement for Romans to desert the altars," a testimony to the Christian emperors' success in recruiting Christians by favoring them for public office. To Flavian he writes during a famine in Rome in 383, a year after Gratian had withdrawn the state subsidies, "Ancestral gods! Grant us pardon for our neglected sacrifices!" With his friend and admirer Protadius, apparently a pagan, he comments sadly on the fact that oracles no longer issue from their traditional sites—the Cumaean cave, the oaks of Dodona, and the crevices of Delphi.[6]

But Symmachus was too immersed in the society of his day to exclude Christians from his acquaintance, and even from his friendship. "You will be surprised to find me recommending a bishop," he writes to his brother Titianus in an early letter; but the bishop had acted like a good citizen when he prevented the leading citizens of African Caesarea from being ruined by the demands of the imperial treasury. Even after his defeat at the hands of Ambrose, Symmachus writes to him on behalf of a certain Marcianus, who had been involved in the failed attempt of a recent usurper. When writing to known Christians such as the aristocratic brothers Olybrius and Probinus, Symmachus is not shy about indicating his own belief in plural gods. "Just as one is permitted to dedicate the antlers of deer in honors of the divinities *(numina)* and to nail boar tusks to doors, so the spoils of the woods are dedicated to the cultivation of friends." The faith of his correspondents, by contrast, rarely emerges from his letters.[7]

Symmachus is not therefore a commander directing a last stand of Roman paganism. He rather sees himself in a long line of Roman aristocrats and senators, tenacious of tradition and regretful of the all-too-visible religious change going on around him, but in no way anticipating the doom of the old gods. The main concern of his last years is not the encroachment of Christianity but the praetorian games of his son Memmius Symmachus, which he lived just long enough to witness. The family of the Symmachi remained among the leaders of western aristocracy into the sixth century, and included the wife of Boethius, the author of the *Consolation of Philosophy.*[8]

A historian of the late fourth century resembles Themistius in combining Greek origins with Roman tradition, though he goes much further than his older contemporary in absorbing that tradition. Ammianus Marcellinus was born in Syrian Antioch about 330, but his history is written in Latin, and (if he is identical with a Marcellinus among the correspondents of Libanius) he enjoyed great success in the Roman capital in the reign of Theodosius. His history lacks its first thirteen books, and so may have lost a preface that elucidated his intended methods and point of view. He appears to have published it in several installments, with the last not long after 390.[9]

Ammianus began his history at the point where Tacitus ended his, in the year 96, and though Greek by origin he places his work in the tradition of Roman historiography. He adheres to "lofty matters" *(negotiorum celsitudines),* and while free with praise and blame, he avoids blatant shows of partisanship or rancor. Though clearly attached to the traditional gods and the customary forms of worship, he treats Christianity with remarkable dispassion. He recounts with seeming approval how the Roman bishop Liberius refused to condemn Athanasius unheard, even when commanded by Constantius. The same emperor "muddled the Christians' unambiguous and uncomplicated religion with his old woman's superstition" (it is true that historians such as Gibbon have used the supposed simplicity of early Christianity as a weapon of irony). He also eschews certain targets that an enemy of Christianity might have exploited. After the great temple of Apollo at Daphne had burned, Julian blamed the Christians, while the historian implies that the fault lay with an itinerant Cynic who had left a candle burning at the god's feet. He mentions several institutions of the church—bishops, synods, buildings, the feast of Epiphany, and even a convent of female monks, "virgins consecrated to divine cult in the Christian manner." By contrast, he nowhere mentions the black-robed monks who excited the disgust of his contemporaries Libanius and Eunapius. Certainly, he shows a bias in favor of prominent pagans. Julian is his hero, though his picture of him is far from unblemished, and his sympathy diminishes as the emperor moves from west to east, and falls under the influence of pretentious philosophers such as Maximus of Ephesus. Similarly, his picture of the great pagan Praetextatus glows in comparison with his picture of the Christian Probus. Nor does he refrain from criticizing Christians. He comments with distaste on their feuds over doctrine, on the riots attendant on the election of Damasus as bishop of Rome, with their toll of 137 dead, and on the luxurious life of city clergy by contrast with the simplicity of their provincial colleagues.[10]

While a modern eye, viewing the future history of Christianity, might consider Ammianus's attitude blind or dismissive, it is not very far from that of a Symmachus, and perhaps of others like him who belonged to the pagan aristocracy of late-fourth-century Rome. One of the greatest, Praetextatus, jokingly remarked to the bishop Damasus, "Make me bishop of the city of Rome and I'll become a Christian straight away." Unlike Libanius or Eunapius, Ammianus does not talk of Christianity as a recent intruder, nor comment on its increasing influence. For him it is a form of cult, widespread and influential, but not a threat to his own values. Whatever the private views of Ammianus the person, Ammianus the author is a religious traditionalist who does not write as one of a threatened minority.[11]

In 391, about the same time as Ammianus was enjoying his success in Rome, Theodosius issued several laws that went far beyond earlier ones in restricting pagan worship and forbidding pagans to hold public office. Soon after there occurred a series of events that have been seen as the death struggle of Roman paganism. Since 388, the junior emperor, Valentinian II, had been ruling from Vienne in southern Gaul with the Frankish general Arbogast as his chief aide *(comes)*. The antipathy between the two ended with Valentinian's mysterious death in 392, probably on Arbogast's orders. Knowing that he could not aspire to be emperor, the Frank turned to a teacher of rhetoric called Eugenius, and elevated him to the purple. At first Eugenius tried to reach an understanding with Theodosius in Constantinople, but when that failed, he entered Italy in 392 and set himself up as a rival emperor. Though originally a Christian, he made common cause with the pagan members of the Senate, appointing the Elder Nicomachus Flavianus consul for 394 and his son the Younger Flavianus, who was also the son-in-law of Symmachus, as his prefect of the city. In the fall of 394, the two sides met on the River Frigidus, at the modern Gorizia Gap, the lowest of the Alpine passes into Italy. On the second day of the battle, September 6, Theodosius's army was completely victorious, the Elder Flavianus committed suicide, and Arbogast was hunted down a few days later. Theodosius forgave the Younger Flavianus, and in 431 the emperor's grandson, Theodosius II, allowed his memory to be rehabilitated.[12]

According to the pagan historian Zosimus, Theodosius followed up his victory by a march on Rome. On arriving, "he convoked the senate, which remained firm in the ancestral customs handed down to it from earlier times and did not choose to side with those who had resorted to contempt for the gods. There he gave a speech, urging them to renounce the 'error,' as he called it, that they had previously followed, and to choose the Christian faith, which promised release from all sin and all impiety. But no-one obeyed his summons, or chose to depart from the traditions that had been handed down to them from the founding of the city, and to prefer an unreasoning assent to such things. For by following those principles, they had lived in a city that had been free from pillage for nearly twelve hundred years, and if they exchanged them for other ones, they did not know what the consequence might be." Theodosius thereupon withdrew all funds for public sacrifice, and thus, in Zosimus's opinion, precipitated the disasters of the following years. The pagan historian has certainly colored the facts, since the Senate contained an influential Christian minority, though several prominent members, among them Symmachus, remained faithful to their inherited religion.[13]

Symmachus died in 401, and thereafter it becomes an increasingly delicate task to judge how far the apparently pagan beliefs expressed by authors such as Claudian, Rutilius Namatianus, and Macrobius corresponded with their behavior. As always, there is potentially a large gap between the implied author of a work and the actual, living writer. Except in rare cases such as Symmachus, it is usually not possible to do more than guess at a writer's actual beliefs, or to assess the strength with which he held them, and one author can differ from another. Those who consider the events of the 390s as marking the end of traditional Roman religion tend to assume that what remained was a form of "cultural" or "erudite" paganism, as if authors could not in real life have quietly venerated pagan gods or believed what they say about them. Concomitant with this view is the supposition that the emperors, or their powerful womenfolk, would not have tolerated pagans in positions of trust. Yet Christian sources continue to refer to pagan officeholders down to the end of the fifth century, and the great turning point is rather in the sixth, and particularly in the reign of Justinian.[14]

Another assumption is that the "triumph of Christianity" had created a Christian audience for new works that would not have been receptive to expressions of paganism. The term "audience" is misleading insofar as, being borrowed from the performative arts, it implies an immediate interaction between author and reader, and that authors wrote with their effect on an "audience" foremost in their minds. Here again each case is different. Claudian can be seen as a "propagandist" who wrote in the full expectation of expressing the views of Stilicho and the western court against such eastern grandees as the praetorian prefect Rufinus and the chamberlain Eutropius, and yet it remains impossible to determine whether he was pagan or Christian. Rutilius makes hostile allusions to both Jews and Christians, and yet the "audience" he seems to envisage for his versified travel diary is the group of his aristocratic friends. Macrobius says that he is writing the *Saturnalia* as a storehouse for the education of his son. Even if that is no more to be taken literally than Catullus's "dedication" of his poems to Cornelius Nepos, it does not strengthen the assumption that Macrobius was "certainly writing for an audience he assumed to be Christian."[15]

In the years after Frigidus, Theodosius and Honorius, his son and successor in the West, tried to conciliate the pagan aristocracy. The Younger Flavianus may have converted to Christianity, and he stayed out of public life for several years while remaining on close terms with Symmachus. Symmachus maintained a frequent correspondence in his last years with three brothers of Gallic origin, Protadius, Florentius, and Minervius, all of whom held high office in 395 and thereafter. They have been branded as time servers who adopted Christianity for their own advancement. But Protadius in particular receives nearly twenty letters from the aging Symmachus, some of them concerning classics of Latin literature such as Caesar, Sallust, and Livy, and he made his own collection of Symmachus's letters. He was also a friend of Rutilius Namatianus, prefect of the city of Rome in 412 and accomplished poet, none of whose known friends can be identified as Christians. Protadius, like Symmachus, can be taken to be an admirer of the republican past, one of those senators who, according to Zosimus, "did not choose to side with those who had resorted to contempt for the gods."[16]

When Zosimus alleges that the Roman Senate feared the consequences of turning Christian, he is preparing the reader for the events with which he was to close his *History,* above all Alaric the Goth's invasion of Italy in 408, his three sieges of Rome, and his sack of the city in August 410. At the time of the invasion, the prefect of the city was a pagan who had been a correspondent and neighbor of Symmachus, Pompeianus. Etruscan soothsayers assured him that they had recently saved the city of Narni by scrutinizing the entrails of animals for omens (haruspicy), and offered to perform the same office for Rome. Both Pompeianus and Pope Innocentius were ready to agree, but when the soothsayers insisted that all the Senate participate, none was found willing to consent. Pompeianus is probably also the prefect, an "extreme Hellene," who proposed to confiscate the property of the pious Christians Pinianus and Melania in order to relieve famine in Rome. This aristocratic couple had sold their vast holdings in Italy and Spain at the approach of Alaric, and while Christians praised God for this timely liquidation, the prefect was torn to pieces by the hungry mob.[17]

Pompeianus's successor was another pagan, Priscus Attalus, a much closer friend of the late Symmachus than Pompeianus and a lover of literature. In late 409, Alaric forced the Senate to make Attalus emperor, much as Arbogast had done with Eugenius eighteen years before, and also had him baptized by a German bishop as an Arian Christian like himself. One of his motives may have been to gain favor both with the Arians of Rome and with the still-powerful pagans. These had inferred from Attalus's past beliefs that he would restore the ancestral rites, and though he did not reign long enough to do so, he took steps to conciliate them by his appointments. His own successor as prefect of the city, Marcianus, had been close to the arch-pagan Praetextatus in the 380s, and his praetorian prefect, Lampadius, may also have been a pagan, as was the consul whom he appointed for 410, Tertullus. Alaric finally lost confidence in his puppet, and after negotiating unsuccessfully with Honorius in Ravenna, besieged Rome for the third time. In August 410, he entered it with his troops and allowed them to sack it for several days.[18]

Alaric's sack of Rome was for Zosimus the first incontrovertible proof that abandonment of the ancestral gods had brought ruin on the western empire. From his viewpoint of the early sixth century, much had happened since that only served to confirm his conclusion, perhaps nothing more clearly than the much more devastating pillage of the city by the Vandals in 455, which extended over two weeks and carried off many of the city's ancient treasures and more than four thousand captives. Among Christians in 410, the reaction was mixed. Jerome was horrified: "My voice is stopped, and sobs interrupt my words as I dictate. The city is captured that captured the whole world, or rather it has perished by hunger rather than the sword, and few have been found to be captured." Augustine, by contrast, held that true Christians lost nothing so long as they did not lose their faith. As for the pagans, those who survived the sack and were now "impudently and boldly insulting Christ's servants" would pay for their obstinacy in hell, when they should rather have learned from the disaster that their gods were powerless to protect them. His associate Orosius compiled his *History against the Pagans* to show that Roman history was a long catalogue of disasters, and that Christians could not take the blame for a further one.[19]

The years immediately following Alaric's sack of Rome in 410 were a time of military and political confusion. By 416, a semblance of order had returned, with the court in Ravenna controlling Italy, southern Gaul, and eastern Spain, while the Visigoths occupied Armorica in northwestern France, the Burgundians the middle Rhineland, the Vandals, Suevi, and Alans southern and western Spain. In 417, the year that Orosius composed his history, a Roman-educated aristocrat returned from Rome to his native province of Narbonese Gaul. Rutilius Namatianus is known almost exclusively from the poem *On His Return,* in which he describes his journey (the poem breaks off in the second book, with the poet still off the Ligurian coast). His father, Lachanius, had risen to be prefect of the city, and the son held the same position in 414. In the course of the poem, he addresses or mentions a number of relatives and friends, some of them with literary pretensions like himself, such as Lucillus, whose satires rivaled those of Turnus and Juvenal. One of these friends, Volusianus, was to be converted on his deathbed in 437, and everything in the poem suggests that the entire circle of the poet's friends was pagan. Thus he describes peasants merrymaking in the countryside around Falesia on the Etruscan coast: "just then it happened that the villages were joyfully cheering their tired hearts around the rustic cross-roads with festive revelry, for on that day Osiris, recalled at last, summons the joyful seeds to new harvests" *(et tum forte hilares per compita rustica pagi / mulcebant sacris pectora fessa iocis. / Illo quippe die tandem reuocatus Osiris / excitat in fruges germina laeta nouas).* Rutilius speaks with distaste of the Jews and their religion, "the root of stupidity" *(radix stultitiae);* of the monks on the island of Capraria—"whether they return to the prisons that punish their own past deeds, or their wretched innards swell with bitter bile" *(siue suas repetunt factorum ergastula poenas, / tristia seu nigro uiscere felle tument);* of a Roman of high birth who had become a hermit on a solitary island—"the unfortunate thinks that the heavenly powers feed on filth, and he punishes himself, more savage than the gods he injures" *(infelix putat illuuie caelestia pasci / seque premit laesis saeuior ipse deis).* In a recently rediscovered passage of the second book, Rutilius praises the patrician general Constantius (brother-in-law of Honorius and briefly emperor in 421) who had defeated the Goths in Gaul and forced them to come to terms, but this is not a sign of Christian sympathies, since as a Gallic aristocrat the poet had every reason to celebrate the savior of his homeland. It is usually and rightly supposed that he was a pagan.[20]

To pose the same question of the author commonly known as Macrobius is to raise different problems of method from those raised by Rutilius. The actual Macrobius, as is now generally agreed after long controversy, had the full name of Macrobius Ambrosius Theodosius, and in conformity with the custom of his day used "Theodosius" as his primary name. At some point in his career, he became a *uir clarissimus et illustris,* and thus a member of the highest ranks of the Roman Senate, and he is also probably the praetorian prefect of 430 known only by the name "Theodosius." The best known of his several extant works, and the most relevant to the paganism of the fifth century, is the *Saturnalia.* This takes a form introduced by Plato in his *Symposium* and often imitated later—a conversation in which a congenial male company discusses learned or abstruse subjects. Rather than describing a single evening, Macrobius imaginatively re-creates a series of conversations held over the course of the ancient Roman holiday in honor of Saturn, the *Saturnalia,* which occupied three days at the time of the winter solstice.[21]

The central figure, and the host of the first of the three days, is Vettius Agorius Praetextatus, one of the most conspicuous Roman senators of the later fourth century and a devotee of many cults, highly praised by Ammianus and a close friend of Symmachus. After Praetextatus, the next two hosts are also prominent pagans: the Elder Flavianus (the ill-fated supporter of Eugenius in 394) and Symmachus. The other guests include several Greeks, among them a Greek philosopher named Eustathius, equally fluent in Greek and Latin, and an ex-athlete turned Cynic from Alexandria called Horus. Almost all the guests are identifiable as actual persons, mainly from the correspondence of Symmachus.[22]

One of them serves as a foil to the others by his ill-mannered bantering, Evangelus. The announcement of his arrival at Praetextatus's house in the course of the first day causes dismay, though the host is too polite to refuse him admittance. He may be identified with an Evangelus known from a letter of Symmachus of 397 as a difficult character. His name, reminiscent of the gospels *(euangelia)*, has led some to see him as the embodiment of a Christian intrusion into a comfortably pagan atmosphere, but this view is untenable. Evangelus is a haughty, even arrogant, Latin-speaker, who owns an estate in Tuscany and riles the Greek guests by asking such questions as whether the chicken came before the egg, unlikely attributes for someone whose Greek name is supposed to suggest Christianity. *Evangelus,* in its Greek form *Euangelos,* is a name of good omen commonly given to pagans. A Roman senator of the name built a temple of Apollo in the late 350s, and might be the father of Macrobius's character.[23]

Unlike Tacitus in his *Dialogus* or Plutarch in his *Convivial Questions,* Macrobius makes no pretense of re-creating an actual occasion. He intends the work as a storehouse of knowledge for his son Eustathius. Hence he does not introduce subjects at random, but arranges them "in a kind of corpus, so that whatever I had noted down indiscriminately and promiscuously to aid my memory should fit coherently together like limbs." Nor is he greatly concerned if some of the characters only came to maturity after the time of Praetextatus: "It did not suit me to reckon up on my fingers the age of those present, having the example of Plato on my side." Whereas Tacitus gives the sixth year of Vespasian's reign as the date of his *Dialogus,* and refers to several recent events, Macrobius gives no obvious date for the *Saturnalia.* Again unlike Tacitus, he makes no claim to have been present on the occasion, or to have had a personal acquaintance with any of his characters. He is also absent from the voluminous correspondence of Symmachus, which covers a period from the 350s to the first years of the next century, and if he was born in the last quarter of the fourth century, he may have known few or none of the persons he depicts.[24]

It has been thought that Macrobius either became a Christian later in life, since otherwise it seemed impossible that he should hold high office in a Christian administration, or that he was a Christian at the time of writing his extant works, even if he reveals his religious position only by subtle hints. For Macrobius, the dialogue form allows the author to hide behind a barrier both of time, since he was evoking an era with which he had little personal connection, and of literary distance, since he does not present himself as a participant. While the actual views of the living Macrobius are beyond recovery, the evidence suggests that he was a pagan Neoplatonist rather than a Christian steeped in Neoplatonic thought such as the young Augustine, or Boethius, married to a descendant of Symmachus, a hundred years later.[25]

A similar attachment to the pre-Christian culture of Rome is observable a generation after Macrobius in Anthemius, a patrician of the eastern Rome and the son-in-law of the emperor Marcian. In 467, Marcian's successor, Leo, chose him to be emperor in the West, hoping thereby to gain the support of the powerful Ricimer, the virtual ruler of Italy, and to destroy the Vandal kingdom in Africa. But the armada that was launched from Constantinople in 468, and was supported by forces from Italy led by the patrician Marcellinus, was a dismal failure, and four years later Anthemius was executed by Ricimer's nephew Gundobad. In a verse panegyric celebrating Anthemius's consulate of 468, the Gallic poet Sidonius Apollinaris expatiates on his Greek and Latin learning. He was familiar, says the poet, with all the Greek philosophers from Thales down to Epicurus and Chrysippus, and with the classics of Latin literature as well. Anthemius appears to have created hopes among devotees of Hellenism that he would revive their cause in the West. One of these, the patrician Severus, returned to Rome from Alexandria, where he had been studying philosophy, and was made consul in 470. Marcellinus, commander of Italian forces in the Vandalic campaign, is a more certain pagan, though probably western in origin. He had been ruling Dalmatia as an independent principality for many years, and, according to the Neoplatonist Damascius, he was not only a pagan, but a skilled diviner and a patron of philosophers. Like Anthemius, he fell prey to the jealousy of Ricimer and was murdered in 468.[26]

Though there may have been no overt pagans in the Roman Senate by the end of the century, some senators remained attached to the traditions of their pagan predecessors. Pope Gelasius, in office from 492 to 496, tried early in his tenure to put an end to celebrations of the Lupercalia, a rite that was believed to go back to the founding of Rome or even further. This provoked a reaction from some senators, of whom one, Andromachus, publicly accused the pope of endangering the city by suppression of a rite that protected it from disasters. (This recalls Alaric's siege of Rome, when the city prefect obtained Pope Innocentius's uneasy acceptance of Etruscan haruspicy.) From Gelasius's reply, Andromachus and others seem to have tried to find a compromise between the prevailing Christianity and the appearance of paganism by observing the shadow *(imago)* of the rite, but this compromise only enabled the pope to argue that such a degradation must bring more misfortune, not less. In this shadow form, so he argued, those of the senatorial class did not personally run about the city naked, as their ancestors had done: instead they were "neither Christians nor pagans," who "have lowered *(reduxistis)* your supposedly venerable and salutary cult to ordinary, vulgar people." It has been suggested that the senators hired actors merely to mime the rite, but that fails to take account of the seriousness of the announcement with which Gelasius concludes: "Finally, as far as I am concerned, no one who is baptized, no one who is a Christian, may perform this rite, but only pagans, to whom alone it belongs. I am obliged to declare that such things are destructive and fatal to Christians. Why do you blame me if I declare that a rite that does no good for those who profess belief in it should be forbidden to those who profess themselves Christian? Certainly I will clear my own conscience: let those who fail to obey just admonitions look after themselves." From all this it appears that a rite to promote fertility had become a secular festival, and had persisted in this altered form to Gelasius's day. His confessed inability to control those who were not true Christians suggests that it continued later.[27]

It is not surprising that this blend of paganism and Christianity persisted in Rome. An author known as "Aethicus" writing no earlier than the fifth century describes a custom whereby the Roman people, together with the prefect of the city or the consul, went down to the sea between Ostia and Portus "to celebrate Castor and Pollux in a joyful ceremony," presumably a ritual to mark the opening of the sailing season. Similarly John the Lydian, writing under Justinian, describes a defunct festival of Syrian origin, the Maioumas, in which the senators went down to Ostia and threw one another into the sea. In Constantinople, festivals of pagan origin continued well into the Middle Ages. The "Trullan" Council of 692 laid down that the faithful must not celebrate the Kalends on January 1 *(Kalendae),* the Wishes for the Emperor *(Vota)* on January 3, Mars's birthday on March 1, and the *Brumalia,* a twenty-four-day bout of eating and drinking in November and December. It is in the continuance of such festivals rather than in literature that the borderline practices of "ordinary, vulgar people" can be discerned.[28]

It has often been observed that Christianity began as an urban religion and made its way only slowly into country towns and villages. This was especially true in the less urbanized West, where the word *paganus* appears to have evolved from its original sense of "country dweller" or "peasant" to "pagan." Yet city and countryside were not separate entities. In both East and West, cities had "territories" *(territoria, chôrai),* areas that could extend over hundreds of square miles, and the towns and villages situated on the territory were "attributed" to the principal city. Village life and city life were conjoined both by commercial exchange and by the maintenance of plural domiciles, especially by the wealthy. Thus when Amantius, a fourth-century bishop of Ruthena (Rodez, Aveyron), smashed a pagan statue in the city, he was attacked by a "sacrilegious mob [eager] to avenge its divinity." Finding him unmoved, the rioters sent a message to "to a certain man, who far excelled the rest in the splendor of his birth, honor, titles, wealth and authority." Calling together a troop of his slaves, he drove to the city in his chariot of office, but at the gates his horses "grew as stiff as senseless statues" (such "paralysis miracles" are not infrequent in hagiography), and he was forced to beg the holy man for forgiveness.[29]

Priests and bishops often had to combat pagan practices in their "flocks." Gregory of Tours, narrating the life of a third-century saint, Symphorianus bishop of Augustodunum (Autun), tells how the city had an image of "Berecinthia" (Cybele). The bishop met some peasants "when they were carrying this in a cart for the safety of their fields and vineyards, in the wretched way of pagans." He prayed God to "enlighten their eyes," and when his prayers produced the requested miracle, they sought out the local priest and "were converted to unity with the church." Sulpicius Severus in his biography of Martin of Tours reports a similar custom in the next century: "The peasants *(rustici)* in their miserable madness used to carry idols of their demons, covered in a white cloth, around their fields." Even when celebrating a Christian saint, "rustics" could revert to pagan practices. Such were the peasants who used to gather at the tomb of Hilary, a third-century bishop of Poitiers, and, in addition to feasting over several days, threw cloths and figures made of cheese, wax, or bread into a nearby lake. Thus "the foolish populace was becoming entangled in error" *(involvebatur insipiens populus in errore)* until a priest built a basilica on the site and put an end to its practices.[30]

The obstacle in the way of such crusading clergy was sometimes not only the conservatism of the peasantry, but the indifference of Christian landlords unwilling to upset their tenants. Maximus, bishop of Turin about 400, addresses several of his sermons to such landlords. "Apart from a few religious persons, scarcely anyone's farm is unpolluted by idols, scarcely anyone's estate is immune from the cult of demons. Everywhere the Christian eye is offended. . . . Let us then take care both of ourselves and those who are ours *(nostri).*" Though "sacrilegious people" have performed a ritual of purification *(lustrum),* those in a position of responsibility say, "I don't know; I didn't order it; it's not my business; it doesn't affect me." "How many times," asks the bishop, "has God ordered that idols should be destroyed, and yet we never consent to be careful in this respect? We have always overlooked, always neglected. Lately an imperial order has admonished us. See what a derogation of Divinity it is when human power has to reinforce it." "Some days ago, my brothers, I urged your Charity, as religious and holy men, to remove all pollution of idols from your property, and uproot all the error of paganism from your lands. It is not right that you who have Christ in your hearts should have Antichrist in your cottages, that when you worship God in church your people worship the Devil in their shrines. . . . When you enter a hut you will find yellowed turf and dead coals—a worthy sacrifice to demons. . . . If you go out to an estate, you see wooden altars and stone images—a suitable offering, when offerings are made to unfeeling gods on rotting altars."[31]

Caesarius, bishop of Arelate (Arles) in the early sixth century, faced similar obstacles. Even in the city, women refused to ply their looms on Thursdays *(quinta feria).* Certain members of the congregation made vows to trees, prayed beside springs, or observed omens sent by the devil. "What is worse, some people, miserable wretches, not only refuse to destroy pagan shrines, but neither fear nor blush to rebuild those that have been destroyed. If someone thinking of God tries to burn the trees of fanatics, or scatter and destroy the altars of devils, such people grow angry and insane, and burn with extreme fury, so much that they either dare to murder those who for the love of God try to overturn sacrilegious idols, or perhaps do not hesitate to think of killing them." Caesarius urges his listeners to do all they can to destroy such traces of paganism, even if they become latter-day martyrs.[32]

In some regions, the worship of pagan deities seems to have ebbed without also carrying away customs that Christian authorities regarded as pagan, for example, the naming of days of the week by gods such as Mars and Venus, or by their Germanic equivalents such as Thor and Freia. A late-sixth-century sermon written by Martin, bishop of Braga in Galicia (now northwestern Portugal), is entitled *On the Correction of Peasants (De correctione rusticorum),* and gives a curious picture of a community nominally Christian, but still attached to observances that in the eyes of the bishop broke the covenant of baptism. He begins with a rapid survey of world history, starting with the creation of the world and moving on successively to the fall of the evil angels, the creation of man in Adam and Eve, and the Flood. Thereafter the Devil and his servants, the demons, began to deceive humankind by demanding worship and taking the names of wicked humans, "so that one called himself Jupiter, who had been a magician and was defiled by such adulteries that he married his own sister, called Juno," while others were Mars, Mercury, and Venus. These and other false gods continue to do harm to "ignorant rustics," who name the days of the week in their honor. "What madness it is that a person baptized in the faith of Christ should not observe the Lord's Day *(dies dominicus),* but say that he observes the day of Jupiter, Mercury, Venus and Saturn!" Another error of "ignorant peasants" is to suppose that the year begins on January 1, when Scripture says that God divided the light and the darkness, so that they ought to know that the true date is the spring equinox on March 25. Worse still is the error of those who observe days in honor of moths and mice. They think that one day's food will satisfy these creatures' hunger for the rest of the year, but so meager an offering will not induce them to spare bread or clothing. It is another form of devil worship to pay attention to omens, since demons have no knowledge of the future, which only God has. When a Christian has received baptism, he has made a solemn covenant with God.

> How then do some of you, who have renounced the devil, his angels, his worshipers and his evil deeds, revert to worshiping the Devil? Lighting candles by rocks, trees, springs, and at cross-roads—what is that if not

> worship of the Devil? To observe divination, omens, days named for idols—what is that if not worship of the Devil? To observe the festival of Vulcan *(Vulcanalia)* and first days of the months *(Kalendae),* to adorn tables, set up laurel-branches, watch your step, to throw fruit and wine on the log in the fire, to throw bread into a spring—what is that if not worship of the Devil? For women to invoke Minerva over their looms, to observe Venus' day for weddings, to watch what day to go out—what is that if not worship of the Devil? To cast a spell on herbs for harmful purposes and to invoke the names of demons while doing so—what is that if not worship of the Devil? And so on for many other things that it would take too long to mention. Why, you do all those things after renunciation of the Devil, after baptism. By returning to the worship of demons and the evil deeds of demons, you have betrayed your faith and broken the covenant that you made with God. You have dismissed the sign of the Cross, and you pay attention to other signs of the devil through birds, sneezes and much else.

Martin's sermon continued to be copied and translated for centuries afterward. Borrowings have been traced as late as an Anglo-Saxon sermon of Aelfric, abbot of Eynsham, *On False Gods (De falsis diis),* about the year 1000, and they suggest that the practices which he denounced, or similar ones, continued well into the Middle Ages. Western Europe never dropped the custom of naming days of the week after pagan gods, whether Roman or Germanic, and only modern Portuguese preserves no trace of it.[33]

Such persistence was all the more to be expected in border regions where the organized Church could maintain control only with difficulty. The abbot Severinus was the spiritual head of a region of Noricum Ripense, on the southern bank of the Danube in modern Austria. Here in the late fifth century he struggled for nearly thirty years to maintain the Catholic faith, with pagans in his own flock and with the German Rugii north of the Danube attached to Arianism. Learning that some of the populace was still performing pagan sacrifices in the fortress town of Cucullis, he ordered that all those attending holy service should bring wax candles and attach them to the walls of the church. He then began to pray with the priests and deacons, "weeping much, and on his knees," whereupon the majority of the candles "were suddenly kindled by divine agency; the rest remained unlighted, being the candles of those who had been polluted by the aforesaid sacrilege, but, wishing to remain hidden, had denied it." Thus the false or halfhearted Christians were shown up, and "by open confession, they bore witness to their own sacrilegious acts." Severinus did not live to see the day when his community was forced to leave their homes on the Danube and to resettle in Italy.[34]

A turning point in the West arrived with the conversion of the "new Constantine," Clovis the Frank, to Catholic Christianity in the late fourth or early fifth century, and with the extension of Frankish rule over much of what is now France. In the reign of Clovis's son Theoderic, Gallus, later to be bishop of Arverna (Clermont-Ferrand), was a deacon in Theodoric's court. When the king visited Cologne, Gallus found that there was a nearby pagan temple in which the locals "gorged themselves on food and drink," worshiped idols, and placed wooden images of body parts which they believed the god to have cured. (This practice continued to be denounced by preachers and church councils, and is still current in southern Europe.) "When the holy Gallus heard of it, he immediately hurried there with another monk, lit a fire (since none of the stupid pagans were present), and set the temple ablaze. Seeing the smoke of the temple rising to the sky, they looked for the person responsible for the fire and chased him with drawn swords. When the king heard from the threats of the pagans what had happened, he mollified them with gentle words and so calmed their wicked fury." There is a patent contrast with Eugippius and his uneasy dealings with the Arian kings north of the Danube. Now a Catholic king with pagans among his subjects intervenes to protect a priest who burns down a pagan shrine. By the end of the century, a diplomatic pope could negotiate with kinglets of Gaul and plant Christianity in southeastern Britain. "Christendom" was coming into existence.[35]

CHAPTER TEN

The East

IN THE EAST as in the West, there is a difference in the progress of Christianity as between cities and countryside, but in the East progress was slowed or hastened by conditions that did not apply in the West. On the one hand, the long intervals of peace with Persia, and the finally successful repulse of Huns and other invaders, gave time for Christianity to put down roots in regions that had been strongly pagan. Yet the prestige of Hellenic culture, acknowledged by Church Fathers such as Gregory of Nyssa, enabled the pagan intelligentsia of cities like Athens and Aphrodisias, though embattled, to stand fast. In the provinces of the eastern Mediterranean, the non-Greek cults of gods such as the moon-god Sin in Carrhae (Harran) and Baal in Heliopolis (Baalbek) were equally resistant. Egypt, as much a special case in Late Antiquity as it had been for Herodotus nearly a millennium before, contained Hellenized elites in cities such as Alexandria, Antinoopolis, and Panopolis, and also preserved local cults in towns such as the obscure Pneuit in Upper Egypt. Here Christianity had a champion in Shenute, abbot of the White Monastery at Atripe (Athribis), close to the local capital at Panopolis (Akhmim), and his battles with both landowners and peasants encapsulate the persistence of paganism at different social levels. But regional differences were large, and it is best to treat the advance of Christianity in four separate areas: Greece, Asia Minor, the eastern provinces of Syria and Mesopotamia, and Egypt.

From large cities down to small villages, Greek and non-Greek communities typically had a divinity to which the population had a proprietorial attachment. Athens derived its name from Athena, the goddess of wisdom, who presided from the citadel of the Acropolis. Here pagan intellectuals combined a devotion to Athena and other gods with the cultivation of characteristically Greek fields of culture—philosophy; rhetoric, the professors of which were usually styled "sophists" *(sophistai);* literature, where they were similarly called *grammatikoi;* and medicine. Though the religion of those below the educated classes is less easy to discern, the evidence of Christianity at all levels is sparse before about 450. "Throughout the 4th century and well into the 5th, Athens was to all intents and purposes a pagan city."[1]

The intellectual heart of Athenian culture was philosophy, especially as represented by the revived Platonism that began with Plotinus in the third century and has been known since the nineteenth as "Neoplatonism." There seems no longer to have been an official chair of philosophy, as there had been in the imperial period, whereas the city still maintained salaried professors of rhetoric and literature. The Platonic school had six successive heads or "scholarchs." The first of these was Plutarch (not to be confused with his earlier namesake, the biographer and Platonic philosopher), who founded the school in the late fourth century and died about 434. He was succeeded for a few years by Syrianus, whose own successor, Proclus, had a long and influential tenure before his death in 485. Thereafter the history of the school becomes hard to follow, but there were two and perhaps three scholarchs, Marinus, Hegias, and Isidore, before the last, Damascius, who left Athens for Persia in 531. Of these, Marinus wrote a still extant biography of Proclus, and Damascius a rich biography of Isidore, which though lost survives in many later excerpts and quotations. The school survived on its considerable endowment and teaching income, which in Proclus's day amounted to a thousand gold pieces *(nomismata),* enough to give teachers and students "leisure and calm" for their pursuits. In addition to its own wealth, it contributed to the civic economy by attracting students from all parts of the Greek world. Yet Damascius's biography of Isidore is also an acerbic requiem for a school that had long been in decline.[2]

Unlike rhetoric, which taught the technique of public speaking, philosophy was inseparable from questions of belief such as the creation of the cosmos and the role of fate in human lives. All the scholarchs were Hellenes in belief and practice, and so (as far as can be told) were all of the students. The Alexandrian school, by contrast, an offshoot of the Athenian one, had two scholarchs who converted to Christianity or made an accommodation with it, and in the sixth century produced a great Christian thinker in John Philoponus, a fellow pupil with Damascius of the pagan Ammonius. Again unlike Alexandria, where a Christian mob lynched the mathematician and philosopher Hypatia in 415, in Athens there is little sign of antagonism between pagans and Christians. The turbulent events of Zeno's reign (474–491) seem to have had little effect on the Athenian philosophers, but implicated several of those in Alexandria. The Athenian Platonists did not flaunt their religion, being content to retain their own beliefs, to worship discreetly within doors at home, and to frequent such shrines as had not yet been closed or stripped bare. When Damascius refers to the new religion, he uses guarded periphrases such as "the outside creed," "the prevailing doctrine," "the inevitability *(anankê)* that has laid low everything ancient," and deplores the conversion to "others" of an Alexandrian contemporary.[3]

The Athenian Neoplatonists have left their mark on the city's material remains. Plutarch appears in a fragmentary inscription that also mentions Telesphoros, the child-god who was the son of Asclepius and the goddess of Health (Hygieia). When he needed a cure, he slept in Asclepius's sanctuary, and heard the god speak in his own voice. A recently published funerary epigram refers to Syrianus's descent from heaven and his return there after death. A house on the south side of the Acropolis, discovered in 1955, may have belonged to Proclus, perhaps an inheritance from his two predecessors. His biographer, Marinus, says that it was near the shrine of Asclepius and was just visible from the Acropolis, and objects found in or near it suggest a philosophical connection, among them a broken verse inscription in which the word "wisdom" *(sophiê)* survives. In its east wall was an apse with a shrine of the Great Mother of the Gods, to whom Proclus had a special devotion.[4]

Another large house, of about the same period, lavishly laid out and furnished, stood on the north slope of the Areopagus. A supply of water from a nearby spring fed a shrine of the nymphs and several cisterns. This house too has been identified as the residence of a philosopher, perhaps Damascius, though the owner could have been the influential Theagenes in the mid-fifth century or some other some rich Athenian. At a date around 500, the owners suddenly abandoned the house and hid some of the statuary in two wells, including a statuette of Hermes, and the new owners transformed it radically for Christian use.[5]

By the last quarter of the fifth century, the Neoplatonic tradition was in decline at Athens. Proclus expressed a fear before his death that the "golden chain" reaching back to Plato might leave the city. His successor, Isidore, observed to a brilliant young pupil, Hegias, that philosophy was on the brink of extreme senility. It is unclear whether Hegias became scholarch, but according to Damascius he used his wealth to restore ruined shrines of Attica and to flaunt his paganism, and by so doing brought philosophy into great disrepute. In 529, the ardently orthodox Justinian forbade the teaching of law and philosophy at Athens. This measure is usually connected with a general law in which the emperor excluded pagans from teaching altogether unless they underwent baptism, the penalty being exile and confiscation of their property. According to the historian Agathias, a party of seven philosophers including Damascius and his pupil Simplicius set out for Persia, hoping to find a more favorable atmosphere at the court of the new king, Kosrow (Chosroes) I. Disappointed by their reception, they returned to the Roman Empire under the terms of the Eternal Peace signed by Justinian and Kosrow in 532, though Agathias does not say where they settled on their return, and the thesis that Simplicius settled in Carrhae (Harran) near the border with Persia is no longer tenable.[6]

The decline of Athenian Neoplatonism was accompanied and perhaps hastened by the removal or destruction of traditional objects and places of worship. During Proclus's tenure, Christian authorities removed the cult statue from the shrine of Asclepius, the very place where the god had tended Plutarch. Soon also the celebrated gold-and-ivory statue of Athena in the Parthenon disappeared, its destination unknown. About the same time, Pheidias's bronze statue of Athens that had stood for centuries in the open air on the Acropolis was transported to Constantinople.[7]

There had long been an affinity between philosophy and rhetoric, since philosophers expounded their ideas as much by lecturing to crowds of students as by writing, and some works of the Athenian Neoplatonists survive only in the form of lecture notes taken down by their listeners. Several of the philosophers mentioned by Damascius studied with "sophists," and he himself had taught rhetoric for many years before turning to philosophy. In fifth-century Athens, certain sophists seem to have enjoyed as much renown as the philosophers whom Damascius celebrates, though they appear less often in the written record. Two of them, Plutarch (if he is different from the Neoplatonist) and Apronianus, honor the governor Herculius with inscribed epigrams about the year 410, and another inscription shows the same Plutarch using his wealth to enhance the festival of the Panathenaea. A sophist contemporary with these was Leontius, who held the official chair of rhetoric. He was sufficiently eminent for his daughter Athenais to catch the eye of Theodosius II and to become his wife, whereupon she received baptism and took the name Eudocia. The historian Olympiodorus, who had engineered Leontius's appointment, describes in detail the elaborate ceremonies of induction which new holders of the chair underwent. The eminent sophist Lachares earns a passing mention from Damascius, but Marinus in his *Life of Proclus* is more generous, saying that Lachares was a fellow student of Proclus under Syrianus, and that his fame as a sophist equaled Homer's as a poet.[8]

Another branch of culture, lower than philosophy and rhetoric in prestige but still with eminent representatives, was the interpretation of literature *(grammatikê),* sometimes called "poetics" *(poêtikê)* because of its concentration on poetry. This too seems to have been largely a pagan preserve. For pagans, Homer, Hesiod, Pindar, and other early poets provided much of the underpinning of their religious beliefs, and the correct understanding of their writings was an essential tool. Pagan intellectuals set out their beliefs in poetry, so that Marinus for instance published his biography of Proclus both in verse and in prose. A *grammatikos* by the name of Philtatios, like Leontius a client of the influential Olympiodorus, taught the Athenians how to use the correct amount of glue when making books, and received an official portrait as his reward. Some fifty years later, Pamprepius, also celebrated as a poet, became the city's official *grammatikos,* and, according to Damascius, set out to rival everyone in erudition except Proclus and the other philosophers. His later career took him into the sphere of high politics, and in Damascius's opinion was ruinous for the cause of Hellenism.[9]

As happened in other regions, erudite pagans from the city were sustained by the cults of the surrounding territory, which their interest helped to perpetuate. The most famous of all such cults in Attica was that of Demeter and Kore in Eleusis, some twelve miles to the west of Athens, though with its sumptuous buildings and large personnel, Eleusis was far from rural. The hierophant was the most prestigious of the several officials of the sanctuary, and the next-to-last incumbent was a theurgic philosopher named Nestorius, the grandfather of the Neoplatonist Plutarch. Nestorius initiated the strongly pagan Eunapius into the Mysteries, and predicted to him the approaching end of the sanctuary. In Eunapius's view, the prophecy came true when "black-robed" monks allowed Alaric and his forces to break through the historic barrier of Thermophylae and to ravage southern Greece in 395. Christians began to use Eleusis for their own worship in the fifth century, and not later than the beginning of the sixth they built a church at what had been the entrance to the sanctuary.[10]

Other sacred places less exposed than Eleusis survived for a while, especially the sacred caves concealed in the several mountains of Attica. A cave on Mount Parnes had been sacred to Pan and the Nymphs from classical times, and was filled with dedications. One of the last known worshipers was Nicagoras, a son of the same Platonic philosopher Nicagoras who explored the burial places of the Egyptian kings in the reign of Constantine. The son, conducting his pilgrimages nearer home, climbed up to the Cave of Pan no fewer than twelve times and recorded his visits in verse. Eventually Christians discovered the site, and smashed the modest sculptures to pieces.[11]

Athens was not the only city that kept up the tradition of Hellenic culture in old Greece, but appears to done so with more success than others. Corinth, to which Paul had directed two of his letters, was the capital and business center of the province, and by reason of its two ports had a more mixed population than Athens. Defending the Corinthian Aristophanes to Julian, Libanius can call him "a Hellene, that is, one of your favorites, . . . a man attached to learning, an initiate, a foster-son of Peirene, a Dorian, a Corinthian." Yet when the pagan temples of Corinth were destroyed by earthquakes in the later fourth century, they were not rebuilt, and the city began to be ringed about by imposing churches. Pagans now worshiped less obtrusively at natural springs, where they jostled with Christians.[12]

Like Greece, Asia Minor shows Christianity advancing at an unequal pace in different regions, with paganism more tenacious in rural districts and in cities with a strong tradition of Hellenic culture. The transition from paganism to Christianity is best observed at Aphrodisias in eastern Caria, situated in a broad valley some twenty miles south of the Upper Maeander. Its original nucleus was a rural shrine of Aphrodite, transformed into a city in the second century BCE, and by Late Antiquity Aphrodisias rivaled Athens and Alexandria as a center of intellectual paganism (though its archaeological and literary record is much richer than that of other centers such as Heliopolis in Syria). Like Athens, it had a great goddess to give its pagan community a religious focus, as well as other divinities of the city and the region. One of these was Apollo, who had a cave in the valley of the Maeander called "Apollo's Halls" (Apollônos Aulai). The Neoplatonist Isidore and his pupil Asclepiodotus were nearly drowned in the Maeander when on a pilgrimage to this ancient cult site, but were saved when Asclepiodotus uttered a secret formula.[13]

The reemergence of philosophy in fifth-century Aphrodisias begins with Asclepiodotus's father-in-law, the elder Asclepiodotus, who belonged to the aristocracy of the city and appears in inscribed epigrams as one of its wealthy benefactors. His son-in-law, the Younger Asclepiodotus, is said by Damascius to have caused "a religious revival in the city of Aphrodite." Late Antique Aphrodisias has left even stronger traces of its paganism than Athens. The chief witness is the so-called Atrium House, a large residence that appears to have had an annex for teaching or for public lectures, and which might have belonged to the Elder Asclepiodotus. It was adorned with portraits of famous men of antiquity and of contemporary persons. The identifiable subjects include Pindar, renowned both as a poet and a source of knowledge about the antique gods, Socrates and Aristotle with their two most famous pupils, Alcibiades and Alexander, and the Pythagorean philosopher and wonder worker Apollonius of Tyana. The contemporary portraits represent an older and a younger philosopher and a youth who may have been a deceased pupil. The portraits appear to date to the fifth century, and in the sixth or seventh they were roughly prised from their niches and dumped in an alley behind the house, much as the statuary of the House of Proclus and of "House C" at Athens was smashed or hidden. The so-called "Triconch House," remodeled and sumptuously decorated about 400, previously identified as the bishop's palace, now appears to have been a secular building, perhaps the house of a wealthy pagan.[14]

Aphrodisians still proclaim an attachment to paganism and its gods in the sixth century. A certain Pytheas, a senator of Constantinople who continued to reside in his native city, showered it with benefits. A statue set up in his honor calls Aphrodisias "the city of the Paphian goddess and of Pytheas" and praises his unstinting generosity. A verse epitaph honors a young woman, linked to families of Constantinople and Alexandria, who died at eighteen and was now "dwelling with the immortals." Another woman also died at eighteen in the reign of the fiercely Christian Justinian. "She was of well-famed prudence and similarly of noble fame, always engaged in prudent labors. May you arrive, Euphemia, in the choir of the blessed gods." These texts give no sign that members of Aphrodisian society, at least if they were able to commission or write elegant epigrams, shrank from displaying their attachment to the old gods.[15]

Christians often thought of pagans and Jews together as enemies of the faith, and pagans sometimes drew on Jewish knowledge for their attacks on Christianity. A sign of the relative weakness of Christianity in Aphrodisias is perhaps to be seen in the clear traces of a vibrant Jewish community there. The site has produced one of the longest of Jewish inscriptions, which may have stood in the local synagogue. It is a stone nearly three meters tall, carved on two sides with texts of different dates. The earlier list, of the fourth or early fifth century, contains a list divided into two parts. All those named in the first part are full Jews, some of whom are listed by their profession, "goldsmith," "retailer," "confectioner." This first part is followed by a second, with the annotation: "And all who were god-fearers." This much-disputed term appears to designate those persons who were attracted to Judaism but, if male, had not submitted to circumcision. The first nine are of "councilors" *(bouleutai)*, while among the rest some are mentioned only with their single names or their patronymic, others again with their professions, but in this part of the list the professions include not only tradesmen but also two entertainers, an athlete *(athlêtês)* and a comedian *(gryllos)*. The inscription on the other face is shorter, and is probably of the fifth century. It begins with an invocation that appears to mean "God, the helper of café-owners" *(patellades)*, after which it lists "scholars" *(philomatheis)* who have built some kind of memorial for the community. This list mentions no professionals except for an official in the imperial service *(palatinos)*, and while the majority are Jews, there are three converts *(prosêlytoi)* and two "god-fearers." Aphrodisias still had a large Jewish community in the fifth century, and most "god-fearers" were probably pagans who were drawn to Judaism, some to the extent of undergoing conversion, though some may have been Christian. Those who were tradesmen must have been at a lower social level than their contemporaries who professed their beliefs in elegantly composed verses, and yet

Aphrodisian pagans could shelter the Jews in their midst or actually become converts.[16]

Despite this persistence of paganism in Aphrodisias, as at Athens a turning point seems to have arrived in the later fifth century. An Aphrodisian called Paralios who was converted to Christianity in Alexandria wrote to his pagan brothers at home, and reminded them of the hopes they had entertained that Illus would succeed in his revolt against Zeno. "Remember," he wrote, "how many sacrifices we offered as pagans in Caria to the pagan gods, when we asked the supposed gods, while cutting up livers and examining them by magic, to tell us whether with Leontius, Illus and Pamprepius and all those who rebelled with them, we would defeat the emperor Zeno, who enjoyed a pious end. We obtained a mass of oracles and of promises at the same time, according to which the emperor Zeno could not resist their attack, and that the moment had come when Christianity would dissolve and disappear and the pagan cults be restored. But the outcome showed that these oracles were mendacious, as with the oracles given by Apollo to Croesus and Pyrrhus of Epirus."[17]

Archaeology shows the determination of the now dominant Christians to overwrite the city's pagan past. Probably about 500, the great temple of Aphrodite, the city's pagan heart, was converted into a church. The temple erected in honor of the first emperors was approached by a long double-sided portico, on both sides of which were reliefs showing members of the imperial house and various divinities and personifications. Christians now defaced the more obtrusively pagan images, such as those of Zeus, Hera, and Aphrodite, but left untouched ones that represented personifications like Victory (Nike) and Health (Hygieia), or heroes like Heracles, Achilles, and Prometheus. Such personifications and heroic figures gave no offense to most Christians, who as good citizens may have wished to deface their monuments as little as possible. Sometime in the seventh century, the city's name was changed from Aphrodisias, with its connotations of the Greek goddess of love, to Stauropolis, "City of the Cross." The change signaled the triumph of Christ in a city once devoted to Aphrodite.[18]

The cave called "Apollo's Halls" to which Isidore and Asclepiodotus made their pilgrimage was in the foothills of the Messogis, the formidable mountain range lying between the valleys of the Maeander and the Cayster. This remote region, in whose recesses were pockets of excellent agricultural land, was well suited to support a conservative rural peasantry.

About twelve years after closing the schools of Athens in 529, Justinian moved to root out pagan practices in western Asia Minor, and especially the Messogis, with the help of a miaphysite Syrian bishop, John of Ephesus. As a historian and hagiographer, John has left detailed accounts of his mission, and claims to have converted seventy thousand persons. For three decades, he and his coworkers labored to destroy temples, images, and altars and to cut down sacred trees. At Pepouza in Phrygia, the cradle of the heresy called Montanism, they destroyed a reliquary containing the bones of the founders, Montanus, Maximilla, and Priscilla, and turned the Montanists' meeting place into a church. An inscription from Sardis in Lydia shows that an imperial official named Hyperechius imprisoned or exiled "unholy and polluted Hellenes," possibly in connection with this same campaign. A recent discovery in the Messogis has revealed a church built on the ruins of a temple of Zeus or Heracles, and a village named "Monastir" may preserve the name of a monastery that was one of John's proudest achievements.[19]

Christianity was born in Judaea when the region was an appendage of the province of Syria, and the name "Christians" was first used for worshipers of Jesus in Antioch, the Syrian capital. The provinces of the eastern Mediterranean were also the first in which the Christian word was spread. Yet as elsewhere the progress of the new faith was laborious. Gaza in Palestine can be observed changing from a largely pagan city about 400 to a capital of Christian culture, strongly tinged with Hellenism, a century later. Carrhae on the border with Persia remained defiantly pagan as late as the reign of Justinian and until the Arab conquest. In country districts, old cults continued to flourish, and Christian communities could scarcely be distinguished from pagan.

Gaza was situated at the junction of important land routes, and possessed a port called Maiouma. The city's first major bishop, Porphyrius, is commemorated in a biography by his deacon Mark, and though the work is sometimes unreliable in detail, it illustrates the difficulty of converting a pagan population into a Christian one even in Palestine. According to Mark, when Porphyrius arrived in 395, there were only 280 Christians, while there were eight flourishing temples, the chief of them consecrated to the rain-god Marnas. The decisive moment came seven years later, when the bishop petitioned the strong-willed empress Eudoxia, and after obtaining her influence and financial support, destroyed the "inner temple" of Marnas and built a Christian church in its stead, leaving the surrounding portico intact. Though his biographer claims that Porphyrius converted many pagans, they may still have been in the majority when he died in 420.[20]

Gaza continued to produce notable pagans late into the fifth century, among them a rhetor called Zosimus, who was executed in the reign of Zeno. Yet by now it had became a center of Christian culture, and produced three important sophists, Procopius and Aeneas in the last quarter of the fifth century and Choricius in the first quarter of the sixth. A feature that unites all three is the ease with which they move between pagan and Christian modes of expression. Procopius's panegyric of the emperor Anastasius, composed about the year 500, avoids any overt reference to Christianity, praising the emperor as a descendant of Heracles and speaking of "the holy city" to avoid the un-Greek name Jerusalem. Almost all of Aeneas's twenty-five letters are addressed to Christians, but he can refer to "libations to Hermes" or "the mysteries of the gods" without giving offense, since Hermes was accepted as the personification of eloquence, and "the gods" are the Muses, who for Christians were merely a personification of the arts. Choricius champions mime, a form of drama which Christian preachers had denounced for centuries, and in his peroration gives an encomium of Dionysus as a benefactor of mankind. As the leading sophist of Gaza, a secular official on excellent terms with the ecclesiastical and secular powers, Choricius defends this popular entertainment by arguing that it promotes harmless amusement, not public immorality.[21]

While Gaza appears to have become largely Christian by the late fifth century, Carrhae in Osrhoene, on the border of the Roman Empire with Persia, was able to maintain its traditional cults, thanks largely to its strategic position. Like Gaza before the arrival of Porphyrius, Carrhae had a civic god who provided a religious focus and a bulwark against Christianity, the moon-god Sin. Sin's great temple may have been demolished in the reign of Theodosius I, but (even if it was not rebuilt, as it may have been) the city had a plethora of other cults. While nearby Edessa had been a Christian stronghold since the early third century, Carrhae was still predominantly pagan in 549, when it welcomed the Persian king Kosrow (Chosroes). The emperors ruling from Constantinople perhaps felt it unwise to enforce their religion in a city essential for the defense of the border with Persia.[22]

About the same time as Procopius of Gaza was composing orations in praise of the city's bishops, the same Isidore who had visited "Apollo's Halls" in Caria toured the countryside of Syria in the company of his pupil Damascius, a native of Damascus. In their journey they visited Bostra, where Isidore encountered the Arabian god whose Greek name, Theandrios or Theandrites ("God-Male"), he interpreted as inspiring a manly life. In the Decapolis of southern Syria, the two visited a chasm "roofed over on every side with rocks and with certain wild plants growing from the rocks," and containing a waterfall that they identified with the River Styx. Farther south, in the region of Petra, they collected legends of the ancient Nabataean god Dusares.[23]

Even when country districts had been nominally converted, their faith could be very superficial. John of Ephesos preserves an account of a pastoral community east of the Euphrates. In this mountainous district a wandering missionary named Symeon came across shepherds living in widely scattered homesteads. Finding that they had no church and did not take communion, he asked if they were Christians, Jews, or pagans, to which they replied that they were indeed Christians, but lived on the mountains "like animals." Symeon reconsecrated a neglected church, tonsured the children over the objections of their parents, and gave the community instruction until he had "converted them from the error of their apostasy to proper rules of life, both bodily and spiritual."[24]

The contrast between city and country is nowhere more stark than in Egypt. Alexandria was still the administrative capital, and the bishop of Alexandria had ecclesiastical sovereignty over all of Egypt, though it was now divided into several provinces. Church building in Alexandria began already in the 320s, and the city's several strong-willed bishops, including Athanasius, Theophilus, and Cyril, were eloquent and sometimes vigorous enemies of paganism. The foundation of monasticism is traditionally associated with Antony, born about 250 in Middle Egypt, and monks *(monachoi)* start to be mentioned in Egyptian papyri about the year 300. Monks were to play a large part in the enforcement of Christianity in the fourth and fifth centuries, in Egypt as well as in neighboring Syria.[25]

One of the most famous of these crusading monks is Shenute, abbot of the White Monastery at Atripe (Athribis) in Upper Egypt. The monastery was about seven miles from Akhmim, known by its Greek name as "Panopolis," the capital of the administrative district or "nome." Shenute left a large body of letters and sermons, some of them still unpublished, which are foundational texts of Coptic Christianity. In addition, a biography of Shenute survives in several versions and several languages, and is commonly attributed to his successor as abbot, Besa. This contains much that is valuable, but also a large dose of the miraculous, as when Shenute, summoned against his will to Constantinople, travels there and back by air, riding on a cloud. Despite this abundance of evidence, much about Shenute is uncertain, including his dates of birth and death, but the time of his major activity appears to have been about 430 to 460.[26]

Paganism was one of Shenute's chief preoccupations, and on two social levels. Besa mentions as his chief adversary a landowner called Gesios, who continued to worship the old gods and to study classic texts of Late Antique religiosity such as Plato and Philostratus's *Life of Apollonius of Tyana*. On one occasion, Shenute found him worshiping in a ruined temple of Atripe. On another, the abbot and several of his monks made the journey to Panopolis, broke into Gesios's house, and smashed some statues and carried off others, posting on his door as they left a notice detailing his "disgrace and infamy." It was not merely Gesios's paganism that enraged the abbot, but his exploitation of the poor, whom he forced to buy bad meat and spoiled wine, and to contribute to the upkeep of the local bathhouse, which they never used. After Gesios's death, Shenute had a vision of him in hell, with his tongue tied to his big toe and in eternal torment. Shenute had also to contend with traditional cults, especially in the nearby village of Pneuit, where he and his monks smashed the images. This raid appears to have caused as much alarm among local Christians as among pagans, and the "priests of idolatry" charged Shenute before the military governor at Antinoe, but he justified his actions so eloquently as to receive acquittal.[27]

At the same time as being a great Christian city, and after 451 the spiritual capital of anti-Chalcedonian belief, Alexandria was the second pole of Hellenic culture after Athens. In the fourth century, philosophy seems to have had no major representative there, and none of the Alexandrian philosophers noted by Eunapius seem to have attained much eminence. But about 400, just when the Neoplatonist Plutarch was reviving the cause of philosophy in Athens, Alexandria produced the brilliant Hypatia, who, according to the church historian Socrates, "succeeded to the Platonic school going back to Plotinus." Even Damascius admits that his hero Isidore was overshadowed in Alexandria by the memory of Hypatia.[28]

In the fifth century, relations between the Neoplatonic schools of Athens and Alexandria were close. Plutarch's successor, Syrianus, was from Alexandria, as was Isidore. Syrianus's pupil Hermeias returned to his native Alexandria after studying in Athens, and there received a civic salary as professor of philosophy. On his death, his widow took their two sons back to Athens to study with Proclus. The more talented of the two, Ammonius, became the leading Neoplatonist of Alexandria later in the century, and his many pupils included Damascius and the great Christian philosopher John Philoponus. Ammonius is also the subject of an unflattering portrait from another of his pupils, the Christian Zacharias of Mitylene. He describes Ammonius "sitting on a high platform" *(bêma)* as he expounded the doctrines of Aristotle, while outside the lecture hall the west wind blew softly and the Nile flowed in high-summer spate. Polish archaeologists have excavated some twenty-five lecture halls in a quarter of modern Alexandria called Kom el-Dikka. One of these has a set of steps leading up to a platform for the professor, an exact illustration of Zacharias's portrait of Ammonius. In the 480s, the philosopher was implicated in a shadowy intrigue called by Damascius "the Ammonius affair," from which he escaped by reaching an accommodation with the Christian authorities.[29]

Zacharias's caustic comment on Ammonius's "sophistic" style of lecturing again shows the link between philosophy and rhetoric. Isidore, who was later to be scholarch in Athens, was a poor speaker, and yet when he taught in Alexandria, professors of rhetoric and poetry attended his lectures in order to sharpen their powers of reasoning. Damascius's professor of rhetoric, Theon, was the son of another such professor, and Damascius himself studied the subject for three years under Theon and taught it for nine more. Severus, later miaphysite bishop of Antioch, came to Alexandria while still a pagan to study rhetoric, where his fellow student Zacharias was to be his future biographer. The scholarly study of poetry, an Alexandrian specialty since the Hellenistic period, still survived. Isidore tried to write poetry, but his pupil Damascius claims to have corrected his teacher's metrical errors.[30]

Much as cultured paganism at Athens passed through a crisis in the third quarter of the fifth century, with the closing of the Asclepieion and the removal of cult statues, so also an obscure chain of events led to the arrest and torture of Alexandrian pagans under the emperor Zeno (474–491). For much of his reign, the emperor was confronted both by external enemies and by a series of revolts. The first of these occurred soon after his accession, when Verina, the widow of his predecessor, Leo I, proclaimed her brother Basiliscus emperor, and Zeno had to take refuge in his native Isauria. Five years later, Marcianus, Leo's son-in-law, attempted a coup in Constantinople, but the energetic master of the offices, another Isaurian named Illus, foiled the plot, and Marcianus was imprisoned in the Isaurian fortress of Papyrius. According to Damascius, Zeno now became mistrustful of Illus and sent him away from the capital as supreme military officer *(magister utriusque militiae)* of the eastern provinces, in which position he began a revolt of his own in 484. Having Verina in his power, since she too had been imprisoned in Isauria, he used her authority to elevate a young soldier named Leontius as a puppet emperor. Within a few months the revolt collapsed, but the rebels held out for another four years in Papyrius.[31]

Though a Chalcedonian Christian, Illus had long been under the influence of Pamprepius, the pagan poet of Egyptian origin who had once been Athens's official *grammatikos*. After studying with Proclus in Athens, Pamprepius moved to Constantinople, where his flamboyant paganism in this deeply Christian city soon drew attention. Illus, now at the summit of his power, took Pamprepius into his patronage, and managed to get him a public salary and a series of official positions. When Illus began his revolt, Leontius appointed Pamprepius as his master of the offices, and in that position he was thought to have influenced both Illus and Leontius in the direction of paganism. Within the confines of Papyrius, he soon lost his influence and was executed, his body thrown over the ramparts.[32]

The events of 484 led some pagans to hope for a revival of the ancient religion, a hope immediately frustrated but destined soon to revive. In his hostile account of Pamprepius, Damascius calls him "an effective tool of the Necessity that runs counter to the good," referring to what he calls "the Ammonius affair." This appears to have grown out of disturbances narrated by Zacharias in his *Life of Severus*. Paralios, mentioned above as a pagan from Aphrodisias in Caria, came to Alexandria to study under Horapollon, whom Zacharias unkindly describes as a *grammatikos*. When Paralios was visiting his brother Athanasios, a monk in the nearby monastery of Enaton, Athanasios and his fellow-monk Stephanos began to undermine his beliefs, and urged him to test their arguments on a group of pagan philosophers, including Horapollon and Isidore. This led to an incident, trivial in its origins, but destined to have drastic consequences. The Elder Asclepiodotus of Aphrodisias, a prominent pagan, had married his daughter to his younger namesake, a native of Alexandria who had settled in the city, but the marriage proved barren. The Younger Asclepiodotus claimed that the goddess Isis had appeared to him in a vision, and promised to grant him children if he visited the site of her shrine at Menouthis, a short distance east of Alexandria. Returning to Alexandria with his wife, he was persuaded by dream interpreters at Menouthis to copulate with an idol of the goddess and then to have intercourse with his wife, and thus to father the desired heir; but this recourse failed, and the priest at Menouthis advised him to substitute the child of a village priestess. Returning to Alexandria with his alleged heir, Asclepiodotus gave great joy to the pagan party. Paralios was at first inclined to believe the supposed miracle, but his Christian associates persuaded him to make his own enquiries at Menouthis, and when he had done so and exposed the fraud, he returned to Alexandria and began to mock the pagan establishment. During one of Horapollon's Friday lectures, when most of the Christians were absent, the pagan students fell on Paralios and beat him up, so that he now took refuge with the Christians. The affair came to the attention of the patriarch, Peter Mongos (mentioned by Damascius as "a reckless and evil man"), who demanded that the prefect investigate, but the prefect was a secret pagan, and his chief of staff an open idolater. When he ordered Paralios to bring an official complaint before his court, the Christian party objected that the chief of staff, being a pagan, was debarred from public office. As he still hesitated to act, a band of Christian students streamed out to Menouthis, conducted a search, and found pagan idols carefully concealed in private house. Some they burned on the spot, while the rest they loaded onto twenty-four camels before bringing them back to Alexandria together with the priest. Here they forced him to explain before a crowd of mocking Christians which demons they represented, after which they burned these idols too.[33]

Perhaps alerted by the events, the emperor sent an agent named Nicomedes to Alexandria with orders to arrest Ammonius, the city's leading Neoplatonist, and his confederate, the *grammatikos* Harpocras. Isidore, who was still in Alexandria, tried to forewarn Harpocras, but his letter was intercepted, and Nicomedes used it to locate two other philosophers, Heraiscos and his nephew Horapollon, and to torture them for information about Isidore and Harpocras. Damascius, at this time a young student of Ammonius, may have been involved, since his younger brother Julian tried to make his escape, but was arrested and tortured.[34]

The family of Heraiscos and Horapollon illustrates the complex links between Greek literature and philosophy, Egyptian religion, and Christianity. The family originated from the Panopolite nome of Upper Egypt, the same district in which Shenute had been so active in his long career as abbot of the White Monastery. An earlier Horapollon was a professor of literature *(grammatikos),* and his sons Asclepiades and Heraiscos were both eminent philosophers. Heraiscos wrote a work on Egyptian philosophy that he dedicated to Proclus, and his nephew, the younger Horapollon, is the author of an extant key to Egyptian hieroglyphs, which combines a number of correct equivalents with a larger number of fantastic ones. By the 490s, he had become a convert to Christianity, whether from political pressure, economic motives, or inner conviction. In an extant petition to a local official, copied by a later hand, he accuses his estranged wife of stealing his property.[35]

Though Christianity was now supreme in Alexandria and other cities of Egypt, the situation was different where imperial and ecclesiastical power was weaker. Considering the territory south of the First Cataract not valuable enough to deserve protection, Diocletian had withdrawn the boundary northward to Syene (Assouan), and permitted the nomadic Blemmyes and other tribes to worship their gods on the island of Philae, a concession that they retained until the reign of Justinian. In the fifth century, the bishop of Syene petitioned Theodosius II begging for help: "I and my churches are in the middle of the accursed barbarians, and we cannot stand the sudden attacks of the Blemmyes, the Annoubadae, and those allied with them, since there is no soldier guarding our region." About a century later, the city of Ombos, downriver from Syene, petitioned the military governor, Flavius Marianus. The details are unclear, but some "bold and slippery" man *(mataios kai olisthêros),* "half-barbarian and half-pagan" *(mixhellên kai mixobarbaros),* has "disavowed the Christian reverence and worship *(sebas kai thrêskos),* and consecrated shrines *(sêkoi)* to demons and idols *(xoana).*" These actions have caused the Blemmyes, "who had been turning to acknowledge the eternal God," so that they are now helping him pillage the citizens' property and extort money from the public treasury.[36]

Paradoxically, despite the much greater political and military disruptions of the West, where Rome was several times sacked, and where German tribes occupied part or all of the former western provinces, Christianity's progress, though no less uneven, was in the end to prove more durable than in the East. In the East, the emperor was a defender of the faith, hedged with divinity but not ordained, even if like Constantine he thought of himself as "bishop of those outside." After the Council of Chalcedon in 451, the emperors ruling from Constantinople had sometimes to use armed force in order to impose their views in miaphysite regions such as Egypt. They could stray from Chalcedonian orthodoxy, as Anastasius was deemed to have done, and even Justinian in his last years. By contrast, the West had a single ecclesiastical authority, the bishop of Rome, who could enforce and propagate the faith even when dealing with many sources of secular power. As the Germanic kingdoms abandoned Arianism and embraced Trinitarian orthodoxy, the pope's spiritual hand was strengthened. Gregory the Great's diplomatic campaign, easing the passage of Augustine through Gaul and into southeastern Britain, occurred only a few years before Muhammad received his summons from the angel Gabriel, a summons that was to affect the East much sooner than the West, and to have more profound and more permanent consequences.

CHAPTER ELEVEN

Conclusion: The Persistence of Paganism

THERE ARE NO census figures to record how fast the conversion of the Roman Empire to Christianity occurred. In Egypt, where conversion may have been unusually rapid, it has been estimated that pagans enjoyed a large majority in 300, had lost it by 325, and were a small minority by 400. In that year, a group of monks visiting Egypt from Palestine found not a single pagan in the city of Oxyrhynchus. By 600, the portion of remaining pagans within what had been the borders of the empire must have been relatively small.[1]

The numerical change is only one of several in this same period, and no less decisive are the political and social ones. Politically, the effect of Constantine's conversion was to nationalize Christianity—not to compel conversion or to execute or exile nonbelievers, but to put the new religion on an official basis by providing subsidies for church buildings and ecclesiastical personnel, by giving separate jurisdiction to bishops, and by the emperor's personal intervention in church councils. Socially, favor to Christians in filling offices and the gradual extrusion of non-Christians from the civil and military service reinforced the other effects of imperial policy.

Yet Christianity followed its own destiny in partial independence of imperial favor or supervision. Emperors labored in vain to limit and to heal doctrinal division: Constantine's efforts at Nicaea were followed by those of Constantius at Serdica, Theodosius I at Constantinople, Theodosius II at the "Robber Council" of 449, and by the Unity Decree (Henôtikon) of Zeno and Justinian's legislation against perceived heretics. Emperors could do even less to limit divergences from orthodoxy among peoples outside their control. In the fourth century, the Goths and other German confederations adopted Arian Christianity, and when Arianism became officially heretical in 381, the split served only to reinforce political and military hostility.

In the same time period of 300 to 600, the Roman Empire underwent its own transformation, and Constantinople lost much of western and central Europe together with northwest Africa in the fifth century, though it recovered parts of Italy, Spain, and Africa in the sixth. On the eastern frontier, war with Persia recurred in every century from the third to the seventh. Three kings, Shapur I, Kosrow I, and Kosrow II took Syrian Antioch, one of the great centers of Christianity. Much of Mesopotamia, including another Christian center, Nisibis, was ceded to Persia in 363, and the conflict only ended with Heraclius's victory over the Persians in 628. In the following year, the first clash between Constantinople and the rising power of Islam occurred at Mut'a east of the Dead Sea, but the Byzantine defeat on the River Yarmuk in 636 began the inexorable advance of Islam over the eastern and much of the western empire.[2]

It has been said that Christianity "destroyed" paganism. Gibbon entitled his twenty-eighth chapter "The Final Destruction of Paganism," which he saw as a process begun by Constantine and ended by Theodosius I within the space of less than a century. Yet, in another sense, paganism was indestructible, in that it had never really existed except as an entity in the eyes of its opponents. Believers in the old gods continued to worship even within the borders of the empire, though largely in fringe regions such as Osrhoene, southern Egypt, and Sardinia. Outside the areas of direct imperial control, but in doctrinal communion with the great metropolitan centers of Rome, Constantinople, Alexandria, and Antioch, independent states had already adopted or begun to adopt the new faith as their national religion. Such were Ethiopia and Armenia in the fourth century and the kingdom of Anglia in the seventh. As Christianity spread and became "Christendom," so it widened its contacts with the pagans on its edges, an ever-receding horizon of disbelief.[3]

Where states were not in such communion, for instance, the German tribes that remained Arian, their policies made them act much as if they had been pagan, to the grief of their Catholic neighbors. The struggles of the abbot Severinus on the south bank of the Danube in the late fifth century failed to stamp out paganism even in his own flock, and the kingdom of the Arian Rugii to the north of the river veered between tolerance and hostility. After his death, the remaining congregation retreated to a new home near Naples.[4]

The problems faced by Constantinople were different and graver. Here the enemies included Huns, Avars, Persians, and, from the seventh century, the Arabs with their new and vigorous faith. Persian invasions often carried off both pagans and Christians, and the treatment of both groups could sometimes be lenient, at other times harsh. After taking Antioch in 540, the Persian king Kosrow I settled his captives in a new city called "Kosrow's-Better-Antioch" (Weh-Andiok-Kosrow), also known as "The Roman Town" (Rumagan), and provided the new city with Hellenic amenities such as a hippodrome and public baths. Persia had political motives for weakening resistance by leniency, and also for welcoming groups in disfavor with Constantinople. It had long sheltered a Jewish population, had fostered the spread of Manichaeism, and from 431 onward welcomed Nestorius and his followers after they had been condemned as heretics (the Nestorian church went on, as did Manichaeism, to spread as far as China). By contrast, when the second Kosrow took Jerusalem in 614, he is said to have slaughtered many Christians and to have carried others off into captivity, though later Christian accounts may have exaggerated the destruction.[5]

The establishment of Arab rule over much of the old Roman Empire, at first over the eastern provinces and later as far as Spain, was similarly not fatal to Christianity, but decline was inevitable. "Among (the causes) were certainly the grinding burden of the poll tax, the fierce rivalries between Christian sects, often eager to appeal to the Muslim authorities for support against their hated opponents, and the tendency of ambitious figures in the Christian community to convert for career reasons." The history of Christianity in the Arab world partly replicated the history of paganism after the conversion of Constantine.[6]

Even before the coming of the Arabs, more flagrantly pagan practices such as animal sacrifice and idolatry had died out in the eastern provinces under the attacks of churchmen such as Cyril of Alexandria and of emperors such as Justinian, rather as the polytheism of pre-Islamic Arabs withered under the monotheism of the Prophet. But perceived paganism persisted, especially as the doctrinal fissures between Rome and Constantinople, latent since the fourth century, widened into an abyss. The iconoclastic controversy was one of the most damaging of such disputes. John of

Damascus attacked the iconoclasm of the emperor Leo III, but also compiled a catalogue of one hundred heresies of which Islam was the last. His account curiously mixes paraphrases of the Qur'an with hostile speculation. The "Saracens" had long been idolaters, he claimed, until a false prophet named Mamed rose up and preached that there was only one God, forming his own heresy partly from the Old and New Testaments, and perhaps from information provided by an Arian monk. John goes on to charge that the Prophet's writings contained absurdities about God the Son. For instance, they said that when He went to heaven, God asked him if He had ever claimed to be the Son of God, and He replied: "Have pity on me, Lord: you know I never said that, and that I am not too proud to be your servant. Transgressing humans have written that I made this claim, and they have lied against me and are in error." In a separate treatise, John devised a series of answers for the faithful to give when "Saracens" attacked their beliefs. Christians like John now found themselves a minority in an empire that had its own, vigorous religion, where they were classed with the Jews as a "People of the Book."[7]

In the Latin-speaking lands where the word *paganus* was born, "pagans" dwindled to a remnant, preserved here and there in country districts. Paganism can be said to die out in the sense that gods condemned by the Church ceased to receive overt worship. In some former provinces such as Britain, this did not happen until well after they had been lost to the Roman Empire, and here the empire may be said to have died before paganism. In a broader sense, that of attachment to old rituals or habits that shocked ecclesiastics such as Martin of Braga, the disappearance of paganism was never fully complete. Perception also caused Christians to see other Christian sects as impure and virtually pagan. In the third century, the followers of the Roman priest Novatian broke away from the established Church because of its perceived weakness in time of persecution, and these called themselves by the Greek word for "pure," *Katharoi*. The Donatists in Africa similarly considered their church "pure" because of its stand in the Diocletianic persecution. The medieval Cathars were "pure" for the different reason that, like the Manichaeans before them, they had a dualistic view of the parallel existence of good and evil, some even holding that the Devil was a Son of God. In the Reformation, Protestants held that Rome had become infected with paganism. In late-sixteenth-century England, Puritanism sprang from a belief that the Anglican Church had moved too close to Rome. In the eighteenth century, Protestants of the Enlightenment such as Gibbon held that the Church of St. Peter, by its cult of Mary and the saints, its use of pomp, imagery, and incense, had become imbued with the very paganism it had seemed to destroy.[8]

In the Anglophone society of past centuries, especially the nineteenth, the term "heathen" designated those other than Jews who lacked knowledge of Christianity and offered a harvest of souls ripe for conversion. The term "heathen" has faded away, not because no such persons remain, but because it implies a superiority of Christianity to other religions such as Islam. Insofar as British missionary movements were bound up with empire, the disappearance of "heathens" also reflects a geopolitical change in a world where imperialism carries a negative charge. So also ancient paganism was a specter that vanished only when it ceased to haunt the minds of its opponents.[9]

APPENDIX

TIMELINE

NOTES

INDEX

APPENDIX

Was Macrobius a Christian?

Until 1938, the author of the *Saturnalia* and the *Commentary on the Dream of Scipio* was generally known as Macrobius, and was thought to have lived approximately at the beginning of the fifth century. The manuscripts of the *Commentary* call him "Macrobius Ambrosius Theodosius, v(ir) c(larissimus)," and he was identified with the Macrobius who was *vicarius* of the Spains in 399 and proconsul of Africa in 410. He was also identified with the *praepositus sacri cubiculi* of the same name attested in 422, but such officials were eunuchs, whereas Macrobius the author had a son. Since his works, it was argued, showed him to be a pagan, he must have been converted to Christianity after writing them, the unspoken assumption being that a high administrator in this period can only have been a Christian.[1]

In 1938, Santo Mazzarino briefly advanced a new proposal. Observing that the conventions of the fifth century suggested that Macrobius's principal name was "Theodosius," Mazzarino identified him with a praetorian prefect of that name attested in 430. His thesis was revived and reinforced by Alan Cameron in 1968, and was strengthened in 1982 when an inscription showed that the author's son Eustathius, to whom he dedicated the *Saturnalia,* was prefect of the city of Rome at an unknown date between 457 and 472, and had the names "Fl(avius) Macrobius Plotinus Eustathius." This view has now gained general, though not universal, acceptance.[2]

This redating makes more urgent the question of Macrobius's religious affiliation, since it entails that he lived a generation later than had been believed, and at a time when Christianity was even more entrenched in the Roman Empire than before. C. W. Hedrick in 2000 revived the argument from Macrobius's official position, applying it to the situation of the 430s: "Given [Macrobius's] prominent position at the court of Galla Placidia in 430, it seems certain that he must have been a Christian." In recent years, P. Lebrecht Schmidt has proposed that the combination of "Theodosius" and "Ambrose," names of the emperor who came to power in 379 and of the bishop of Milan from 384, "obviously allows the inference of a Christian origin and a corresponding way of life transmitted to the son from his father; hence it is correspondingly certain that he was born after 379" (lässt offensichtlich auf christliche Herkunft und ein entsprechendes, dem Sohn durch den Vater mitgegebenes Lebensprogramm schliessen: ein Geburtsjahr nach 379 ist damit ebenfalls sicher). Alan Cameron, who has done more than anyone to advance understanding of Macrobius and the *Saturnalia* in recent decades, firmly rejected the thesis of Macrobius's Christianity in 1967 and again in 1977, but has now modified his earlier position: "[Macrobius is] surely not a pagan," "if a pagan, . . . not writing with a specifically pagan agenda." In his new Loeb text of the *Saturnalia,* Robert Kaster has called him "probably a Christian and certainly writing for an audience he assumed to be Christian."[3]

Kaster has set out the arguments for Macrobius's Christianity as follows:

1. "The name 'Theodosius' is hardly found among the Roman elite before the reign of Theodosius the Great: since Macrobius was given the name about the same time that the latter was closing the temples and forbidding the cult of the traditional religion, the parents who named him after the emperor are very unlikely to have been 'pagans.' "

2. "Macrobius held one of the very highest positions in what was, by 430, a thoroughly Christianized imperial administration."

3. "Macrobius has a character say, 'I too once snatched my hand out from under the teacher's rod, I too have heard lectures on the pontifical law' (3.10.2). . . . The man who wrote those words had no personal experience of the ways in which the lore and practices of the traditional religion were transmitted, but simply used the analogy of the literary culture's institutions—or the analogy of Christian catechistic practices."

4. "Another speaker, referring to the cycle of market days, is made to say, 'The festivals held every ninth day provide the opportunities for the *pagani* and *rustici* to gather for purposes of trade or to see to their personal affairs' (1.16.6). In their original senses, the terms *pagani* and *rustici*

were essentially synonyms ('people of the countryside,' 'peasants'): Macrobius here used the second to gloss the first because he anticipated that his Christian audience would understand *pagani* in the pejorative, sectarian sense it had come to have."

5. "Among the witticisms attributed to Augustus . . . is the following: 'On hearing that the son of Herod, king of the Jews, had been slain, when Herod ordered that all boys in Syria under the age of two be killed, Augustus said, 'It's better to be Herod's pig than his son' (2.4.11). Herod the Great did kill his oldest son and heir apparent shortly before his own death in 4 BCE, which could easily have prompted Augustus's remark. But that murder had nothing to do with the event it is tied to here, the Slaughter of the Innocents, which Matthew alone of the Evangelists recounts (2.16–18) and—as has long been noted—Macrobius alone of secular authors mentions. The witticism in its present form can derive only from a Christian source, and Macrobius assumed that his Christian audience will need no explanation."

To take these arguments in turn:

1. The name "Theodosius." This rests on the assumption that Macrobius must have been born about 390 to be urban prefect in 430. But his successor, the Younger Nicomachus Flavianus, had held public office for more than fifty years before becoming prefect. If Macrobius was from Africa, as has often been thought, his name might equally well be derived from Theodosius's father, who had brilliantly suppressed the revolt of Firmus there in 374. The name "Theodosius," "God's Gift," had been in use since the fourth century BCE, and the *Lexicon of Greek Personal Names* lists thirty-nine examples from Attica alone. "Ambrosius," derived from the mythical food of the gods, is another name with a very long history, even if rarer than "Theodosius," with the earliest example in Attica being from the sixth century BCE.[4]

2. Though the large majority of "administrators" were Christian by 430, pagans were not excluded. The highly aristocratic Rufius Antonius Agrypnius Volusianus, the last pagan in a family that was now Christian, was prefect of the city of Rome from 417 to 418, praetorian prefect from 428 to 429, and still a pagan when he was sent on a delicate diplomatic mission to Constantinople in 436. When he fell ill, his niece, the great

Christian benefactress Melania, begged the patriarch of Constantinople, Proclus, to help in converting him to Christianity. The dying man declared, "If Rome had three men such as Proclus, there would be no pagans there."[5]

3. The sentence translated by Kaster as "I too once snatched my hand out from under the teacher's rod, I too have heard lectures on the pontifical law" (3.10.2) can be more literally translated as "We (*or* "I") too once withdrew our hands from beneath the rod, we (*or* "I") too have listened to pontifical law" (*cepimus iuris pontificii auditum*). For *auditus* in Macrobius, the *Thesaurus Linguae Latinae* (1.2.1298, 54–56) cites the phrases *ut auditu uestro recreer* (1.24.21) and *rerum talium capiuntur auditu* (7.1.9), the first of which Kaster translates as "so that I can be refreshed by hearing you" and the second as "are beguiled by the things they hear." The speaker here, "We (*or* "I") too once withdrew our hands from beneath the rod," is Evangelus, whose role in the work is that of the ill-mannered skeptic. He is opening an attack on the previous speakers after their praise of Vergil's sacral expertise, and he does so by quoting the jurist Ateius Capito's treatise *On the Law of Sacrifices (De iure sacrificiorum)* and an unnamed work of the antiquarian Cornelius Labeo. Elsewhere he addresses Symmachus as a social equal and perhaps a coeval: "No, Symmachus, when we were boys we admired (Vergil) uncritically, and neither our teachers nor our age allowed us to consider his faults" (*immo, Symmache, cum pueri essemus sine iudicio mirabamur, inspicere autem uitia nec per magistros nec per aetatem licebat, Sat.* 1.24.6). If Evangelus "heard" these works in school, it would follow that young aristocrats of the fourth century studied priestly antiquities among their school subjects, and there is no need to imagine formal "lectures" on pontifical law.

Kaster's final two arguments assume what they were meant to prove, that Macrobius was writing for a Christian "audience." Argument 4 does not seem very strong. As Kaster observes, "*pagani* and *rustici* were essentially synonyms": if Macrobius was afraid that Christians might misunderstand the doublet *pagani itemque rustici,* he had only to use the simple *rustici.* Argument 5 is trickier. A more literal translation of the relevant sentence is: "When [Augustus] had heard that, among the boys in Syria whom Herod, king of the Jews, had ordered to be put to death before their second birthday, his son too had been killed, he said, 'It is better to be Herod's pig than his son'" (*cum audisset inter pueros quos in Syria Herodes rex Iudaeorum intra bimatum iussit interfici filium quoque eius occisum, ait, "melius est Herodis porcum esse quam filium," Sat.* 2.4.11). Macrobius's telling of the story implies both that Herod's order had applied to Syria, and that his son was one of those killed in infancy. In historical fact, Herod ordered the death of his sons Alexander and Aristobulus about 7 BCE and of his eldest son, Antipater, a few days before his own death. The Gospel of Matthew (2.16–18) says that Herod ordered the massacre of all children "in Bethlehem and its neighborhood, of the age of two years or less," and says nothing about Syria or about a son of Herod. According to Josephus, the dying king also summoned "all the notable men of the nation," one from each household, had them imprisoned in the hippodrome of Caesarea, and ordered his sister Salome and her husband to have them all shot down after his death; as soon as he had died, the couple countermanded his orders and sent the prisoners home. Where out of this farrago of rumor Macrobius picked up the detail of "the boys in Syria whom Herod had ordered to be put to death before their second birthday," which he then tied to the death of the king's unnamed son, it is now impossible to say. So far from requiring "no explanation," a Christian audience might well have been surprised at his divergences from an account they presumably knew by heart.[6]

It is agreed on all sides that Macrobius's extant works make no overt reference to Christianity. The part of the *Saturnalia* that has seemed to offer the clearest view of his beliefs is the long discourse on the sun-god given to the aristocrat Praetextatus in the first book (1.7.7–23). This is one of the longest speeches in the entire work, and being spoken by the chief interlocutor, it is presumably meant to have a special prominence. Praetextatus is replying to an observation of Avienus, author of the extant *Fabulae*.[7] "Do not think, my dear Avienus, that the flock of poets, when they speak of the gods, do not for the most part borrow the seeds of philosophy from hallowed spaces *(adyta)*. When they identify almost all the gods, those beneath the heaven at least, with the sun, it is not empty superstition but divine reason that supports them." Praetextatus goes on to prove his position, first enumerating the many names and powers of Apollo, and then showing that he is also Liber or Dionysus, Mars, Mercury, Asclepius (who is both the son of Apollo and identical with him), and Hercules, after which he adduces a series of non-Roman gods such Sarapis, Adonis, and Attis. He then argues that "all the signs of the zodiac are rightly ascribed to the nature of the Sun," until finally he returns to three gods, Pan, Saturn, and "Jupiter himself, the king of the gods," whom he holds to be identical with the sun. When Praetextatus has finished, "all had their faces turned to him, and expressed their admiration by their astonishment. One praised his memory, another his learning, all his piety *(religio),* saying that he had a unique knowledge of the secret nature of the gods, since he alone by his genius could both conceive the divine by his intellect and express it by his genius." It is hard to see the audience as merely admiring Praetextatus's erudition and eloquence, and not endorsing the substance of his views.[8]

The doctrines that Macrobius makes Praetextatus express were not such as to offend a "Christian audience," but also not likely to suggest that the author was one of them. While Christians held that the sun was one of God's most glorious creations, they were adamant that it was an object devoid of intelligence and not, as some pagans held, an intelligent being. They might also have felt uneasy at hearing that Asclepius was "both the son of Apollo and identical with him." Asclepius was a god who gave especial offense to Christians because of his supposedly miraculous powers, and so casually to assimilate a father-god with his son would have sounded alarming in the 420s and 430s, when the relation of God the Father to God the Son was the subject of fierce debate between Rome, Constantinople, and Alexandria. In the *Commentary,* Macrobius argued strongly for the eternity of the universe, another position that Christians rejected as contradicting their belief in the finite nature of Creation.[9]

Praetextatus's long discourse, a kind of "aretalogy" or prose hymn to the sun-god, recalls the *Hymn to King Helios* written by an emperor who had appointed him to one of his earliest offices, Julian. Julian's conception is very different, and philosophically more sophisticated. His sun emanated from the primal Good residing at the ineffable heart of the Universe. "He proceeded as One from One from the one intelligible cosmos as King Helios." He is identical with the other gods, and yet mystically they are extensions of him, so that "there are gods that are of one kind and nature as Helios, who encapsulate the undefiled nature of the god, multiplied in the cosmos, but existing about him in a single nature." Praetextatus's discourse shares certain details with Julian's. Both cite the same oracle, ascribed by Julian to Apollo and by Praetextatus to Orpheus, "There is one Zeus, one Hades, one Helios Sarapis." Julian never talks in terms of Mithras, even though he was an initiate, and speaks only of Helios, equating him with the Invincible Sun *(anikêtos Hêlios)* whose cult was celebrated at Rome on December 25, immediately after the Saturnalia. Mithras is likewise missing from Praetextatus's discourse in the *Saturnalia,* even though the actual Praetextatus was a Mithraic initiate. Rather than ascribing this omission to Macrobius's ignorance, it is more likely that he did not choose to exalt a god who, unlike Sol, lacked an established place in the Roman pantheon.[10]

If the actual Macrobius was a pagan, he might had the conservative, "Roman" stance of a Symmachus, the more adventurous devotion of a Praetextatus, or a purely philosophical and contemplative *religio animi.* Now that his son is known to have had the names "Macrobius Plotinus Eustathius," it can perhaps be inferred that he himself was a pagan Neoplatonist in an era when Neoplatonism was being revived in Athens by the scholarch Plutarch and his successors. As for his son's name "Plotinus," not only is it "vanishingly rare in the Roman aristocracy" and "utterly appropriate for the son of a Neoplatonist," as Kaster has observed, but "Eustathius" is also the name of a pagan Neoplatonist active under Constantius II and Julian, and of a philosopher who appears in the *Saturnalia.*[11]

Timeline

233–ca. 306:	**Porphyry,** Neoplatonist and author of *Against the Christians*
300–310 (approx.):	Council of Elvira (Spain) condemns wall paintings in churches
312:	Battle of the Milvian Bridge and conversion of Constantine
313–ca. 393:	**Libanius**
Ca. 317–ca. 388:	**Themistius**
325:	Council of Nicaea draws up first agreed statement of Christian faith (Nicene Creed)
330–400 (approx.):	**Ammianus Marcellinus**
Ca. 340–401:	Q. Aurelius **Symmachus**
341:	First antipagan legislation under western emperor Constans
348–466 (alleged):	**Shenute, abbot of the White Monastery**
354–430:	**Augustine, bishop of Hippo**
361–363:	Reign of **Julian** the "Apostate"
365–435 (approx.):	**Isidore of Pelusium**
379:	Accession of Theodosius I
380–400 (approx.):	Plutarch becomes first head (scholarch) of the Neoplatonic school at Athens
381:	Theodosius summons Council of Constantinople, which condemns Arianism; he initiates a series of antipagan laws

384:	Third *Report (relatio)* of **Symmachus**
391:	Christians led by Theophilus, bishop of Alexandria, destroy temple of Serapis
Ca. 393–ca. 466:	**Theodoret of Cyrrhus**
394 (September):	Battle of River Frigidus
395:	Death of Theodosius: Roman Empire divided between his sons Arcadius and Honorius
399:	Eastern emperor Arcadius orders the destruction of rural temples
410:	Alaric and his Gothic army sack Rome
415:	Philosopher and mathematician Hypatia lynched by Alexandrian Christians
417:	**Orosius** completes his *History against the Pagans;* **Rutilius Namatianus** returns to Gaul, later making the journey the subject of his poem *On His Return*
430–440 (approx.):	**Macrobius,** *Saturnalia*
431:	Council of Ephesus condemns Nestorius for allegedly maintaining the separation of the divine and human natures in Christ
Ca. 435:	Proclus succeeds Plutarch as Neoplatonic scholarch
435:	Theodosius II and Valentinian III forbid animal sacrifice and order closing of pagan temples
438:	Publication of the *Theodosian Code*
451:	Council of Chalcedon adopts formula of "Christ in two natures," which leads to schism with believers in Christ's single nature (miaphysites)
482–488:	Revolt of Illus, supported by soothsayer Pamprepius, against the emperor Zeno
485:	Death of Proclus; Neoplatonic school of Athens begins to decline
486–488 (approx.):	Violent attack on pagans in Alexandria and Menouthis, followed by inquisition into Alexandrian Neoplatonists ("Ammonius affair")
492–496:	**Gelasius,** bishop of Rome, forbids Christians from celebrating Saturnalia
Ca. 511:	**Eugippius,** *Life of St. Severinus*

529:	Justinian bans teaching of philosophy in Athens and forbids "Hellenes" from holding public office
531:	**Damascius** and other philosophers leave Athens for Persia
540–593 or 594:	**Gregory of Tours**
542:	**John of Ephesus** begins his thirty-year campaign of converting pagans of Asia Minor
575–600 (approx.):	**Martin of Braga,** *On the Correction of Peasants*
579:	Last known inquisition into paganism in upper ranks of society at Antioch and Constantinople
597:	Mission of Augustine, first bishop of Canterbury, to Anglia (southeastern Britain)
636:	Muslim Arabs defeat eastern Romans at Battle of River Yarmuk
675–753:	**John of Damascus**
692:	"Trullan" Council attempts to suppress pagan practices

Abbreviations

AnchBibDict	D. N. Freedman, ed., *The Anchor Bible Dictionary* (New York: Doubleday, 1992)
Barrington Atlas	R. J. A. Talbert, ed., *Barrington Atlas of the Greek and Roman World* (Princeton: Princeton University Press, 2000)
Bibliotheca Sanctorum	*Bibliotheca Sanctorum* (Rome: Istituto Giovanni XXIII, 1961–1970)
Brown, *Augustine*[2]	P. L. R. Brown, *Augustine of Hippo: A Biography,* 2nd ed. (Berkeley: University of California Press, 2000)
Brown, *Eye of the Needle*	P. L. R. Brown, *Through the Eye of the Needle* (Princeton: Princeton University Press, 2012)
Cameron, *Last Pagans*	A. Cameron, *The Last Pagans of Rome* (New York: Oxford University Press, 2011)
CAH	*The Cambridge Ancient History,* 2nd ed.
CIL	*Corpus Inscriptionum Latinarum*
CQ	*Classical Quarterly*
CRAI	*Comptes Rendus de l'Académie des Inscriptions et Belles-Lettres*
CSCO	*Corpus Scriptorum Christianorum Orientalium*
CSEL	*Corpus Scriptorum Ecclesiasticorum Latinorum*
DACL	F. Cabrol and H. Leclerq, eds., *Dictionnaire d'archéologie chrétienne et de liturgie*
Danker, *Lexicon*	F. W. Danker, ed., *A Greek-English Lexicon of the New Testament and Other Early Christian Literature,* 3rd ed. (Chicago: University of Chicago Press, 2000)

Daremberg-Saglio	Ch. Daremberg and E. Saglio, eds., *Dictionnaire des antiquités grecques et romaines d'après les textes et les monuments*
DPhA	R. Goulet, ed., *Dictionnaire des philosophes antiques* (Paris: Éditions du Centre National de la Recherche Scientifique, 1994–)
FGrHist	F. Jacoby, ed., *Die Fragmente der griechischen Historiker*
GCS	*Die Griechischen christlichen Schriftsteller der ersten drei Jahrhunderte*
IG	*Inscriptiones Graecae*
ILS	*Inscriptiones Latinae Selectae*
JRS	*Journal of Roman Studies*
LA Guide	G. W. Bowersock, P. Brown, and O. Grabar, eds., *Late Antiquity: A Guide to the Postclassical World* (Cambridge: Harvard University Press, 1999)
Lampe	G. W. H. Lampe, ed., *A Patristic Greek Lexicon*
LCL	Loeb Classical Library
LSJ	H. G. Liddell, R. Scott, and H. S. Jones, *A Greek-English Lexicon*, 9th ed.
Mansi	Mansi, G. D., ed., *Sacrorum Conciliorum Nova et Amplissima Collectio*
MGH, AA	*Monumenta Germaniae Historica, Auctores Antiquissimi*
MGH, SRM	*Monumenta Germaniae Historica, Scriptores Rerum Merovingicarum*
New Cath. Encycl.	*New Catholic Encyclopedia*, 2nd ed.
Nilsson, *GGR*³	M. P. Nilsson, *Geschichte der griechischen Religion*, 3rd ed. (Munich: Beck, 1967–1974)
Nock, *Essays*	A. D. Nock, *Essays on Religion and the Ancient World*, ed. Z. Stewart (Cambridge: Harvard University Press, 1972)
*OCD*³	*The Oxford Classical Dictionary*, 3rd ed.
ODB	*The Oxford Dictionary of Byzantium*
OGIS	W. Dittenberger, *Orientis Graeci inscriptiones selectae*

PCBE Afrique	A. Mandouze et al., *Prosopographie chrétienne du Bas-Empire 1: Prosopographie de l'Afrique chrétienne (303–533)*
PCBE Asie	S. Destephen, *Prosopographie chrétienne du Bas-Empire 3: Prosopographie du Diocèse d'Asie (325–641)*
PCBE Italie	C. Pietri, L. Pietri et al., *Prosopographie chrétienne du Bas-Empire 2: Prosopographie de l'Italie chrétienne (313–604)*
PG	J.-P. Migne, ed., *Patrologiae cursus completus: Series Graeca*
PL	J.-P. Migne, ed., *Patrologiae cursus completus: Series Latina*
PLRE	A. H. M. Jones et al., *The Prosopography of the Later Roman Empire*
RAC	*Reallexikon für Antike und Christentum*
RE	*Paulys Real-Encyclopädie der classischen Altertumswissenschaft*
Robert, *Hellenica*	L. Robert, *Hellenica: Recueil d'épigraphie, de numismatique et d'antiquités grecques* (Limoges: A. Bontemps, 1940–1965)
Robert, *OMS*	L. Robert, *Opera minora selecta* (Amsterdam: Hakkert, 1969–1990)
SC	Sources Chrétiennes
TheolDict	G. W. Bromiley, ed., *Theological Dictionary of the New Testament* (Grand Rapids: Eerdmans, 1964–1976)
TRE	*Theologische Realenzyklopädie* (Berlin and New York: W. de Gruyter, 1977–2007)

Notes

1. The Perception of Paganism

1. Acts 17.16–34. For "devout" as the meaning of *deisidaimôn* here, Danker, *Lexicon* 216; for an extended discussion, D. B. Martin, *Inventing Superstition* (Cambridge: Harvard University Press, 2004), 5–8. "Him therefore whom": some manuscripts and translations give "that therefore which." On Paul in Athens, see now A. Kaldellis, *The Christian Parthenon: Classicism and Pilgrimage in Byzantine Athens* (Cambridge: Cambridge University Press, 2009), 53–59. Pseudo-Dionysius: A. Kahzdan and B. Baldwin, "Dionysios the Areopagite, Pseudo-," *ODB* 1.629–630.

2. "The most ancient . . .": Libanius, *Orations* 13.18. On Athens' continued attraction for tourists and students, Kaldellis, *Christian Parthenon,* 19–23.

3. Jews and Hellenes: Acts 18.4, 19.17. In both places, current English versions translate "Jews and pagans" or "Jews and Gentiles." On *Hellênes* in intertestamental Jewish and early Christian texts, Danker, *Lexicon* 318. Council of Nicaea: Socrates, *Ecclesiastical History* 1.23.7. Christian "Hellenes": G. W. Bowersock, *Hellenism in Late Antiquity* (Ann Arbor: Michigan University Press, and Cambridge: Cambridge University Press, 1990), 11–13.

4. *Ethnos:* Danker, *Lexicon* 276. Jesus: Matt. 28.19. Huns: *Trullan Council* (691 CE), *Canons* 37, 39 (Mansi, 11.959).

5. Idols: Acts 15.20. Constantine's father: Eusebius, *Life of Constantine* 1.17. "Those outside": *Life of Constantine* 4.24, with the discussion of A. Cameron and S. G. Hall, *Eusebius: Life of Constantine* (Oxford: Clarendon Press, 1999) 320, "one of the most famous and puzzling statements in the *VC*." Gregory of Nyssa never uses "Hellenic," but only "outside," in his essay entitled *To the Young on How to Profit from Hellenic Literature.*

6. On the difficult question of the division of "Illyricum" (approximately the Balkans including Greece), V. Grumel, "L'Illyricum de la mort de Valentinien Ier (375)," *Revue des Études Byzantines* 9 (1951): 5–46.

7. Military sense of *paganus:* C. Mohrmann, "Encore une fois: *Paganus,*" *Vigiliae Christianae* 6 (1952): 109–121 = *Étude sur le latin des chrétiens* 3 (Rome: Edizioni di storia e letteratura, 1965), 277–289; so also Brown, in *LA Guide* 625

and *Eye of the Needle* 102; Cameron, *Last Pagans* 22–25. *Pagani* as "people of the place": P. Chuvin, *A Chronicle of the Last Pagans* (Cambridge: Harvard University Press, 1990), 9, "*pagani* are quite simply 'people of the place,' town or country, who preserved their local customs." On *pagani et montani* in Cicero, *De domo* 74, see the commentary of R. G. Nisbet (Oxford: Clarendon Press, 1939), 137–38.

8. Law of 399: *Theodosian Code* 16.10.16. Prudentius: *Against Symmachus* 1.449. Orosius: *History,* Preface 9. Rutilius Namatianus: *On His Return* 1.373. Cf. Cameron, *Last Pagans* 19nn38–39.

9. Caesarius, *Sermon* 54.1; Gelasius, *Against Andromachus* 30. On "instruction" ("catechism"), see Chap. 8.

10. For excellent objections to "polytheism" as a substitute for "paganism" in modern discourse, Cameron, *Last Pagans* 25–32. In defense of "henotheism" as a term of analysis, as opposed to "pagan monotheism" or "inclusive monotheism," C. Addey, "Monotheism, Henotheism and Polytheism in Porphyry's *Philosophy from Oracles,*" in S. Mitchell and P. Van Nuffelen, eds., *Monotheism between Pagans and Christians in Late Antiquity,* 149–165 (Leuven: Peeters, 2010).

11. Cf. G. Dagron, "L'Empire romain d'Orient au IVe siècle et les traditions politiques de l'Hellénisme: Le Témoignage de Thémistios," *Travaux et Mémoires* 3 (1968): 1, "Whatever you call it, this opposite of Christianity is a convenient notion, indispensable even, but dangerous, not very historical, and with no historical content. It is night to explain the day" (my translation). For the argument that "paganism" is not only a Christian concept but the outcome of a dialectical process between Christians and non-Christians, P. Van Nuffelen, "Eusebius of Caesarea and the Concept of Paganism," in L. Lavan and M. Mulryan, eds., *The Archaeology of Late Antique "Paganism,"* 89–109 (Leiden: Brill, 2011).

12. Spectrum: Cameron, *Last Pagans* 176–77. Cameron's placing of both "time-servers" and "sincere believers who were nonetheless not interested in . . . details of theology" in the category of "center-Christians" also combines two very different groups: a "time-server" like Domitius Modestus (*PLRE* 1.608, Modestus 2) is different from a cultivated *littérateur* like Ausonius (*PLRE* 1.140–141, Ausonius 7). Pagans in Augustine's audience: *Cum pagani ingrederentur* = F. Dolbeau, "Nouveaux Sermons de saint Augustin pour la Conversion des Païens et des Donatistes," *Revue des Etudes Augustinennes* 37 (1991): 53–78. Aristocrats: Index s.v. Volusianus.

13. "Faith": A. H. M. Jones, *The Later Roman Empire, 284–602: A Social, Economic, and Administrative Survey* (Oxford: Blackwell, 1964), 943, "Paganism was not a heroic faith, and could boast few martyrs"; R. MacMullen, *Christianity and Paganism in the Fourth to Eighth Centuries* (New Haven: Yale University Press, 1997), 72, "Taken as a whole system, paganism worked."

14. Cf. Gibbon, *Decline and Fall,* chap. 28 at end (2.96–97 Womersley), "Introduction of pagan ceremonies," with n. 90, "The imitation of Paganism is the subject of Dr. Middleton's agreeable letter from Rome," referring to Conyers Middleton, *A letter from Rome, shewing an exact conformity between popery and paganism: or, The religion of the present Romans to be derived entirely from that of their heathen ancestors* (London: W. Innys, 1729).

2. Constantine

1. This is a bare summary of a complicated period: an excellent brief treatment is Averil Cameron in A. K. Bowman et al., eds., *The Cambridge Ancient History* 12 (Cambridge: Cambridge University Press, 2005), chap. 4; of the many books, the latest is D. S. Potter, *Constantine the Emperor* (Oxford: Oxford University Press, 2013).

2. Lactantius: *On the Deaths of the Persecutors* 44.4–5 (ed. J. Moreau, SC 39 [Paris: Éditions du Cerf, 1954]). For the date of this work, T. D. Barnes, *Constantine and Eusebius* (Cambridge: Harvard University Press, 1981), 13–14; on Lactantius's account of Constantine's dream, ibid. 43. Eusebius: *Life of Constantine* 2.49 (his father's piety), 1.27–31 (Constantine's vision).

3. Constantius: *PLRE* 1.227–228, Constantius 12. Sun-god (Sol): Nilsson, *GGR*[3] 2.507–519 and 572. Eusebius, *Life* 1.17.2–3. Against the notion of Constantius's Christianity, K. M. Girardet, "Christliche Kaiser vor Konstantin d. Gr.?" in P. Kneissl and V. Losemann, eds., *Imperium Romanum: Studien zu Geschichte und Rezeption*, 299–305 (Stuttgart, F. Steiner Verlag, 1998).

4. Anastasia: *PLRE* 1.58, Anastasia 1. For this view, e.g., Barnes, *Constantine and Eusebius* 4, "The Jewish and Christian overtones of the name point unmistakably to the religious sympathies of Constantius"; for the contrary view, Girardet, "Christliche Kaiser" 303; Potter, *Constantine* 63–64.

5. For editions, translations, and commentaries, see the list in the front matter of this volume.

6. *Panegyric of 297* (IV (8) Galletier): 4.3 (benefits), 17.1 (victory). *Panegyric of 307* (no. VI (7) Galletier): 3.3 (Constantius among the gods), 14.3 (listening to speech).

7. *Panegyric of 310* (VII (6) Galletier): 21.4–5. On the location, probably Grand in the Vosges, Nixon and Rodgers, *In Praise* 248n91; *Barrington Atlas* 11F 4 (Grannum).

8. *Panegyric of 313* (IX (12) Galletier): 2.5 (supreme divinity), 25.4 (statue), 26.1 (vagueness). On this well-known way of addressing gods, E. Norden, *Agnostos Theos: Untersuchungen zur Formengeschichte religiöser Rede* (Leipzig: B. G. Teubner, 1923), 144–147.

9. Nazarius: (X (4) Galletier), 14–15. On the speaker, *PLRE* 1.618–619; Nixon and Rodgers, *In Praise* 335–336 (a "temporizer"). His daughter may have been Christian: *PLRE* 1.296, Eunomia 1.

10. For such epiphanies in historical time, L. Robert, *Études anatoliennes* (Paris: de Boccard, 1937), 460–461, 520–21; in general, E. Pax, "Epiphanie," *RAC* 5.842–844; A. Henrichs, "Epiphany," *OCD*[3] 546.

11. The inscription, *CIL* 6.1139 (*ILS* 694): new edition, *CIL* 6.8.2, p. 4328. Cf. N. H. Baynes, *Constantine the Great and the Christian Church*, 2nd ed. (London: Oxford University Press, 1972), 68, "The expression may be regarded as evidence that pagans in Rome knew of Constantine's belief that his victory had been the result of divine intervention." For a similarly ambiguous use of *diuinitas*, cf. Symmachus's general invitation to his son's praetorian games, *Letters* 8.71–72, *praefato diuinitatis fauore, diuinitatis honore praemisso*.

12. Donatism: Brown, *Augustine*[2] 208–221; T. E. Gregory, *ODB* 1.650; W. Frend, *LA Guide* 417–419. Council of Constantinople: A. Papadakis, "Constantinople I," *ODB* 1.512; H. Leppin, *TRE* 33.255–257. Christian sects: e.g., Celsus quoted by Origen, *Against Celsus* (H. Chadwick, transl., *Origen: Contra Celsum* [Cambridge: Cambridge University Press, 1953]), 3.12, 5.63.

13. Arius: V. C. De Clercq, "Arianism," "Arius," *New Cath. Encycl.* 1.660–664, 685–686. Arianism among Germans: O. Pritsak, "Goths," *ODB* 2.862; A. Kazhdan, "Ulfilas," *ODB* 3. 2139.

14. Notably the martyrdom of Saint Sabas in 372: H. Delehaye, *Analecta Bollandiana* 31 (1912) 216–221, 288–291; J.-M. Sauget, *Bibliotheca Sanctorum* 11.531–533.

15. Eusebius, *Life of Constantine* 4.25.1 (laws), 3.26 (Jerusalem), 3.56 (Aegeae), 3.58 (Heliopolis), 2.56.1 ("I wish . . ."), with the commentary of Averil Cameron and S. G. Hall, *Eusebius: Life of Constantine* (Oxford: Clarendon Press, 1999).

16. Nicagoras: *OGIS* 721; Baynes, *Constantine* 83–84; K. Clinton, *The Sacred Officials of the Eleusinian Mysteries* (Philadelphia: American Philosophical Society, 1974), 64–66; T. D. Barnes, *Constantine: Dynasty, Religion and Power in the Later Roman Empire* (Chichester, UK: Wiley-Blackwell, 2011), 192–194. Cf. F. Millar, "P. Herennius Dexippus: The Greek World and the Third-Century Invasions," *JRS* 59 (1969): 17, "The event must surely signify an attempt by Constantine to show favour to, and win the favour of, the established pagan aristocracy of Athens in the period after his victory over Licinius." Praxagoras: *FGrHist* 219 T 1; Barnes, *Constantine: Dynasty, Religion and Power* 195–197. Ablabius: *PLRE* 1.3–4, Ablabius 4. Note the second-century *dadouchos* Praxagoras: Clinton, *Sacred Officials* 61–63.

17. Eunapius, *Lives of the Philosophers* 6.2. For Sopater: *PLRE* 1.846, Sopater 1; Barnes, *Constantine and Eusebius* 252–253. Cf. Eunapius's similar story of the pagan Eustathius almost persuading the Persian king to become a philosopher until prevented by the Magi, *Lives* 6.5.8.

18. *CIL* 11.5265 (*ILS* 705). D. S. Potter, "Constantine and the Gladiators," *CQ* 60 (2010): 596–606, argues that Constantine did not ban all gladiatorial combat but only the practice of condemning convicts to fight as gladiators *(damnatio ad ludum);* M. Clauss, "Kein Aberglaube in Hispellum," *Klio* 93 (2011): 429–445, argues that by *superstitio* Constantine chiefly means haruspicy.

19. F. M. Stenton, *Anglo-Saxon England,* 2nd ed. (Oxford, 1947), 112–113.

20. Sozomen, *Ecclesiastical History* 2.8.1; G. Klinge, "Armenien," *RAC* 1.678–689; G. Fowden, *Empire to Commonwealth: Consequences of Monotheism in Late Antiquity* (Princeton: Princeton University Press, 1993), index s.v. "Armenia, Christianization of"; J.-P. Mahé in G. Dédéyan, ed., *Histoire du peuple arménien* (Toulouse: Privat, 2007), 163–175.

21. Rufinus, *Ecclesiastical History* 10.11. Cf. G. Lordkipanadze and H. Brakman, "Iberia II (Georgien): Christianisierung und Kirchengeschichte," *RAC* 17.40–51; for a comparison with the Christianization of Ethiopia (below), C. Haas, "Mountain Constantines: The Christianization of Aksum and Iberia," *Journal of Late Antiquity* 1 (2008): 101–126.

22. For the conversion of Ethiopia, see now G. W. Bowersock, *The Throne of Adulis: Red Sea Wars on the Eve of Islam* (New York: Oxford University Press, 2013). Rufinus's account: *Hist. Eccl.* 10.9–10.

23. First stage in Greek versions: E. Littmann, *Sabäische, griechische und altabessenische Inschriften: Deutsche Aksum-Expedition* 4 (1913), no. 4 (*OGIS* 200); for the second and fuller version, closely corresponding to those already known in Sabaic and Ethiopic script (Littmann, nos. 6 and 7): É. Bernand, A. J. Drewes and R. Schneider, eds., *Recueil des inscriptions de l'Éthiopie des périodes pré-axumite et axoumite* (Paris: Diffusion de Boccard, 1991), no. 270; T. Eide, T. Hägg, R. Holton Pierce, L. Török, eds., *Fontes Historiae Nubiorum* (Bergen: John Grieg AS, 1998) no. 298 (their translation). Second stage: Littman, *Inschriften* no. 11. Third stage: *Recueil* no. 271; *Fontes* 3, no. 299 (the editors' translation, slightly altered).

24. Invasions of Ardashir and Shapur I and activity of Kerdir: B. Dignas and E. Winter, *Rome and Persia in Late Antiquity: Neighbours and Rivals* (Cambridge: Cambridge University Press, 2007).

3. After Constantine

1. For an excellent discussion of Constantine's policies in regard to paganism, M. Clauss, "Kein Aberglaube in Hispellum," *Klio* 93 (2011): 429–445, esp. 439–440 on the absence of antipagan legislation from his reign.

2. Julian: G. W. Bowersock, *Julian the Apostate* (London: Duckworth, 1978), and now *Gnomon* 84 (2012): 180–181 on the pagan reaction to Julian. Libanius: *Autobiography* (*Oration* 1) 119; H.-U. Wiemer, *Libanios und Julian* (Munich: C. H. Beck, 1995), 360–363. Themistius: C. P. Jones, "Themistius after the Death of Julian," *Historia* 59 (2010): 501–506.

3. For Julian's philosophical thought, and the thesis that by its effect on Gregory of Nazianzus it helped to shape Christian theology, S. Elm, *Sons of Hellenism, Fathers of the Church* (Berkeley: University of California Press, 2012).

4. Maximus of Turin, *Sermon* no. 106.2, p. 418 Mutzenbecher. For a review of imperial legislation against paganism, K. L. Noethlichs, "Heidenverfolgung," *RAC* 13.1149–1176. On the textual problems of the *Theodosian Code*, J. K. Harper, "The *SC Claudianum* in the *Codex Theodosianus:* Social History and Legal Texts," *CQ* 60 (2010): 610–638, esp. 613–617.

5. Constans: *Theodosian Code* 16.10.2 (341), 16.10.3 (342); on the date and addressee of 16.10.3, *PLRE* 1.187–188, Catullinus 3.

6. Constantius: *Theodosian Code* 16.10.4 (= *Code of Justinian* 1.11.1), cf. 16.10.5 and 6. On the date (356, not 346) and the addressee: *PLRE* 1.879–880, Taurus 3. Eustathius: Ammianus, 17.5.15; *PLRE* 1.310, Eustathius 1. Themistius, *PLRE* 1.890. George of Cappadocia: Ammianus Marcellinus, 22.11.7. I incline to think that this refers to the Serapeum, but for discussion, see now C. A. Gibson, "The Alexandrian Tychaion and the Date of Ps.-Nicolaus *Progymnasmata*," *CQ* 59 (2009): 618–621. For a succinct account of Athanasius's vicissitudes: V. C. De Clercq, *New Cath. Encycl.* 1.817–818.

7. Jovian: O. Seeck, *RE* 9 (1916): 2006–2011. Law of toleration: Themistius, *Oration* 5.67 B, 68 D–69 C. Valentinian's policy: Ammianus, 30.9.5; *Theodosian Code* 9.16.9. Law against haruspicy: *Theodosian Code* 9.16.7. Valens and associates of Julian: Secundus, *PLRE* 1.814–816; Sebastianus, *PLRE* 1.812–813. Conspiracy of 371: Ammianus 29.1.5–2.20, cf. N. Lenski, *Failure of Empire: Valens and the Roman State in the Fourth Century A.D.* (Berkeley: University of California Press, 2002), 218–234.

8. Theodosius: *Theodosian Code* 16.10.7 (law of 381), *Theodosian Code* 16.10.9 (law of 385), 16.10.10, 16.10.11, 16.10.12 pr. (laws of 391 and 392). Libanius, *For the Temples* (*Oration* 30): in favor of a date of 390, J. A. Jiménez Sánchez, "Teodosio I, Libanio, y la prohibición de los sacrificios," *Latomus* 69 (2010): 1088–1104.

9. Ruling against destruction: *Theodosian Code* 16.10.8, cf. C. P. Jones, "Three Temples in Libanius and in the Theodosian Code," *CQ* 63 (2013), 839–844.

10. *Theodosian Code* 16.10.13 (Arcadius, 395), 15 (Honorius, 395), 17–18 (Honorius, 399), 20 (Theodosius II, 415), 23 (Theodosius II, 423), 25 (Theodosius II and Valentinian III to the praetorian prefect Isidorus [*PLRE* 2.631–633], 435).

11. *Theodosian Code* 16.10.21 (law of 416), 16.10.22, 16.10.23 (laws of 423). For highly placed pagans in the fifth century, see Chaps. 8, 9, and 10.

12. Previous rulings: *Code of Justinian* 1.11.3, 4, 6 (= *Theodosian Code* 16.10.15, 17, 24). Marcian: *Code of Justinian* 1.11.7; on the recipient, *PLRE* 2.820–21, Palladius 9. Leo: *Code of Justinian* 1.11.8; on the recipient and date, *PLRE* 2.367–368, Dioscorus 5. Anastasius: *Code of Justinian* 1.11.9; Oxyrhynchus Papyri 22.1814; S. Corcoran, "Anastasius, Justinian and the Pagans," *Journal of Late Antiquity* 2 (2008): 183–208, esp. 193–198.

13. *Code of Justinian* 1.5.12.4.

14. John Malalas, *Chronicle* 18.42: Theophanes the Confessor, *Chronicle,* Anno Mundi 6022 (p. 274 Mango and Scott), gives a slightly different version. For the connection of this legislation with *Code of Justinian* 1.11.10, Corcoran, "Anastasius, Justinian and the Pagans" 198–203. Borboritae: G. Bareille, *Dictionnaire de théologie catholique* 2 (Paris: Letouzey et Ané, 1923), 1032–1033.

15. Theophilus: Index s.v. Theophilus. Hypatia: Socrates, *Ecclesiastical History* 7.13.6–7 (enmity of Orestes and Theophilus), 7.15 (murder). *PLRE* 2.575–576 (Hypatia 1), 810–11 (Orestes 100). For this famous incident, M. Dzielska, *Hypatia of Alexandria* (Cambridge: Harvard University Press, 1995), 83–100; E. J. Watts, "The Murder of Hypatia: Acceptable or Unacceptable Violence?," in H. A. Drake, ed., *Violence in Late Antiquity: Perceptions and Practices,* 333–342 (Aldershot, UK: Ashgate, 2005).

16. Eunapius: *Lives of the Philosophers* 6.11.6. *Parabalani:* G. W. Bowersock, "*Parabalani:* A Terrorist Charity in Late Antiquity," *Anabases* 12 (2010): 45–54. Menouthis and Antioch: below, Chaps. 5 and 10.

17. For this term and the Christological issues involved, see Chap. 4.

18. Philosophers: John Malalas, *Chronicle* 18.47. Trials in Constantinople: Theophanes, *Chronicle* Anno Mundi 6022 (p. 274 Mango and Scott), here more accurate than Malalas, *Chronicle* 18.42. Cf. *PLRE* 3.134 (Asclepiodotus 1), 801 (Macedonius 1), 988 (Pegasios 2). John of Ephesos: S. A. Harvey and H. Brakmann, *RAC* 18.553–564: *PCBE Asie* 494–519. Purge of 545/546: *Chronicle of Zuqnîn,* 91–92 Witakowski. Phocas: *PLRE* 2.881–882, Phocas 5. Evagrius: *PLRE* 3.452–453.

19. John of Ephesus, *Ecclesiastical History* 3.27–31, p. 114–121 Brooks; I. Rochow, "Die Heidenprozesse unter den Kaisern Tiberios II. Konstantinos und Maurikios," in H. Köpstein and F. Winkelmann, eds., *Studien zum 7. Jh. in Byzanz,* 120–130 (Berlin: Akademie-Verlag, 1976), calling this "the last wave of pagan trials in the Byzantine realm." *PLRE* 3.737–738 (Iulianus 20), 1119 (Sebastianus 2), 1308–1309 (Theophilus 2).

20. Socrates, *Ecclesiastical History* 7.15.6. On the use of persuasion by Christians, see Chap. 8.

4. God and Other Divinities

1. Psalms: Ps. 81.6, cf. Ps. 49.1, 135.2, "the God of gods." John: John 10.31–39. Augustine: *City of God* 9.23 (ed. D. Wiesen [LCL], 3.240). Paul: 1 Cor. 8.5 ("so-called gods"), 2 Cor. 4.4 ("god of this age").

2. G. Kittel, ed., *Theologisches Wörterbuch zum Neuen Testament* 2 (Stuttgart: Kohlhammer, 1935), 70–80; C. A. Newsom and D. F. Watson, "Angels," *AnchBibDict* 1.248–255; D. F. Watson, "Devil," *AnchBibDict* 2.183–184. Giants: Gen. 6.1–4.

3. I have given a very summary account of these Christological disputes: for further brief treatments, *The Oxford Dictionary of the Christian Church,* 3rd ed. (Oxford: Oxford University Press, 1997), articles "Chalcedon, the Definition of"; "Cyril, of Alexandria"; "Ephesus, Council of"; "Latrocinium"; "Monophysite." In the following, I have used "Chalcedonian" for believers in two natures, "miaphysite" for believers in an undivided nature. On the term "monophysite," P. Allen, *TRE* 23 (1994), 219.

4. Angels in later Judaism: L. Robert, *Hellenica* 11/12 (Paris: Adrien-Maisonneuve, 1960), 432–443; J. Michl, "Engel II," *RAC* 5.64–84. Dreams and visions: e.g., Matt. 1.20, Luke 1.11–20, 1.26–38. Jesus in desert: Matt. 4.11. At his tomb: John 20.12. In Acts: 12.7–10, cf. 5.19, 11.13. On the history and etymology of *daimonion,* J. W. Burnet, ed., *Plato's Euthyphro, Apology of Socrates and Crito* (Oxford: Clarendon Press, 1924), 16–17; E. C. E. Owen, "*Daimôn* and Cognate Words," *Journal of Theological Studies* 32 (1931): 133–153.

5. "Gods of the nations": Ps. 95.5. Gadarene swine: Matt. 8.28–32, Mark 5.1–17, Luke 8.26–33. "Beelzeboul": Matt. 9.32–33, Luke 11.14–15.

6. Nock, *Essays* 427, "The sharp anthropomorphism of literature and art was something superimposed, which never wholly mastered the popular mind and which wore thin under the Empire; in those parts of the Graeco-Roman world which lay outside the main stream of intellectual life it had never established itself."

7. Endobellicus: J. Toutain, *Les cultes païens dans l'Empire romain* 3 (Paris: E. Leroux, 1917), 127–131. Dusares: G. W. Bowersock, "The Cult and Representation of Dusares in Arabia," *Studies on the Eastern Roman Empire* (Goldbach: Keip Verlag, 1994), 245–252.

8. *Theos* and *deus* etymologically unconnected: P. Chantraine, *Dictionnaire étymologique de la langue grecque,* 2nd ed. (Paris: Klincksieck, 1999), 430. "Henotheism": e.g., Nilsson, *GGR*^{3} 573, Nock, *Essays,* Index s.v. "henotheism."

9. Meaning of *daimôn:* P. Chantraine, *Dictionnaire étymologique* 246: "'Puissance divine,' d'où 'dieu, destin'; le terme s'emploie chez Homère pour désigner une puissance divine que l'on ne peut ou ne veut nommer. . . . Le mot se prête après Hésiode à designer un demi-dieu, un démon; il s'emploie finalement en mauvaise part et fournit au vocabulaire chrétien le terme désignant l'esprit malin." Hesiod: *Works and Days* 122–123. Aeschylus: *Agamemnon* 1468, 1475–76 (transl. E. Fraenkel). *Daimonân:* LSJ s.v. δαιμονάω, δαιμονίζομαι. Demons snuffing up fumes:

H. Chadwick, ed., *Origen: Contra Celsum* (Cambridge: Cambridge University Press, 1953), 146n1.

10. Plato: *Symposium* 202 D-203 A. Xenocrates: fragments 225–230 Isnardi Parente. Plutarch: *Brutus* 36.7. Shakespeare: *Julius Caesar,* act 4, scene 3.

11. Lucian: *Lovers of Lies (Philopseudeis)* 16, cf. 30. Demons black: e.g., Dio Cassius, *Roman History* 67.9, boys painted black acting as *daimonia* at a banquet. The idea of devils as black, "Egyptians," or "Ethiopians," appears earlier in literary texts than in art: e.g., *Passion of Perpetua* 10.6, with the commentary of J. Amat (SC 417.224); Augustine, *City of God* 22.8 (7.224 Wiesen [LCL]); H. Leclercq in *DACL* 4.578–582.

12. Porphyry: fragments in A. Smith, ed., *Porphyrii Philosophi Fragmenta* (Stuttgart: B. G. Teubner, 1993), 351–407; on Zeus, fragment 325 F Smith. Oracles: Nock, "Oracles théologiques," *Essays* 160–168; Robert, "Trois oracles de la théosophie," *OMS* 5.584–615 (*CRAI* 1968).

13. On this much-discussed oracle, also known from an inscribed copy, Robert, "Un oracle gravé à Oenoanda," *OMS* 5.617–639 (*CRAI* 1971). Lactantius: *Divine Institutes* 1.7 (ed. P. Monat, SC 204 [Paris: Éditions du Cerf, 2000]).

14. Dream: Homer, *Iliad* 2.26. Birds: e.g., *Iliad* 24.292. Angels in Syria and Palestine: J. T. Milik, *Dédicaces faites par des dieux* (Paris: Paul Geuthner, 1972), 423–440. In Anatolia: A. R. R. Sheppard, "Pagan Cults of Angels in Roman Asia Minor," *Talanta* 12/13 (1980/81): 77–101; V. Hirschmann, "Zwischen Menschen und Göttern: Die kleinasiatischen Engel," *Epigraphica Anatolica* 40 (2007): 135–146, also arguing for the influence of Persian conceptions. Oracle: Porphyry, fragment 325 F Smith. Iamblichus: *On the Mysteries* 2.3, p. 81 ed. des Places.

15. Democritus: B 18 Diels. Plato: *Meno* 99 C–D. Plutarch: *On the Decline of Oracles (De def. orac.)* 438 B: cf. Philostratus, *Life of Apollonius* 3.38, a *daimôn,* the ghost of a dead man, causes a boy's voice to become deep. Celsus: Origen, *Against Celsus* 7.9, with Chadwick's note, 402n6. Porphyry: fragment 326F Smith. Iamblichus: *On the Mysteries* 2.3, p. 81 ed. des Places, with his note.

16. Plato: *Palatine Anthology* 7.669.

17. Paul: Acts 17.28. Athenagoras: *Petition (Legatio)* 5 (SC 379.84–87).

18. Firmicus Maternus, *Mathesis:* ed. P. Monat (Paris: Les Belles Lettres, 1992–1994). Eulogy of Constantine: *Mathesis* 1.10.14. *On the Error of Profane Religions:* R. Turcan, ed., *L'erreur des religions païennes* (Paris: Les Belles Lettres, 1982). On Firmicus, *PLRE* 1.567–568, Maternus 2; T. D. Barnes, *Constantine: Dynasty, Religion and Power in the Later Roman Empire* (Chichester, UK: Wiley-Blackwell, 2011), 168–170 (arguing that Firmicus's Highest God "can only be the God of the Christians").

19. Carpocrates: M. Smith, *Clement of Alexandria and a Secret Gospel of Mark* (Cambridge: Harvard University Press, 1973), 266–278 (discussion), 295–350 (testimonia); C. Scholten, "Karpokrates," *RAC* 20.174–186. Irenaeus: *Against Heresies* 1.25 (A. Rousseau and L. Doutreleau, eds., SC 264.332–344). Clement: *Miscellanies (Stromateis)* 3.2 (O. Stählin, ed., *Clemens Alexandrinus* 2^2, GCS 52 (15) [Berlin: Akademie-Verlag, 1960], 197–200). For similar acts of heroization, C. P. Jones, *New Heroes in Antiquity: From Achilles to Antinoos* (Cambridge: Harvard University Press, 2010), chap. 5, "Private Heroes."

20. Secret Gospel: Smith, *Clement of Alexandria;* for this as a fabrication of Carpocrates himself, K. Jaroš, "Zur Textüberlieferung des Markusevangeliums," *Aegyptus* 88 (2008): 109–113.

21. In favor of a single cult of *Theos Hypsistos,* S. Mitchell, "The Cult of Theos Hypsistos," in P. Athanassiadi and M. Frede, eds., *Pagan Monotheism in Late Antiquity,* 81–148 (Oxford, UK: Clarendon Press; New York: Oxford University Press, 1999), and "Further Thoughts on the Cult of Theos Hypsistos," in S. Mitchell and P. Van Nuffelen, eds., *One God: Pagan Monotheism in the Roman Empire,* 167–208 (Cambridge: Cambridge University Press, 2010). Contrast Nock, *Essays,* 425, "*Hypsistos* was a term in use, vague enough to suit any god treated as the supreme being"; Nilsson, *GGR*² 664: "Ὕψιστος ist ein Adjectiv, das jedem grossen Gott beigelegt werden konnte; es gibt keine Gewähr dafür, dass so bezeichnete Götter einander nahe standen." Melchizedek: Gen. 14.18.

22. Gregory of Nazianzus, *Oration* 18.5 (*PG* 35.990–991); Gregory of Nyssa, *Against Eunomius* 2.37 (W. Jaeger, ed. [Leiden: Brill, 1960], 2.327). Gregory's expression "some god" (*theon tina*) shows that he is referring only to the Hypsistians, since he cannot question the identity of the Jewish and Christian god.

23. Epiphanius, *Medicine Chest* (*Panarion*) 80.1–2 (first Messalians), 3–11 (second) (K. Holl, ed., *Epiphanius* 3², GCS [Berlin: Akademie-Verlag, 1985], 485–496). On the Messalians, A. Guillaumont, *Dictionnaire de spiritualité* 10 (Paris: Beauchesne, 1980), 1074–1083; K. Fittschen, *Der Neue Pauly* 8 (Stuttgart: J. G. Metzler, 2000), 39–40. Lupicinus: *PLRE* 1.520–521, Lupicinus 6.

24. Lamps in religion: Nilsson, *GGR*² 2.374–377.

25. Gregory of Nyssa, *To the Hellenes, on Plural Ideas (Ad Graecos de communibus notitiis),* ed. F. Mueller (Leiden: Brill, 1958), 3.1.19–33; *To Ablabius (Ad Ablabium, quod non sunt tres Dei),* 3.1.37–57.

5. Idolatry

1. Commandments: Exod. 20.3–4: Ps.: 113.12. Isa.: 44. 9–20. Wisd. of Sol.: 14.12–16. On this last work, see D. Winston, "Solomon, Wisdom of," *AnchBibDict* 6.120–127.

2. Acts 15.6–21. For this problematic account, C. B. Cousar, "Jerusalem, Council of," *AnchBibDict* 3.766–768.

3. "You cannot drink": 1 Cor. 10.21. "Sacrificed to idols": 1 Cor. 10.27–28. Letter to Romans: Rom. 1.18–32, esp. verses 23, 25; cf. Tertullian, *On Idolatry* 1.3. "Be sure of this": Eph. 5.5, cf. Col. 3.5; cf. K. S. Frank, "Habsucht," *RAC* 13.238–239.

4. E. Kitzinger, "The Cult of Images before Iconoclasm," *Dumbarton Oaks Papers* 8 (1954): 123. Animated statues: Ch. Picard, "Statue," in Daremberg-Saglio 4.1473n21. Lucian: *Lovers of Lies (Philopseudeis)* 20–21. Apollodorus: Cassius Dio, *Roman History* 69.4–3.5. Theurgy: K.-H. Uthemann, "Theurgy," *ODB* 3.2074.

5. On Christian opposition to idolatry: Kitzinger, "The Cult of Images"; N. H. Baynes, "Idolatry and the Early Church," in *Byzantine Studies and Other Essays* (London: Athlone Press, 1955), 116–143; H. L. Kessler, "Iconoclastia," *Enciclopedia dell'arte medievale* 7 (1996), 276–282. Accusations of cross worship ("staurolatry"): Minucius Felix, *Octavius* 9.4, 12.4, 29.6; S. Heid, "Kreuz," *RAC* 21.1129. Helena: R. Klein, "Helena," *RAC* 14.367–372.

6. Christian building: C. H. Kraehling, *The Christian Building, Dura-Europos Final Report VIII, 2* (New Haven: Yale University Press, 1967). Synagogue: Kraehling, *The Synagogue: Dura-Europos Final Report VIII, 1* (New Haven: Yale University Press, 1956), esp. 340–346 for the question of the paintings in connection with the prohibition of images. On both sets of paintings, T. K. Thomas in J. Y. Chi and S. Heath, eds., *Edge of Empires: Pagans, Jews and Christians at Roman Dura-Europos*, 44–49 (New York: Institute for the Study of the Ancient World, 2011). For the distinction between two- and three-dimensional representation, see below.

7. Council of Elvira, *Canon* 36 (Mansi 2.11; *PL* 84.306): *placuit picturas in ecclesia esse non debere, ne quod colitur et adoratur in parietibus depingatur.* In favor of interpreting the canon as embracing all representation, H. Koch, *Die altchristliche Bilderfrage nach den literarischen Quellen* (Göttingen: Vandenhoeck & Ruprecht, 1917), 31–41; for a narrower interpretation, C. Murray, "Art and the Early Church," *Journal of Theological Studies* 28 (1977): 303–345. Note A. Grabar, *L'Iconoclasme byzantin: Dossier archéologique* (Paris: Collège de France, 1957), 77–78, "On ne finira jamais de discuter sur le point exact de la deuxième partie de ce texte." Iliberris: *Barrington Atlas* 27 B 4.

8. Good Shepherd and Daniel: Eusebius, *Life of Constantine* 3.49 (rightly interpreted by Baynes, "Idolatry" 122). *Fastigium: Liber Pontificalis*, ed. L. Duchesne (Paris: de Boccard, 1955) 1.172, on which I follow R. Grigg, "Constantine the Great and the Cult without Images," *Viator* 8 (1977): 9–12; L. A. Hughes, "Illusive Idols and the Constantinian Aesthetic," *Latomus* 70 (2011): 478–492, supports the evidence of the *Fastigium*. Bishop Eugenius: R. Merkelbach and J. Stauber, eds., *Steinepigramme aus dem griechischen Osten* 3.80 (Munich: B. G. Teubner, 2001); *PCBE Asie* 281–283, Eugénios 1. Priest Eugenius: Merkelbach and Stauber 3.82–83; *PCBE Asie* 287, Eugénios 11.

9. A. Grabar, *The Beginnings of Christian Art, 200–395* (London: Thames & Hudson, 1967), 269: "The new faith dealt the death blow to this form of art, hitherto preponderant throughout the Roman Empire. No written records explain its abandonment, which was, however, so general and so abrupt that there must have been some sort of prohibition, probably an unwritten one."

10. Constantia: see below. Statuette: Grabar, *Beginnings* 269–70. Tomb of Bassus: Grabar, *Beginnings* 246–248; E. S. Malbon, *The Iconography of the Sarcophagus of Junius Bassus* (Princeton: Princeton University Press, 1990); *PLRE* 1.155, Bassus 15. Sacred objects: e.g., Grabar, *Beginnings* 270–274, reliquary casket in Brescia.

11. Hinton St. Mary mosaic: S. Pearce, "The Hinton St. Mary Mosaic Pavement: Christ or Emperor?," *Britannia* 39 (2008): 193–218. *Kourotrophos:* T. Hadzisteliou Price, *Kourotrophos: Cults and Representations of the Greek Nursing Deities* (Leiden: Brill, 1978). Paphos mosaic: G. W. Bowersock, *Hellenism in Late Antiquity* (Ann Arbor: University of Michigan Press, 1990), plate 1.

12. Text: Mansi 13.313; *PG* 20.1545–1550; translation by Cyril Mango, *The Art of the Byzantine Empire* (Englewood Cliffs, NJ: Prentice-Hall, 1972), 16–18. Constantia: *PLRE* 1.221, Constantia 1. On this letter, Baynes, "Idolatry" 121–22; for doubts of its authenticity, Murray, "Art and the Early Church" 326–328.

13. Epiphanius to John of Jerusalem: Baynes, "Idolatry" 126–128; I have translated the Greek text as cited by Nicephorus (P. Maas, *Kleine Schriften* [Munich: Beck, 1973], 437–445) rather than Jerome's free translation, *Letter* 51.9 (*CSEL*

54.411–412). For the lost texts, K. Holl, "Die Schriften des Epiphanius gegen die Bilderverehrung," *Gesammelte Aufsätze zur Kirchengeschichte* 2 (Tübingen: J. C. B. Mohr, 1928), 351–358; Kitzinger, "Cult of Images" 93n28.

14. Nilus, *Letter* 4.61 (*PG* 79.577–80); translation in Mango, *Art of the Byzantine Empire* 32–33. Olympiodorus: *PLRE* 2.799, Olympiodorus 3. For this sense of *pêxasthai*, cf. *Themistius* 310d, 2.115 ed. Downey; for *historia*, E. A. Sophocles, *Greek Lexicon of the Roman and Byzantine Periods* (repr., New York: Frederick Ungar, 1957), 1.607.

15. Mosaic scenes: K. M. Dunbabin, *The Mosaics of Roman North Africa* (Oxford, UK: Clarendon Press; New York: Oxford University Press, 1978), Index s.v. "Hunting scenes," "Marine scenes," "Seasonal Plants." Cross: Grabar, *L'Iconoclasme* 135, 153–155. Cf. the mosaic cross placed by Leo III in the apse of Hagia Irene, Istanbul: Kessler, "Iconoclastia" 280.

16. Text in F. Diekamp, *Analecta Patristica* (Rome: Pontificale Institutum Orientalium Studiorum, 1938), 127–129; cf. Baynes, "The Icons before Iconoclasm," *Byzantine Studies* 226–229. Hypatios: *PCBE Asie* 457–469, Hypatios 4, esp. 467. Julianus of Adramyttion: *PCBE Asie* 561, Ioulianos 11.

17. Eusebius: *Ecclesiastical History* 7.18.1–3 (672 ed. Schwartz; 2.176 ed. Oulton [Loeb]). Philostorgius: *Ecclesiastical History* 7.3 (78 ed. Bidez-Winkelmann). Images bleeding, etc.: Kitzinger, "Cult of Images" 100–101, cf. 117, "Among the broad masses the concept that divine forces were present in religious images was deeply rooted in the pagan past."

18. Theodosius: *Theodosian Code* 16,10.8, 10,15: further bibliography in R. Delmaire, ed., J. Rougé, transl., *Code Théodosien, Livre XVI* (SC 508), 434nn1–2. Statues in Africa and Italy: C. Lepelley, "Le Musée des Statues divines: La Volonté de sauvegarder le Patrimoine artistique païen à l'Époque théodosienne," *Cahiers Archéologiques* 42 (1994): 1–15. Arcadius: *Theodosian Code* 16.10.16. See now also L. Lavan, "Political Talismans? Residual 'Pagan' Statues in Late Antique Public Space," in L. Lavan and M. Mulryan, eds., *The Archaeology of Late Antique "Paganism,"* 439–477 (Leiden: Brill, 2011), and B. Caseau, "Religious Intolerance and Pagan Statuary," ibid. 479–502.

19. G. Deligiannakis, "Christian Attitudes towards Pagan Statuary," *Byzantion* 78 (2008): 142–157.

20. Zacharias of Mytilene, *Life of Severus* pp. 27–29 Kugener. See further below, Chaps. 7 and 10.

21. Tomis: D. M. Pippidi, *Scythica Minora* (Bucharest: Editura Academiei; Amsterdam: Adolf M. Hakkert, 1975), 294–295. For similar caches: A. Frantz, *The Athenian Agora: Late Antiquity,* A.D. *267–700* (Princeton, NJ: American School of Classical Studies at Athens, 1988), 88.

22. A. Ambrogi, "Sugli Occultamenti antichi di Statue: Le Testimonianze archeologiche a Roma," *Römische Mitteilungen* 117 (2011): 511–566.

23. P. Martin, "Discours de Jacques de Saroug sur la Chute des Idoles," *Zeitschrift der deutschen morgenländischen Gesellschaft* 29 (1875): 140–141.

24. For Leo's measures, M. V. Anastos, "Leo III's Edict against the Images in the Year 726–27 and Italo-Byzantine Relations between 726 and 730," *Byzantinische Forschungen* 3 (1968): 5–41; cf. Grabar, *L'iconoclasme* chap. 5, "L'Art et les Empereurs iconoclastes"; Mango, *Art* 151–52. John of Damascus, *On the Divine*

Images: *PG* 94.1231–1420. Attacks on the emperors: 1281C, 1285A, 1296C, etc. Hellenes: 1255 D-1257 A, cf. 1303 B. "Our Saintly Fathers": 1293D–1296A.

6. Sacrifice, Blood, and Prayer

1. Tertullian: T. D. Barnes, *Tertullian: A Historical and Literary Study* (Oxford: Oxford University Press, 1971), 55–56 (dates of his works), 93–96 *(On Shows)*. "Do you want . . .": *On Shows* 29.5, *vis autem et sanguinis aliquid? Habes Christi.*

2. On the issue of sacrifice generally, the bibliography is vast, with general agreement that no one theory or definition can cover all the phenomena: D. Hicks, "Sacrifice," in *International Encyclopaedia of the Social and Behavioral Sciences* 20 (2001), 13439, "The term sacrifice is best regarded as a polythetic category which includes heterogeneous modes of behavior motivated by intentions of variable kinds"; cf. H.-J. Klauck, "Sacrifice and Sacrificial Offerings (NT)," in *AnchBibDict* 5, 891: "It is impossible to do justice to the N[ew] T[estament] evidence if it is judged in the light of a general concept of sacrifice as a phenomenon in the history of religion." For Jewish sacrifice, E. G. Hirsch, "Sacrifice," *Jewish Encyclopedia* 10, 615–623; A. Rainey and A. Rothkoff, "Sacrifice," *Encylopaedia Judaica* (2nd ed.) 17, 639–649; G. A. Anderson, "Sacrifice and Sacrificial Offerings (OT)," *AnchBibDict* 5, 870–886; for Christian sacrifice: Klauck, "Sacrifice" 886–891; for Greco-Roman sacrifice: L. Ziehen, "Opfer," *RE* 18.1 (1939): 579–627; J. Rudhardt and O. Reverdin, eds., *Le Sacrifice dans l'Antiquité,* Entretiens Hardt 27 (Geneva: Fondation Hardt, 1981); for animal sacrifice, M.-Z. Petropoulou, *Animal Sacrifice in Ancient Greek Religion, Judaism, and Christianity, 100 BC to AD 200* (Oxford: Oxford University Press, 2008), with an interesting overview of research since the sixteenth century in chapter 1; for sociological theories of sacrifice, Hicks, "Sacrifice," 13439–13441; for the varieties of sacrifice across cultures, A. M. Porter and G. M. Schwartz, eds., *Sacred Killing: The Archaeology of Sacrifice in the Ancient Near East* (Winona Lake, IND: Eisenbrauns, 2012).

3. Homer, *Odyssey* 11.23–320. *Enagismos:* Nock, *Essays* 591–593. On the comparative unimportance of blood in Roman sacrifice, Nock, *Essays* 599n90.

4. Blood in Greek sacrifice: Nock, *Essays,* 592: "When animals were offered in sacrifice with participation, *thysia,* their blood was shed with due solemnity, at or before an altar. Often it was caught in a bowl, and what fell on the altar was not cleared away—any more than the ashes of the sacrificial fire were removed." Sale of meat: G. Berthiaume, *Les Rôles du Mágeiros* (Leiden: E. J. Brill, 1982), 44–59. Pliny: *Letters,* 10.96.10. Augustus: Suetonius, *Life of Augustus* 35.3.

5. Meaning of *thysia:* LSJ s.v. *thysia* 3, "festival at which sacrifices were offered": cf. Eusebius, *Life of Constantine* 3.15.1, the banquet given by Constantine to the bishops after Nicaea a "*thysia* appropriate to God." Women at public banquets: P. Schmitt Pantel, *La cité au banquet* (Rome: École française de Rome, 1992), 397–399: "leur exclusion du banquet public reste la règle." Cleanax: *Supplementum Epigraphicum Graecum* 32 (1982) 1243 (R. A. Kearsley in *New Documents Illustrating Early Christianity* 7 [North Ryde, N. S. W., Australia: Macquarie University, 1994], 233–241).

6. Pythagoras: K. von Fritz, "Pythagoras," *RE* 24 (1963), 193. Empedocles: fragment 128 Diels, from Theophrastus, *On Piety,* fragment 12, lines 9–19 ed. W.

Pötscher, Theophrastus: *Peri Eusebeias* (Leiden: Brill, 1964). Porphyry: J. Bouffartigue, ed., *Porphyre: De l'abstinence* (Paris: Les Belles Lettres, 1977); translated by G. Clark, *Porphyry: On Abstinence from Killing Animals* (Ithaca, NY: Cornell University Press, 2000).

7. Libanius: *Oration* 17.4 (Norman's translation). Ammianus: 22.12.6 (Julian in Antioch), 22.14.3 (taunts), 25.4.17 (obituary).

8. Salutius ("Sallustius"): A. D. Nock, ed., *Sallustius: Concerning the Gods and the Universe* (Cambridge: Cambridge University Press, 1926), 15–16 (Nock, lxxxiii–lxxxvi: Nock's translation). For Julian's friend, and the correct form of his name, G. W. Bowersock, *Julian the Apostate* (London: Duckworth, 1978), 125. On philosophical opposition to animal sacrifice, see below.

9. Julian and the Temple: Bowersock, *Julian* 88–90, 120–122. *Against the Galilaeans:* 354C, 356C = Stern, *Greek and Latin Authors* 527 (Greek). *Letter to the Jews:* Stern 559–568. Gentile sacrifice: Rothkoff, "Sacrifice" 647.

10. Moses's covenantal sacrifice: Exod. 24.4–8. Blood in Temple sacrifice: Lev. 1.11, 1.15, 3.9, 3.13, etc. Jesus and the Passover sacrifice: John 11.55–12.1. End of sacrifice: Josephus, *Jewish War* 6.94; G. G. Stroumsa, *The End of Sacrifice: Religious Transformations in Late Antiquity* (Chicago: University of Chicago Press, 2009), though I do not accept all his arguments. Denunciation by Prophets: Rainey, "Sacrifice," 644.

11. "Institution": Mark 14.22–24. Covenantal sacrifice: Exod. 24.4–8. Paul: 1 Cor. 11.24–25: added from Paul to the text of Luke 22.19. Paul on participation: 1 Cor. 10.16–17. I have followed Nock's analysis of the "Institution," *Essays,* 104–116.

12. John 6.25–59, esp. 6.49–51, 55–56. On *trôgô:* Danker, *Lexicon,* 1019. Pagans: Macarius of Magnesia, *Discourse* 3.15.1, citing John 6.53.

13. "Sacrifice pleasing to God": Eph. 5.2. Heb.: 9.14, 9.26, 13.12 (Christ as offering), 9.11–13, 10.19–21 (Christ as high priest). John: 1.29 (Jesus as Lamb), 19.31 (Day of Preparation): cf. Hirsch, "Sacrifice," 627. On the vexed question of the day of the Crucifixion, H. L. Strack and P. Billerbeck, *Kommentar zum Neuen Testament*^{2} 2 (Munich: C. H. Beck, 1956), 812–853. Rev. 7.14.

14. *Teaching of the Apostles* 14.1 (*Didachê*, SC 248,192). Lack of discussion in early centuries: G. Bareille, *Dictionnaire de théologie catholique* 5 (1913), 1121–1122.

15. *ta sa ek tôn sôn:* G. Downey, "The Inscription on a Silver Chalice from Syria," *American Journal of Archaeology* 55 (1951): 351: I. Ševčenko, "The Moses Cross at Sinai," *Dumbarton Oaks Papers* 17 (1963): 393–394.

16. Paul, 1 Cor. 8.4 (Deut. 6.7), 8.13 (meat), 10.19–21.

17. "Apostolic Decrees": Acts 15.20, 15.29, 21.25. *Pnikton:* Danker, *Lexicon,* 838. Tertullian: *Apology* 9.13–14. Apostolic Canons: *Apostolic Constitutions* 8.47.63 (no meat containing blood), 8.47.53 (meat and wine on holy days) (SC 336, 298, 296). On the Apostolic Canons, A. Schminck, *ODB* 1.141.

18. Perpetua: J. Amat, ed. *Passion de Perpétue et de ses compagnons,* SC 417 (1996), with full bibliography; J. N. Bremmer and M. Formisano, eds., *Perpetua's Passions: Multidisciplinary Approaches to the Passio Perpetuae et Felicitatis* (Oxford: Oxford University Press, 2012). Saturus: *Passion of Perpetua* 21.1–5. Demons in bathhouses and good-luck wishes: K. M. D. Dunbabin, "*Baiarum grata volup-*

tas: Pleasures and Dangers of the Baths," *Papers of the British School at Rome* 57 (1989): 6–46, esp. 18–19 on good-luck wishes.

19. Cult of relics: A. Angenendt, "Reliquien/Reliquienverehrung," *TRE* 29 (1998), 69–74. "We become more numerous . . .": Tertulllian, *Apology* 50.13, cf. 21.25; the same idea in Basil of Caesarea, *Letter* 164 (*PG* 32, 636A), "the blood of martyrs watering the church fed athletes of the truth in growing numbers." Ambrose: *Letter* 73 (18), 11.

20. Pliny: *Letters* 10.96.5. Decius: G. Clarke, *CAH* 12 (2005) 625–635, with 627n106 on certificates.

21. Eusebius: *Ecclesiastical History* 8.1.2, *hê peri to thuein agônia.* Diocletian's sacrifice: Lactantius, *On the Deaths of the Persecutors* 10 (SC 39, 88–89). On the Great Persecution and its aftermath down to 324, Clarke, *CAH* 12 (2005) 647–665. Magistrates tiring of bloodshed: Eusebius, *Ecclesiastical History* 8.12.8.

22. Eusebius: *Life of Constantine* 2.45.1; see now A. D. Lee in N. Lenski, ed., *Cambridge Companion to the Age of Constantine* (Cambridge: Cambridge University Press, 2006) 173–174. Law against haruspicy: *Theodosian Code* 9.16.1–2, cf. Lee, 172.

23. Law of 356 or 357: *Theodosian Code* 16.10.4, also 16.10. 6. Constantius and the Altar of Victory: Symmachus, *Third Report* 6, Ambrose, *Letter* 73 (18) 32.

24. On Gratian's religious policies and the question of the altar, J. Curran, *CAH* 13 (1998), 104–108; Cameron, *Last Pagans* 33–56 (highly skeptical of traditional views); Brown, *Eye of the Needle* 103–109. Ambrose on Christian virgins: *Letter* 73 (18) 11–12.

25. "Why do you bloody me . . . ?": *Letter* 73 (18) 7 : compare Theophrastus, *On Piety,* fragment 7, lines 16–21 Pötscher, "If we sacrifice by destroying animals that do no wrong, we too do wrong"; also Plutarch, *Convivial Questions* 8.8.3 (*Plutarch's* Moralia 8.180, LCL). "The manner of your sacrifices . . .": *Letters* 73 (18) 7. Psalm 95: *Letters* 72 (17) 1. "It is tolerable . . . ?": *Letter* 73 (18) 31, cf. 72 (17) 9 (Ambrose's second word for ash, *favilla,* denotes ash carried by wind or smoke). Christian virgins: *Letter* 73 (18) 11–12. Eugenius: *Letter* 10 (57).

26. Tertullian: *On Shows,* 12 (M. Turcan, ed., *Tertullien: Les spectacles,* SC 332 [Paris: Éditions du Cerf, 1986]). Prudentius, *Against Symmachus* 1.380–382. Honorius: C. P. Jones, "The Organization of Spectacle in Late Antiquity," in J. Nelis-Clément and K. M. Coleman, *L'Organisation des Spectacles dans l'Empire romain, Entretiens Hardt* 58 (Vandoeuvres, Switzerland: Fondation Hardt, 2012), 316. Cyril: *Against Julian,* PG 76, 697B. On pagan and Christian criticism of gladiatorial spectacle, W. Weismann, "Gladiator," *RAC* 11 (1985), 38–43.

27. Law of 391: *Theodosian Code* 10.10; cf. Ambrose, *Letter* 73 (18) 7. Theodosius's subsequent laws: *Theodosian Code* 10.11, 10.12, 10.14. Theodoret: *Cure of Pagan Maladies* 7, esp. 7.49 (SC 57). In general, K. W. Harl, "Sacrifice and Pagan Belief in Fifth- and Sixth-Century Byzantium," *Past and Present* 128 (1990): 7–27.

28. Gregory, *Letter* 5.38.

29. Nicholas's sacrifices: I. Ševčenko and N. P. Ševčenko, *Life of Nicholas of Sion* (Brookline, MA: Hellenic College Press, 1984; H. Blum, ed., *De vita Nicolai Sionitae* [Bonn: Habelt, 1997]), chaps. 54–57, cf. L. Robert, *Hellenica* 10 (1955), 199–200, comparing the activity of earlier pagan benefactors. Accusations: *Life of Nicholas,* chap. 53. Gregory: *Letter* 11.56.

30. *Second Alcibiades:* translation by W. R. M. Lamb, LCL *Plato* 8 (London, 1927), 226–273; for a recently published papyrus, *The Oxyrhynchus Papyri* 76, 5080.

31. Jewish Prayer in the Bible: I. Abrahams, *Encyclopedia Judaica* (2nd ed.), 16, 456–458, citing Deut. 21.7–8, 26.1–15. Paul: 1 Tim. 2.1–15; on this letter, J. D. Quinn, *AnchBibDict* 6, 561. Lord's Prayer: Matthew 6.9–13; Luke 11.2–4; J. L. Houlden, *AnchBibDict* 4: 356–362. "Waffle" *(battologein):* Danker, *Lexicon* 172. *Epiousios:* Danker, *Lexicon* 377–378.

32. Cato: *On Agriculture* 132.1. Arval Brothers: M. Beard, J. North, and S. Price, *Religions of Rome I: A History* (Cambridge: Cambridge University Press, 1998), 194–196, 353.

33. Gethsemane: Matt. 26.39; Mark 14.35; Luke 22.41. Tertullian, *On Prayer:* ed. G. F. Diercks, *Tertulliani Opera* 1, *Corpus Christianorum, Series Latina* (Turnholt: Brepols, 1954), 255–274; translated by E. J. Daly, *Tertullian: Disciplinary, Moral and Ascetical Works, The Fathers of the Church* 40 (New York: Fathers of the Church, Inc., 1959), 153–188.

7. Debate

1. Paul before Areopagus: Acts 17.17–20 (I have translated *sebomenoi* as "worshipers": the meaning of this and cognate terms such as *theosebeis* is debated, but it must refer to gentiles well disposed toward the synagogue; cf. Acts 18.7, "Titius Justus, a worshiper of God"). Acts as apology: L. Alexander, "The *Acts of the Apostles* as an Apologetic Text," *in Apologetics in the Roman Empire,* ed. M. J. Edwards et al., 15–44 (Oxford: Oxford University Press, 1999).

2. The classic collection of "fragments" is by A. Harnack, "Porphyrius, 'Gegen die Christen,'" *Abhandlungen der Königlichen Preussischen Akademie der Wissenschaften, Philosophisch-Historische Klasse,* No. 1 (Berlin, 1916); recent translation by R. M. Berchman, *Porphyry against the Christians* (Leiden: Brill, 2005). The debates about the attribution of fragments, date, and historical setting have still not reached any firm conclusion: e.g., T. D. Barnes, "Scholarship or Propaganda? Porphyry, *Against the Christians* and Its Historical Setting," *Bulletin of the Institute of Classical Studies, London,* 39 (1994): 53–65.

3. Eusebius, *Gospel Preparation* 1.2–4 (J. Sirinelli and É. des Places, eds., *Eusèbe, Préparation évangelique,* SC 206 [Paris: Éditions du Cerf, 1974]) = fragment 1 Harnack. Arnobius, *Against the Gentiles* 1.1–26. Jerome, the only external source for Arnobius's date, places him under Diocletian: Le Bonniec, edition of Arnobius, 7–8.

4. R. Lim, "Christian Triumph and Controversy," in *LA Guide* 196–218.

5. Christ as interlocutor: *Discourse* 2.18.1–7; 3.13, 23–26. The Jews as interlocutors: 2.30.3–11.

6. *Discourse* 2.20.1 ("Sneering"), 2.28.1 ("When this man . . .": the text is uncertain), 4.25.1 ("the Hellene").

7. *Discourse* 2.23.6 ("stale and discordant"), 3.15.1–6 (Jesus), cf. John 6.53.

8. For an overview of the relation between Cyril's work and Julian's, J. Quasten, *Patrology* 3 (Utrecht: Spectrum, 1966), 129–130; for editions of Cyril and the fragments of Julian, see Authors. On the earlier replies to Julian by Diodorus of Tarsus

and Theodore of Mopsuhestia, F. Thome, *Historia contra Mythos* (Bonn: Borengässer, 2004).

9. *Against Julian* 512 A (polytheism), 697 B (gladiatorial games), 874 B (priests of Cronos), 697 D–700 C (human sacrifice), 813 C, 816 B–C (plural gods).

10. Augustine, *Letters* 132 (Augustine to Volusianus), 135 (Volusianus to Augustine), 136 Marcellinus to Augustine), 137 (Augustine's lengthy reply); cf. Brown, *Augustine*[2] 300–303. On Volusianus's deathbed conversion, below, Chap. 8.

11. The *Letters* are still not fully edited; for editions, see Authors. On Isidore: J.-M. Sauget, "Isidoro di Pelusio," *Bibliotheca Sanctorum* 9.968–971; U. Treu, "Isidor II (von Pelusion)," *RAC* 18 (1998): 982–1001. On the function and status of *scholastikoi,* H. G. Ioannidou in E. W. Handley et al., eds., *The Oxyrhynchus Papyri* 59 (London: British Academy, 1992), 166, "The term denotes a man with legal training. *Scholastici* acted as courtroom lawyers, judges, municipal and imperial officials"; I. Andorlini, "Paganesimo e Cristianesimo nell'Egitto del IV secolo d. C.," *Anabases* 12 (2010) 17, with further bibliography. Volusianus: Augustine, *Letters* 136.2. Maximus: Isidore, *Letters* 1.96 (*PLRE* 2.746, Maximus 10). Olympiodorus: 4.27, cf. 2.256, 4.186 (possibly identical with the Alexandrian philosopher, *PLRE* 2.799, Olympiodorus 2). Antiochus: 3.7, cf. 5.1 (*PLRE* 2.104, Antiochus 8). Harpocras: 2.228 (*PLRE* 2.528, Harpocras 1). Ammonius: 1.21, 2.166 (*PLRE* 2.70, Ammonius 1). Casius: 2.146, 149, referring to Demosthenes, *Speeches* 1.20 (*PLRE* 2.263, Casius).

12. Nilus: Isidore, *Letters* 5.21 (*PLRE* 2.784, Nilus 1). "Oracle" (i.e., saying of Jesus): Matt. 5.28. Andromachus: *Letters* 5.75, cf. 5.42.

13. Domitius: *Letters* 4.30, 5.5, 5.528 (*PLRE* 2.371, Domitius 1). Sons: 5.163, 164. Diogenes: 3.389 (*PLRE* 2.360, Diogenes 3). *Magistriani:* S. Barnish in *The Cambridge Ancient History* 14 (Cambridge: Cambridge University Press, 2008), 172.

14. Nilus: B. Baldwin and A. Kazhdan, "Neilos of Ancyra," *ODB* 2.1450; on his addressees, Alan Cameron, "The Authenticity of the Letters of St Nilus of Ancyra," *GRBS* 17 (1976): 181–196. Aeneas: *Letters* 2.280 (*PLRE* 2.16, Aeneas 1). Hephaestus: 1.6 (*PLRE* 2.538). Chryseros: 2.42 (*PLRE* 2.297, Chryseros 2). Apollodorus: 1.75 (*PLRE* 2.119, Apollodorus 3). Comasius: 2.73 (PLRE 2.305, Comasius 2). Alexander: 2.49 (*PLRE* 2.56, Alexander 7).

15. Menander: Nilus, *Letters* 2.32 (*PLRE* 2.754, Menander 1). Taurianus: *Letters* 2.178 (*PLRE* 2.1055).

16. B. Baldwin, "Theodoret of Cyrrhus," *ODB* 3.2049; Y. Papadogiannakis, *Christianity and Hellenism in the Fifth-Century Greek East* (Cambridge: Harvard University Press, 2012). *Cure* 1.54 (blind faith), 2.56 (three gods), 2.87 (angels), 8.11 (relics), 12.27 (monks), 6.87 (idolatry), 8.22 (Asclepius), 8.33 (libations), 9.28 ("all that is Greek"), 10.50–58 (idolaters); *Commentary on Isaiah* 2.18–19 (SC 276.206).

17. Count Dionysius: *Letters* 17 (*PLRE* 2.364, Dionysius 6). Uranius governor of Cyprus: *Letter* 76 (*PLRE* 2.1186, Uranius 2). Palladius: *Letter* 12 (*PLRE* 2.820, Palladius 6). Isocasius: *Letters* 27, 28, 44 (pupils), 38 (wood carver) (*PLRE* 2.633, Isocasius).

18. Aeneas of Gaza: B. Baldwin, *ODB* 1.41; A. Segonds, *DPhA* 1.82–87. M. F. Colonna, ed., *Teofrasto* (Naples: S. Iodice, 1958); E. Watts, "An Alexandrian

Christian Response to Fifth-Century Neoplatonic Influence," in A. Smith, ed., *The Philosopher and Society in Late Antiquity: Essays in Honour of Peter Brown* (Swansea: Classical Press of Wales, 2005), 215–219.

19. Zacharias: B. Baldwin and S. H. Griffith, *ODB* 3.2218. Ammonius and Proclus: *On the Creation, PG* 85.1019 A (*PLRE* 2.71–72, Ammonius 6, 915–919, Proclus 4). Gessius: *PG* 85.1059 A (*PLRE* 2.511, Gessius 3); Watts, "An Alexandrian Christian Response," 219–222.

20. 1021 C (new church), 1028 A (Ammonius's throne), 1057 B (end of first day), 1060 A (Gessius), 1062 A (Muses), 1105 B (Gessius's assent), 1118 B (Ammonius silenced), 1141 B (final prayer). On the lecture halls discovered at Kom el-Dikka in Alexandria, see below, Chap. 10.

21. Damascius, *Life of Isidore* 65 (*PLRE* 2.790, Odaenethus).

22. Pseudo-Dionysius: R. Roques et al., "Denys l'Aréopagite," *Dictionnaire de spiritualité* 3 (Paris: Beauchesne, 1957), 244–429, esp. 252 on the identification with Severus; P. E. Rorem, *LA Guide* 410–411. Boethius: F. Vernet, *Dictionnaire de spiritualité* 1 (1937), 1739–1745; *PLRE* 2.233–237, Boethius 5; J. J. O'Meara, *LA Guide* 344–345. On the comparable transmission of Greek philosophy to the Arab world, R. Goulet and U. Rudolph, eds., *Entre Orient et Occident,* Entretiens Hardt 57 (Geneva: Fondation Hardt, 2011).

8. Conversion

1. Mark: 16.16. Matt.: 28.19. Conversions in Acts: 11.21, 15.3, 15.19, 26.18.

2. Paul in Athens: Acts 17.33, 34. Agrippa: Acts 26.28: on this controversial passage, Danker, *Lexicon* 791, πείθω 1 b.

3. Clement: *Second Letter of Clement* 17.1. *Catêchêsis:* O. Pasquato and G. Brakmann, "Katechese," *RAC* 20 (2004), 422–496. Constantine: Eusebius, *Life of Constantine* 4.61.2–3, with Cameron and Hall, 341–342, also discussing instruction and baptism in the fourth century.

4. Aug., *Conf.* 1.17–18 (delayed baptism), 3.7 *(Hortensius),* 3.10 (Manichaeism), 5.13 (abandonment of Manichaeism), 5.23–24 (Ambrose), 5.25 (catechumenate), 8.29 (voice in the garden), 9.14 (baptism). On Augustine's conversion: Brown, *Augustine*[2], chaps. 8–12. Patricius: *PCBE Afrique* 833–834, Patricius 2. Monica: *PCBE Afrique* 758–762.

5. Simplicianus and Victorinus: Augustine, *Conf.* 8.3–5. Marius Victorinus: *PLRE* 1.964, Victorinus 11; *PCBE Italie* 2289–2293. Simplicianus: *PCBE Italie* 2075–2079.

6. *Conf.* 9.22 (Patricius), 9.5 (Verecundus; *PCBE Italie* 2265–2266).

7. Volusianus: [Gerontius], *Life of Melania* 50–55; *PLRE* 2.1184–1185, Volusianus 6; *PCBE Italie* 2340–2341. Cameron, *Last Pagans* 196–197, argues that "there is no evidence that Volusianus was ever a committed pagan," but this goes directly against the evidence of [Gerontius].

8. *Augustine, Conf.* 9.6. Nebridius: *PCBE Afrique* 774–776. Cf. Brown, *Augustine*[2] 57, 128–129.

9. Augustine: *Conf.* 5.24. Ethiopian: Acts 8.27–39 (vs. 37, in which Philip asks the eunuch if he believes, was presumably interpolated because the original text did not mention catechism). Gregory of Nyssa, *Life of Gregory the Thaumaturge:*

PG 46.908D–909B (Phaedimus), 913D (prevalence of demons, Gregory's resolution), 916 A–917C (first miracle), 921 D–924 A (first day), 924 A–B (church), 953D (seventeen unbelievers).

10. Augustine's toothache: *Conf.* 9.12. Sozomen: *Ecclesiastical History* 5.15.15, p. 216 Bidez-Hansen. Hilarion: Jerome, *Life of Hilarion* 14; *PLRE* 1.414, Helpidius 4.

11. Sulpicius Severus, *Life of Martin* 17.1–4. Cf. *PLRE* 1.873, Taetradius (otherwise unknown). On Martin, see now K. Rosen, "Der heilige Martin—Bischof, Arzt und Missionar," *Jahrbuch für Antike und Christentum* 52 (2009): 61–80.

12. In general, J. Hahn, S. Emmel, U. Gotter, eds., *From Temple to Church: Destruction and Renewal of Local Cultic Topography in Late Antiquity* (Leiden: Brill, 2008); L. Lavan and M. Mulryan, eds., *The Archaeology of Late Antique "Paganism"* (Leiden: Brill, 2011).

13. Severus, *Life of Martin* 13–14 (tree, Levrosum: *Barrington Atlas* 14 G 2), 15.4 (effect of Martin's teaching).

14. Sozomen, *Ecclesiastical History* 7.15.13–15. Cf. D. Feissel, "Bulletin épigraphique," *Revue des Études Grecques* 100 (1987): 374, no. 501 (mosaic inscriptions mentioning him).

15. Rufinus, *Ecclesiastical History* 11.22–23; Eunapius: *Lives of the Philosophers* 6.11.1; E. J. Watts, *Riot in Alexandria* (Berkeley: University of California Press, 2010), 192–196. Evagrius: *PLRE* 1.286, Evagrius 7. Romanus: *PLRE* 1.769, Romanus 5. Gibbon: *Decline and Fall,* chap. 28 (2.84–85 ed. Womersley).

16. On the archaeology of the Serapeum and the Christian buildings, J. S. McKenzie, S. Gibson, and A. T. Reyes, "Reconstructing the Serapeum in Alexandria from the Archaeological Evidence," *Journal of Roman Studies* 94 (2004): 73–121. Cross: Rufinus, *Ecclesiastical History* 11.29. Coptic cross *(croix ansée):* H. Leclercq in *DACL* 3.3120–3123. Nilometer: Rufinus, *Ecclesiastical History* 11.30, cf. F. E. Engreen, "The Nilometer in the Serapeum at Alexandria," *Medievalia et Humanistica* 1 (1943): 3–13. Canopus: Rufinus, *Ecclesiastical History* 2.26.

17. Rufinus, *Ecclesiastical History* 11.28.

18. Gregory of Nyssa, *Life of Gregory the Miracle-Worker, PG* 46.953 B–C.

19. Augustine: *Letter* 29.9 (LCL, *Letter* 10; Baxter's translation, slightly adapted). Gregory the Great to Augustine of Canterbury: *Letters* 11.56 (ed. Hartmann, *MGH, Epist.* 2.331).

20. Augustine, *Against Faustus* 20.4 (*PL* 42.370). Gifts *(strenae):* e.g., Maximus of Turin, *Sermon* 98.2. On the date of Easter: J. Ford, "Easter Controversy," *New Cath. Encycl.* 5.13–14; on the date of Christmas, S. K. Roll, "Christmas and Its Cycle," *New Cath. Encycl.* 3.551–554.

21. Sozomen: *Ecclesiastical History* 2.5.6. On pagans in high office down to 455: R. von Haehling, *Die Religionszugehörigkeit der hohen Amtsträger des Römischen Reiches* (Bonn: R. Habelt, 1978), with the reservations of T. D. Barnes, "Statistics and the Conversion of the Roman Aristocracy," *JRS* 85 (1995): 135–147.

22. Sozomen 2.5.7–8. Porphyry: Mark, *Life of Porphyry* 58, 64, 72; N. Belayche, "Pagan Festivals in Fourth-Century Gaza," in B. Bitton-Ashkelony and A. Kofsky, eds., *Christian Gaza in Late Antiquity* (Leiden: Brill, 2004), 5–22; C. Thiersch, "Zwischen Hellenismus und Christentum—Transformationsprozesse der Stadt Gaza vom 4.–6. Jh. n. Chr.," *Millennium: Jahrbuch zu Kultur und Ge-*

schichte des ersten Jahrtausends n. Chr. 5 (2008): 57–91. On Porphyrius, see further, Chap. 10.

23. D. Feissel, "L'Adnotatio de Constantin sur le Droit de Cité d'Orcistus en Phrygie," *Antiquité Tardive* 7 (1999): 255–267, discussing *Monumenta Asiae Minoris Antiqua* 7.305. Nacoleia and Orcistus: *Barrington Atlas* 62 E 3, F 3.

24. Gregory the Great, *Letters* 6.49 (plan of converting Angles), 8.29 (conversion of 10,000 Angli), 11.35 (Bertha), 11.37 (Aethelbert), 11.48 (Brunigild), 11.56 (Mellitus). *PLRE* 3.248–251 (Brunichildis), 227–228 (Bertha), 20 (Aethelbert). Narrative version in Bede, *Ecclesiastical History* 3.23–33, who alone gives the detail of Augustine's initial discouragement.

25. Nino: chap. 2. Ireland: J. Stevenson, "Ireland," *LA Guide* 514–515.

26. Riot in Constantinople: Evagrius, *Ecclesiastical History* 3.44 (ed. G. Sabbah), SC 542 (Paris: Éditions du Cerf, 2011). For the Christological issue, G. Downey, *A History of Antioch* (Princeton: Princeton University Press, 1961), 485–486, discussing a similar disturbance in Antioch under Leo I.

27. Homer, *Iliad* 1.8–487. Washing by the sea: 1.312–317; cf. the Achaeans' handwashing before they touch the sacrificial grains, 1.449.

28. Excellent catalogue in G. Petzl, *Die Beichtinschriften Westkleinasiens, Epigraphica Anatolica* 22 (1994), on whose analysis (vii–xviii) I have drawn. The examples that have appeared since do not alter the general picture.

29. Petzl, *Beichtinschriften* no. 3. "Did away with": nos. 37, 72. Innocents: no. 7, 44, 62, etc.

30. Paul: Gal. 5.11, cf. 1 Cor. 1.23. For the pagan attitude to the Crucifixion, compare Lucian, *The Passing of Peregrinus* 11, 13 (LCL, *Lucian* 5.12, 14), "that person they still worship, the crucified human being," "the crucified impostor *(sophistês)*." Christ to Peter: Matt. 16.18–19.

31. Baptism of Christ: Matt. 3.13–17, Mark 1.9–11, Luke 3.21–22, cf. John 1.32–34. Purification of all waters: Maximus of Turin, *Sermon* 13a, 3. Mikveh: D. Kotlar, *Encyclopaedia Judaica* 11.1534–1544. Baptisteries: H. Leclerq, "Baptistère," *DACL* 2.382–469; for examples with several steps, 403, 408, 422. At Dura, the font was 0.955 mm. deep and the candidate had to "mount the outer step, sit on the ledge, swing the feet over the ledge and step down in" (C. H. Kraehling, *The Christian Building, Excavations at Dura-Europos, Final Report* 8.2 [New Haven: Dura-Europos Publications, 1967], 145–151, with plates 10–13).

32. Philostratus: *Life of Apollonius*, e.g., 1.1, 3.21–22 (metempsychosis), *Heroic Dialogue (Hêrôikos)* 2, p. 3 de Lannoy (Protesilaos). Pagan bafflement: e.g., Lucian, *Peregrinus* 13 (LCL, *Lucian* 5.14), "The poor wretches have persuaded themselves that they will be immortal and live for ever, and that is why they despise death."

9. The West

1. Themistius: *PLRE* 1.889–894; for a useful recent discussion, R. Penella, *The Private Orations of Themistius* (Berkeley: University of California Press, 2000), 1–5. Athletic simile: *Oration* 5, 68 D–69 A (but runners do not usually run toward a goal from different directions). Prov. 21.1: *Orations* 7, 89 D; 11, 147 C; 19, 229 A.

2. *Oration* 13, 178 A (the gods), 178 D–179 A (white dress), 180 A–B (prayer).

3. Older view of Symmachus: O. Seeck, *RE* 4 A (1931), 1142, "Verfechter des sinkenden Heidentums"; J. F. Matthews in *OCD*^{3} 1460, "a leading proponent of the pagan religious cause against the Christian emperors." Contrast Brown, *Eye of the Needle* 101, "[Symmachus] was the first member of the Roman nobility whom we can see adjusting to an unprecedented situation." For summaries of his career, Seeck, 1142–1144; *PLRE* 1.865–870, Symmachus 4; Matthews, *OCD*^{3} 1460. Panegyrics: *Oration* 1.1 (all-seeing emperor), 2.18 (emperor closest to god), 2.23 *(caelestes).*

4. *Oration* 2.32. On the emperors as God's vicegerents, D. M. Nicol in *The Cambridge History of Medieval Political Thought* (Cambridge: Cambridge University Press, 1988), 52–53. For *numen,* compare, e.g., *Theodosian Code* 15.4.1.1 (425), "in the games also, (our) images when displayed should only show that our *numen* and our praises flourish in the thoughts of the competitors and in the recesses of their minds" *(ludis quoque simulacra proposita tantum in animis concurrentum mentisque secretis nostrum numen et laudes vigere demonstrent).*

5. Plurality of religions: *Third Report* 7, 8, 19. Ambrose: *Letters* 72, 73 Zelzer = 7, 8 Beyenka.

6. Symmachus to Praetextatus: *Letter* 1.49 (Praetextatus), 1.51 (advancement), 2.7.3 (Flavianus), 4.33.2 (oracular sites). On the recipients, *PLRE* 1.722–724 (Praetextatus 1), 1.347–349 (Flavianus 15), 1.751–752 (Protadius). On Protadius and his brothers Florentinus and Minervius, O. Seeck, *MGH AA* 6.1, cxli–cxliii; the fact that all three held high office after Frigidus does not show that they were or became Christian, as sometimes argued, e.g., by Cameron, *Last Pagans* 188–189.

7. Titianus: *Letter* 1.64 (*PLRE* 1.917–918, Titianus 5). Ambrose: *Letter* 3.33; on Marcianus, *PLRE* 1.555–556, Marcianus 14 (identifying the usurper with Eugenius, though he is more likely Magnus Maximus, Augustus during the period 383–388). Olybrius and Probinus: Letter 5.68 (*PLRE* 1.639–640, Olybrius 2, *PLRE* 1.734–735, Probinus 1).

8. The letters concerning Memmius Symmachus's games are listed in *PLRE* 1.869; *PLRE* 2.1046–1047, Symmachus 10. Boethius: *PLRE* 2.233–237, Boethius 5, and 2.1322, Stemma 22.

9. For brief treatments, O. Seeck, *RE* 1 (1894), 1845–1852; *PLRE* 1.547–548, Marcellinus 15; J. F. Matthews, *OCD*^{3} 73–74. For a vigorous defense of a publication date ca. 390, Cameron, "Nicomachus Flavianus and the Date of Ammianus's Last Books," *Athenaeum* 100 (2012): 337–358. I accept the usual identification of the historian with the Marcellinus of Libanius, *Letter* 1063 Förster; cf. Cameron, art. cit. 355 ("probably correct").

10. Ammianus 26.1.1 ("lofty matters"), 15.7.6–10 (Liberius), 21.16.18 (simplicity of Christianity), 22.13.1–3 (burning of temple), 18.10.4 (convent), 22.5.3–5 (Christian feuds), 27.3.11–13 (riots), 27.3.14–15 (luxury of city clergy).

11. Praetextatus: Jerome, *Against John of Jerusalem* 8, *PL* 23.377C. I accept the argument of L. Cracco, *Il paganesimo romano tra religione e politica (384–394 d. C.), Accademia Nationale dei Lincei, Classe di Scienze morali, Memorie* 8.23.1 (1979), that the so-called *Carmen adversus Flavianum* is in fact directed against Praetextatus; see now also Cameron, *Last Pagans,* chap. 8, "The Poem against the Pagans."

12. Death of paganism: e.g., H. Bloch in A. Momigliano, ed., *The Conflict between Paganism and Christianity in the Fourth Century* (Oxford: Clarendon Press, 1963), 193: "the final conflict between paganism and Christianity, a conflict

which culminates and comes to a dramatic conclusion at the end of the fourth century." The only continuous ancient narrative is Zosimus, *New History* 4.56–59; summaries by O. Seeck, *RE* 2 (1895), 417–419, Bloch in *Conflict* 198–201, J. Curran in *CAH* 13: *The Late Empire* (Cambridge: Cambridge University Press, 1998), 108–110; see also *PLRE* 1.293 (Eugenius 6), 1.345–47 (Younger Flavianus), 1.347–49 (Elder Flavianus).

13. Zosimus, *New History* 4.59.

14. Thus É. Wolff et al., eds., *Rutilius Namatianus: Sur son retour* (Paris: Les Belles Lettres, 2007), xiii, "Rutilius était incontestablement païen . . . Cependant, son paganisme est d'essence plus culturelle que strictement religieuse." Yet Rutilius the author could hardly express his distaste for Judaism and Christianity more plainly: see below.

15. Claudian: A. Cameron, *Claudian: Poetry and Propaganda at the Court of Honorius* (Oxford: Clarendon Press, 1970), chap. 8, "The Pagan at a Christian Court" (but in the index, 498, "perhaps a nominal Christian"). Macrobius: Kaster, *Macrobius* (see "Authors") 1.xxii (henceforth "Kaster"); see further the Appendix.

16. The Younger Flavianus's conversion is inferred from Augustine, *City of God* 5.26, where Augustine says that Theodosius forgave and later honored the sons of his enemies, "who though not yet Christian had fled to the Church (*or* a church)" *(nondum Christianos ad ecclesiam confugientes),* and that he required their conversion *(Christianos hac occasione fieri uoluit).* In favor of his continued paganism, T. Grünewald, "Die letzte Kampf des Heidentums in Rom? Zur postume Rehabilitation des Virius Nicomachus Flavianus," *Historia* 41 (1992): 462–487. For Protadius and his two brothers, above, n. 6. Protadius's successor as prefect of the city, Lampadius, may also have been a pagan: *PLRE* 2.654–655; R. von Haehling, *Die Religionszugehörigkeit der hohen Amtsträger des Römischen Reiches seit Constantins I. Alleinherrschaft bis zum Ende der Theodosianischen Dynastie* (Bonn: R. Habelt, 1978), 398.

17. Rome in 408–410: J. B. Bury, *History of the Later Roman Empire from the Death of Theodosius I to the Death of Justinian*[2] (London: Macmillan, 1923), 1.174–185; sources in *PLRE* 2.43–48. Pompeianus: Cracco Ruggini, *Paganesimo* 120–123; Haehling, *Religionszugehörigkeit* 402–403; *PLRE* 2.897–898, Pompeianus 2. Pagan prefect: Gerontius, *Life of Melania* 19; Brown, *Eye of the Needle* 294–299.

18. Attalus: Haehling, *Religionszugehörigkeit* 403–404; *PLRE* 2.180–181, Attalus 2. Pagan hopes: Sozomen, *Ecclesiastical History* 9.9.1. Lampadius: *PLRE* 2.656, Lampadius 7; Haehling, *Religionszugehörigkeit* 315–316. Marcianus: *PLRE* 1.555–556, Marcianus 14; Ruggini, *Paganesimo* 11 n. 16; Haehling, *Religionszugehörigkeit* 404–405. Tertullus: *PLRE* 2.1059, Tertullus 1.

19. Vandal sack: Bury, *History*[2] 1.325–326. Jerome: *Letter* 127.12 (*CSEL* 56.154, *haeret uox et singultus intercipiunt uerba dictitantis*). Augustine: *City of God* 1.10 (Christians none the worse), 1.1 (punishment of pagans). Cf. Brown, *Augustine*[2] 289: "Rome could be represented as the black sheep of a family of loyal Christianized cities. . . . The Romans, who pinned their faith on false gods, had merely got what they deserved." Orosius: cf. Bury, *History*[2] 1.306–307, "Perhaps it deserves more than any other book to be described as the first attempt at a universal history, and it was probably the worst."

20. Events after 410: Bury, *History*[2] 185–209. Rutilius: *PLRE* 2.770–771; Cameron, *Last Pagans* 207–218. Lucillus: *On His Return* 1.603–604; *PLRE* 2.691. Volusianus: see Index. Falesia: *On His Return* 1. 373–76; for the site, *Barrington Atlas* 41 D 4. Jews: *On His Return* 1.387–398. Monks: 1.439–452. Hermit: 1.517–526. Constantius: fragment B (p. 43 Wolff); *PLRE* 2.321–325, Constantius 17. Rutilius's religion: good summary in E. Doblhofer's edition (*Rutilius Namatianus: De reditu suo* [Heidelberg: C. Winter, 1972–1977]), 1.27–33; Cameron, *Last Pagans* 207–218, concluding that Rutilius "was probably, though perhaps not 'incontestably' a pagan."

21. For Macrobius's life and career, see now the summary of Kaster, 1.xi–xxiv; like Kaster, I accept the identification of the prefect (*PLRE* 2.1101, Theodosius 8) with the author (*PLRE* 2.1102–1103, Theodosius 20).

22. Praetextatus: see Index. Eustathius: *PLRE* 1.311, Eustathius 5, and see Appendix. Horus: *PLRE* 1.445.

23. *Euangelus:* e.g., L. Vidman, ed., *CIL* 6.6 (1980), 254. *Euangelos:* T. Corsten, ed., *A Lexicon of Greek Personal Names* V A, *Coastal Asia Minor* (Oxford: Clarendon Press, 2010), 172. Symmachus, *Letters* 6.7.2; *PLRE* 1.286, Evangelus 1; Cameron, *Last Pagans* 253–254. Senator: *PLRE* 1.286 (Evangelus 2). *Saturnalia* 1.7.1–2 (Evangelus's arrival), 5.2.1, 7.5.1–2, 7.16.1 (questions).

24. Macrobius's intentions: *Saturnalia,* preface. Eustathius: *PLRE* 2.435, Eustathius 7; see further the Appendix. On the dramatic date, Kaster 1.xxiv–xxv; the date of composition is usually placed in the 430s (thus Kaster 1.xvii).

25. See Appendix.

26. Anthemius: O. Seeck, *RE* 1 (1894), 2365–2368; Bury, *History*[2] 1.335–340; *PLRE* 2.96–98. His education: Sidonius, *Poems* 2.156–192 (*MGH, AA* 8.177–178). Severus: *PLRE* 2.1005–1006, Severus 19: Damascius, *Life of Isidore* 77A. Marcellinus: *PLRE* 2.708–710; Damascius, 69. For his paganism, also Count Marcellinus for the year 468 (*MGH, AA* 11.90), *Marcellinus Occidentis patricius idemque paganus.*

27. Gelasius, *Against Andromachus* 23 (the suppression "in my time"), 27 ("shadow"), cf. 3 ("empty figments"), 19 ("neither Christian nor pagan"), 16 ("you have lowered"), 30 (no Christian may participate: the Latin is corrupt and the sense is not fully clear). For discussion, W. M. Green, "The Lupercalia in the Fifth Century," *Classical Philology* 26 (1931): 69, "a performance of the superstitious Christian mob"; N. McLynn, "Crying Wolf: The Pope and the Lupercalia," *Journal of Roman Studies* 98 (2008): 161–175 (actors); so also Cameron, *Last Pagans* 170.

28. Aethicus: A. Riese, *Geographi Latini Minores* (1878) 83.22–24 (cf. *PLRE* 2.19, Aethicus). Maioumas: John the Lydian, *On Months* 4.80 (133.2–8 ed. Wuensch), copied by the Suda, M 47 (3.308–309 ed. Adler); cf. R. Meiggs, *Roman Ostia*[2] (Oxford: Clarendon Press, 1973), 377; G. W. Bowersock, "Maioumas," *LA Guide* 553. Trullan Council: Canon 62 (Mansi 11.971–972). On the Brumalia: J. R. Crawford, "De Bruma et Brumalibus Festis," *Byzantinische Zeitschrift* 23 (1914–1919 [1920]): 365–396.

29. Territory: in the East, e.g., L. Robert, *BCH* 108 (1984): 480–481 = *Documents d'Asie Mineure* (1987) 468–469, "Il arrive fréquemment que des philologues, des historiens et même des épigraphistes n'aient pas assez présent à l'esprit que la cité grecque n'est pas restreinte à la ville et qu'elle ne peut se comprendre

qu'avec son territoire, la *chôra.*" The same applies also to the less urbanized West, on which see A. van Buren, *RE* 8 A (1958), 2090, citing Isidore of Seville, *Etymologies* 15.2.11, *vici et castella et pagi . . . maioribus civitatibus adtribuuntur.* Amantius: [Venantius Fortunatus,] *Life of Saint Amantius* 32–37, *MGH, AA* 4.2.58.

30. Symphorianus: Gregory of Tours, *Miracles, MGH, SRM* 1.2.343–344. Martin: Sulpicius Severus, *Life* 12.2. Hilary of Poitiers: Gregory of Tours, *Miracles, MGH, SRM* 1.2.299.

31. Maximus of Turin: E. Crovella, *Bibliotheca Sanctorum* 9.68–72; C. Sotinel, *TRE* 22 (1992), 304–307. "Apart from a few": *Sermon* 91, extr. 2. "Sacrilegious persons": *Sermon* 106.2. "Some days ago": *Sermon* 107, 1–2.

32. Caesarius: J.-C. Didier, *Bibliotheca Sanctorum* 3.1148–1150; R. J. H. Collins, *TRE* 7 (1981), 531–536. Women weaving: *Sermon* 52.2. Destruction of pagan shrines: *Sermon* 53.1–2.

33. Martin of Braga, ed. C. W. Barlow (see "Authors"); S. McKenna, *Paganism and Pagan Survivals in Spain* (Washington, D.C.: Catholic University of America Press, 1938), 84–107. For the Vulcanalia on August 23, often mentioned in Christian writers of Late Antiquity, W. Eisenhut, *RE* Supplement 14 (1974), 957. For the taboo on stubbing one's foot on a threshold, for example, Ovid, *Amores* 1.12.3–6. Aelfric, *On False Gods:* English translation online at http://faculty.virginia.edu/OldEnglish/aelfric/defalsis.html (accessed 07/30/13). Days of the week: Barlow, 165, observes that "Portuguese is the only Romance language that has retained the use of *feria* with numbers to designate the days of the week."

34. Eugippius, *Life of Severinus* 11. Severinus: D. Ambrasi, *Bibliotheca Sanctorum* 11.965–971. Culcullis: *Barrington Atlas* 19 F 2.

35. Gallus: Gregory of Tours, *Miracles MGH, ARM* 1.2.231; P. Viard, *Bibliotheca Sanctorum* 6.20. Theoderic: *PLRE* 2.1076–1077, Theodericus 6. On Augustine of Canterbury, above, Chap. 8.

10. The East

1. Athens a pagan city: M. Frantz, *Late Antiquity, A.D. 267–700* (Princeton, NJ: American School of Classical Studies at Athens, 1988), 19. In favor of a more precocious Christianization, G. Fowden, "The Athenian Agora and the Progress of Christianity" (review of Frantz, *Late Antiquity*), *Journal of Roman Archaeology* 3 (1990): 494–501. On education in Late Antique Athens, G. W. Bowersock, "The Great Teachers of Late Antique Athens," *Archaiognosia* 14 (2006): 169–182.

2. Scholarchs: successively *PLRE* 1.708 (Plutarchus 5), 2.1051 (Syrianus 3), 2.915–919 (Proclus 4), 2.628–631 (Isidorus 5), 2.725–726 (Marinus), 2.342–343 (Damascius 2); it is disputed whether Hegias (*PLRE* 2.528–529) became scholarch after Marinus's retirement to Alexandria. For the history of the school from the late fourth century to 529, E. Watts, *City and School in Late Antique Athens and Alexandria* (Berkeley: University of California Press, 2006), chaps. 4 and 5. I have used the convenient terms "Neoplatonic" and "Neoplatonist," even though they are modern coinages. Income: Damascius, *Life of Isidore* 102 (henceforth "Damascius, *Life,*" with numbering as in P. Athanassiadi, *Damascius: The Philosophical History* [Athens: Apamea Cultural Association, 1999]). Decline: Damascius, *Life* 150, 151B.

3. On the "Ammonius affair" under Zeno, see below. Damascius: *Life* 78C ("outside creed"), 118B ("prevailing doctrine"), 82B (inevitability), 120B (conversion).

4. Inscription of Plutarch: *IG* 2/3².12767a = 13286. Shrine of Asclepius: Damascius, *Life* 89A. Syrianus epigram: *IG* 2/3².13451. House of Proclus: Marinus, *Life of Proclus* 29. On the house identified as Proclus's, Frantz, *Late Antiquity* 42–44 (in favor); M. di Branco, *La città dei filosofi: Storia di Atene da Marco Aurelio a Giustiniano* (Florence: Olschki, 2006), 152–155 (skeptical).

5. Frantz, *Late Antiquity* 40–41, 44–46, 87–90 ("House C"): Athanassiadi, *Damascius* 342–347, suggesting Damascius as the owner.

6. Damascius, *Life* 98E (golden chain), 150 (senility), 145A–B (Hegias). Closing of school: Malalas, 18.47, p. 379 Thurn; Cameron, "The Last Days of the Academy at Athens," *Proceedings of the Cambridge Philological Society* 15 (1969): 7–29 (skeptical); Frantz, *Late Antiquity* 84–87; E. Watts, "Justinian, Malalas, and the End of Philosophical Teaching in Athens," *JRS* 94 (2004): 168–182; di Branco, *Città* 192–197 (all three less skeptical of Malalas). Against the thesis of M. Tardieu that Simplicius settled in Carrhae, R. Lane Fox, "Harran, Simplicius, and the Late Platonist 'Movers,'" in A. Smith, ed., *The Philosopher and Society in Late Antiquity: Essays in Honour of Peter Brown* (Swansea: Classical Press of Wales, 2005), 231–244.

7. Asclepius shrine: above, n. 4. Chryselephantine Athena (Parthenos): Marinus, *Life* 30: Frantz 57–58. Bronze Athena (Promachos): Frantz, 76–77.

8. Sophist Plutarch: *IG* 2/3².3818 = 13281, 4224 = 13283; *PLRE* 2.893–894, Plutarchus 2 (in favor of identifying him with the scholarch, Frantz, *Late Antiquity* 63–64; so also Bowersock, "Great Teachers" 172–174). Apronianus: *IG* 2/3².4225 = 13284; *PLRE* 2.124, Apronianus 1. Leontius: *PLRE* 2.668–669, Leontius 6. Eudocia: *PLRE* 2.408–409, Eudocia 2. Leontius's inauguration: Olympiodorus, *Fragmenta Historicorum Graecorum* ed. Müller, fragment 28. Lachares: Damascius, *Life* 61, 62 A; *PLRE* 2.652–653, Lachares 2; *IG* 2/3².11952 = 13454.

9. Philtatios: Olympiodorus, Fragment 32 Müller. Pamprepius: Damascius, *Life* 112; on him, see further below.

10. Eunapius, *Lives of the Philosophers* 7.3.1–5; K. Clinton, *The Sacred Officials of the Eleusinian Mysteries* (Philadelphia: American Philosophical Society, 1974), 43. On the site: J. Travlos, *Bildlexikon zur Topographie des antiken Attika* (Tübingen: Wasmuth, 1988), 91–169, esp. 98 on Christian use.

11. Cave of Pan on Parnes: N. Skias, "Τὸ παρὰ τὴν Φυλὴν ἄντρον τοῦ Πανός," *Arkhaiologikê Ephêmeris* (1918): 1–28; for the poem (overrestored), Skias 24–25 no. 12; *IG* 2/3².4831 = 13251. On this and other cave sites in Attica, G. Fowden, "City and Mountain in Late Roman Attica," *Journal of Hellenic Studies* 108 (1988): 56–57.

12. Libanius on Aristophanes: *Oration* 14.27, 64 (*PLRE* 1.106–107); H.-U. Wiemer, *Libanios und Julian* (Munich: Beck, 1995), 127–134. On Late Antique Corinth, R. M. Rothaus, *Corinth, The First City of Greece: An Urban History of Late Antique Cult and Religion* (Leiden: Brill, 2000), 92–104 ("Christianizing the City"), 126–134 ("Nymphs and Angels").

13. Aphrodisias: *Barrington Atlas* 65 A 2. On its importance as a philosophical link between Athens and Alexandria, Bowersock, "Great Teachers" 174–175. Isidore and Asclepiodotus: Damascius, *Life* 82. On "Apollo's Halls" and this incident,

L. Robert, *Bulletin de Correspondance Hellénique* 101 (1977): 86–88 = *Documents d'Asie Mineure* (Athens: École française d'Athènes, 1987), 44–46.

14. *PLRE* 2.160–161 (Elder Asclepiodotus), 161–162 (Younger). Inscriptions of Elder Asclepiodotus: Ch. Roueché, *Aphrodisias in Late Antiquity* (London: Society for the Promotion of Roman Studies, 1989), nos. 53, 54. Damascius on him: *Life* 86B. Atrium House: R. R. R. Smith, "Late Roman Philosopher Busts from Aphrodisias," *JRS* 80 (1990): 127–155. Triconch House: M. L. Berenfield, "The Triconch House and the Predecessors of the Bishop's Palace at Aphrodisias," *American Journal of Archaeology* 113 (2009): 203–229, esp. 221–222.

15. Roueché, *Aphrodisias* nos. 56 (Pytheas), 154 ("dwelling with the immortals"), 157 (Euphemia).

16. Best edition now W. Ameling, *Inscriptiones Judaicae Orientis II: Kleinasien* (Tübingen: Mohr Siebeck, 2004), 71–112 no. 14, esp. 83–85 for this interpretation of the mysterious *patellades*. See also A. Chaniotis, "The Jews of Aphrodisias: Old Evidence and New Problems," *Scripta Classica Israelica* 21 (2002): 209–242, esp. 218 on the dates and 232 on the connection with contemporary paganism.

17. Zacharias, *Life of Severus* p. 40 Kugener. On the revolt of Illus, see below.

18. Conversion of the temple: Roueché, *Aphrodisias* 153–155; Berenfield, "The Triconch House" 211. Sebasteion: R. R. R. Smith, "Defacing the Gods at Aphrodisias," in B. Dignas and R. R. R. Smith, eds., *Historical and Religious Memory in the Ancient World,* 283–326 (Oxford: Oxford University Press, 2012). Final Christianization of Aphrodisias: Roueché, "From Aphrodisias to Stauropolis," in *Wolf Liebeschuetz Reflected, Bulletin of the Institute of Classical Studies, London,* Supplement 91 (2007): 183–192. On church building in and around Aphrodisias, Ö. Dalgiç, "Early Christian and Byzantine Churches," in C. Ratté and P. D. De Staebler, *Aphrodisias V: The Aphrodisias Regional Survey* (Darmstadt: Philipp von Zabern, 2012), 367–39.

19. John of Ephesos, *Lives of the Eastern Saints* pp. 659–60, 681 Brooks; *Chronicle of Zuqnin* pp. 92–93 Harrak; Destephen, *PCBE Asie* 501–504. Hyperechius: *PLRE* 3.606; W. H. Buckler and D. M. Robinson, *Sardis: Greek and Latin Inscriptions* no. 19; Roueché, *Aphrodisias* 147. Converted temple and monastery of Dereira: C. P. Jones, "An Inscription seen by Agathias," *Zeitschrift für Papyrologie und Epigraphik* 179 (2011): 107–115.

20. On Late Antique Gaza, C. Saliou, ed., *Gaza dans l'Antiquité Tardive: Archéologie, rhétorique et histoire* (Salerno: Helios, 2005). Porphyrius: Mark the Deacon, *Life of Porphyrius* 19 (280 Christians), 17, 19, 23, etc. (pagan opposition), 26–27, 33–84 (mission to Constantinople and building of church).

21. Zosimus: *PLRE* 2.1205, Zosimus 2. Procopius: *Opuscula,* pp. 80–104 Amato; cf. C. P. Jones, "Procopius of Gaza and the Water of the Holy City," *Greek Roman and Byzantine Studies* 47 (2007): 455–467. Choricius: pp. 344–380 Förster-Richsteig; G. W. Bowersock, *Mosaics as History* (Cambridge: Harvard University Press, 2006), 62–63.

22. C. P. Jones, "Three Temples in Libanius and in the Theodosian Code," *CQ* 63 (2013): 839–844.

23. Athanassiadi, edition of Damascius, *Life* 134–136, with full commentary; J. Aliquot, "Dans les Pas de Damascius et des Néoplatoniciens au Proche-Orient,"

Revue des Études Anciennes 112 (2010): 363–374. *Barrington Atlas* 69 D 2 (Damascus), D 4 (Bostra), 71 B 1–2 (Decapolis), 71 A 5 (Petra). On Theandrios, G. W. Bowersock, *Studies on the Eastern Roman Empire* (Goldbach bei Aschaffenburg: Keip, 1994), Index s.v. Theandrios: on Dusares, id., "The Cult and Representation of Dusares in Roman Arabia," *Studies* 245–252.

24. John of Ephesus, *Lives of the Eastern Saints,* pp. 229–247 Brooks.

25. C. Haas, "Alexandria," *LA Guide* 285–287; C. Leyser, "Monasticism," *LA Guide* 583–584. For the historical Antony, F. Caraffa, *Bibliotheca Sanctorum* 2.106–114.

26. The classic treatment is J. Leipoldt, *Schenute von Atripe und die Entstehung des national ägyptischen Christentums* (Leipzig, 1903); for an informative, recent treatment, A. G. López, *Shenoute of Atripe and the Uses of Poverty* (Berkeley: University of California Press, 2013), esp. 131–133 (chronology), 134–137 (sources).

27. Gesios: Besa, *Life of Shenute* 88, 125; Shenute, L. 24 = "If the Fox should bark," translated by J. W. Barns in J. Wolski, ed., *Actes du Xe Congrès International de Papyrologues* (Wroclaw: Wydawnictwo Polskiej Akademii Nauk, 1964), 156–159; "Let our Eyes," translated by S. Emmel in J. Hahn et al., eds., *From Temple to Church* (Leiden: Brill, 2008), 182–188. Emmel identifies Gesios with Flavius Aelius Gessius, governor of the Thebaid under Valens (*PLRE* 1.395, Gessius 2), but López, *Shenoute* 133 considers him an otherwise unknown landowner. Gesios and temple of Atripe: López, *Shenoute* 105–106. Raid on his house: L. 24 (p. 44 Wiesmann); López, *Shenoute* 108–120. Pneuit: Shenute L. 25; Besa, *Life* 83; López, *Shenoute* 120–126.

28. Eunapius: *PLRE* 1.46–47 (Alypius 4), 1.75 (Antoninus 7, who taught in Canopus east of Alexandria). Magnus (PLRE 1.534. Magnus 7) was a medical orator ("iatrosophist"). Hypatia: Socrates, *Ecclesiastical History* 7.15; Damascius, *Life* 106B; *PLRE* 2.575–576.

29. *PLRE* 2.547–548 (Hermeias 3), 2.71–72 (Ammonius 6). Zacharias: *On the Creation of the World, PG* 85.1028–1029. Platform: G. Majcherek, "Kom el-Dikka: Excavation and Preservation Work, 2002/2003," *Polish Archaeology in the Mediterranean* 15 (2004): 29–31 (Auditorium K); Bowersock, "Great Teachers" 179–182. "Ammonius affair": see below.

30. Damascius, *Life* 106B (professors attending his lectures), 48A (his poetic efforts), Testimonia III, 81–83 (Damascius's study with Theon). Severus: Zacharias, *Life of Severus* p. 12 Kugener.

31. On these events, J. B. Bury, *History of the Later Roman Empire*² 1.394–399 (London: Macmillan, 1923). Papyrius: *Barrington Atlas* 66 B3.

32. Pamprepius: *PLRE* 2.825–828; E. Livrea, *Pamprepii Panopolitani Carmina* (Leipzig: Teubner, 1979); di Branco, *Città* 160–161.

33. Zacharias, *Life of Severus* pp. 14–37 Kugener. Damascius on Peter Mongus: *Life* 113 I. In general Athanassiadi, *Damascius* 27–29; E. J. Watts, *Riot in Alexandria* (Berkeley: University of California Press, 2010), chap. 1, "The Anatomy of a Riot," and appendix 1, proposing a date of 386.

34. Damascius, 113 D (Pamprepius), 117–121 A ("Ammonius affair"). On Horapollon and his family, see further below.

35. Horapollon I: *PLRE* 2.569, Horapollon 1; *DPhA* 3.806; R. A. Kaster, *Guardians of Language* (Berkeley: University of California Press, 1988), 295–297.

Heraiscus: *PLRE* 2.543–544; *DPhA* 3.628–630. Asclepiades: *PLRE* 2.158–159, Asclepiades 2; *DPhA* 1.620–621. Horapollon II: *PLRE* 2.569–570, Horapollon 2; *DPhA* 3.804–806; O. Masson, "A propos d'Horapollon, l'auteur des *Hieroglyphica*," *Revue des Etudes Grecques* 105 (1992): 231–235; H. J. Thissen, ed., *Des Niloten Horapollon Hieroglyphenbuch* (Leipzig: Saur, 2001).

36. Blemmyes: K. Sethe, *RE* 3 (1897), 566–568; R. B. Hitchner and A. Kazhdan, *ODB* 1.296–297; R. S. Bagnall, *Egypt in Late Antiquity* (Princeton: Princeton University Press, 1993), 146–147. Blemmyes at Philae: Procopius, *Wars* 1.19.27–37 = T. Eide et al., eds., *Fontes Historiae Nubiorum* 3 (Bergen, Norway: University of Bergen, 1998), 1188–1193 no. 328. Petition of Ombos: *P. Cairo Maspéro* 67004; for the governor, Flavius Triadius Marianus Athanasius, *PLRE* 3.145–146, tentatively dating his tenure to 566–568.

11. Conclusion

1. R. S. Bagnall, "Religious Conversion and Onomastic Change in Early Byzantine Egypt," *Bulletin of the American Society of Papyrologists* 19 (1982): 105–124 = *Later Roman Egypt* (Aldershot: Ashgate/Variorum, 2003), chap. 8. Oxyrhynchus in 400: A.-J. Festugière, ed., *Historia Monachorum in Egypto* (Brussels: Société des Bollandistes, 1971), chap. 5 (p. 41–43).

2. Z. Rubin, "Romans and Sasanids," *The Cambridge Ancient History* 14 (Cambridge: Cambridge University Press, 2000), 638–644.

3. Cf. B. Caseau, *LA Guide* 52–53, "Finally, as the sacred geography of the former Roman provinces adapted to the new medieval societies, the religious conquest of new lands started. East of the Rhine and north of the Danube there were still pagans to convert, pagan shrines to desecrate, and new Christian sanctuaries to consecrate with perfumed oil and incense."

4. Severinus: above, Chap. 9.

5. Kosrow I and Kosrow's-Better-Antioch: M. L. Chaumont, "Antioch," *Encyclopaedia Iranica* 2 (1987), 123–124. On Kosrow II and his capture of Jerusalem, G. W. Bowersock, *Empires in Collision in Late Antiquity,* The Menahem Stern Jerusalem Lectures (Hanover, NH: University Press of New England, 2013), chap. 2, "The Persian Capture of Jerusalem."

6. H. Kennedy, "Islam," *LA Guide* 229; similarly J. M. Fiey, "Nasara," *Encyclopaedia of Islam* 7 (1992), 971–972.

7. John on the cult of images: above, Chap. 5. On the hundredth heresy: R. de Coz, ed., *Jean Damascène: Écrits sur l'Islam,* SC 383 (Paris: Éditions du Cerf, 1992), 210–227, esp. section 2, a loose paraphrase of *Sura* 5.116. *Dialogue with a Saracen:* ibid. 228–251.

8. E.g., Spain: S. McKenna, *Paganism and Pagan Survivals in Spain* (Washington, D.C.: Catholic University of America Press, 1938), chap. 5, "Pagan Survivals in Visigothic Spain." Later "heresies": *Oxford Dictionary of the Christian Church*[3] (1997), 301 (Cathars), 499–500 (Donatists), 1165 (Novatians). For Gibbon's appreciation of Conyers Middleton's *Letter from Rome,* see Chap. 1.

9. C. P. Jones, "The Fuzziness of 'Paganism,'" *Common Knowledge* 18, no. 2 (2012): 249–254.

Appendix

1. *PLRE* 2.698 (Macrobius 1, vicar and proconsul), 698–699 (Macrobius 2, praepositus). Thus P. Wessner, *RE* 14 (1928), 170: "da M. in seinen beiden Hauptschriften [the *Saturnalia* and *Commentary on the Somnium Scipionis*] als Heide erscheint, müsste er später zum Christentum übergetreten sein."

2. S. Mazzarino, *Rendiconti Lombardi* 71, ser. 3.2 (1937–38): 255–58; A. Cameron, "The Date and Identity of Macrobius," *JRS* 56 (1966): 25–38; A. Cameron, *Last Pagans* 231–272. Son: *PLRE* 2.435 (Eustathius 7), 436 (Plotinus Eustathius 13); the inscription is now *CIL* 6.8.3, no. 41394.

3. C. W. Hedrick Jr., *History and Silence: Purge and Rehabilitation of Memory in Late Antiquity* (Austin: University of Texas Press, 2000), 79–80; P. Lebrecht Schmidt, "(Macrobius) Theodosius und das Personal der *Saturnalia*," *Rivista di Filologia e di Istruzione Classica* 136 (2008): 50; Cameron, "Macrobius, Avienus, and Avianus," *CQ*, n.s. 17 (1967): 388, "Macrobius was undoubtedly a pagan"; ibid. 399, "A further positive indication of Macrobius' paganism is provided by *Comm.* ii. 10. 5–16, where he defends against objections the Platonic view of the eternity of the Universe—a doctrine wholly unacceptable to Christians"; Cameron, *Christianisme et formes littéraires de l'Antiquité tardive en Occident,* Entretiens Hardt 23 (Vandoeuvres-Geneva: Fondation Hardt, 1977), 26, "I am not (of course) suggesting that Macrobius was himself a Christian, still less that either of his books were in any sense Christian books"; Cameron, *Last Pagans* 265, 272; R. A. Kaster, ed., *Macrobius: Saturnalia,* LCL (Cambridge: Harvard University Press, 2011), xxi–xxiv. The view has not found favor in French-language scholarship: e.g.. M. Armisen-Marchetti, ed., *Macrobe: Commentaire au Songe de Scipion I* (Paris: Les Belles Lettres, 2001), xviii: "Faire de Macrobe un chrétien, même négligent, est aller contre l'évidence."

4. *PLRE* 1.345–347 (Nicomachus Flavianus 14): *consularis Campaniae* before 382, *Praefectus Praetorio* 431–432. Theodosius's father: *PLRE* 1.902–904, Flavius Theodosius 3. *Lexicon of Greek Personal Names* II: *Attica* (Oxford: Clarendon Press, 1994), 24 *(Ambrosios)*, 214 *(Theodosios)*.

5. *Vita Melaniae* 50–55, SC 90.224–239 (*PLRE* 2.1184–1185, Volusianus 6).

6. *PIR* A 498 (Alexander), 748 (Antipater), 1050 (Aristobulus). Matt.: 2.16–18. Josephus: *AJ* 17.177–181, 193. According to Cameron, *Last Pagans* 271, "It must be a Christian adaptation of an original joke alluding to Herod's well-attested execution of three of his adult sons." But why should Christians "adapt" the story in a way that conflicted with the gospel?

7. Avienus, identical with the fabulist "Avianus": Cameron, "Macrobius, Avienus," 385–399; *PLRE* 2.191–192; Lebrecht Schmidt, "(Macrobius) Theodosius," 57–76; Kaster, 1, p. xxx.

8. Speech of Praetextatus: 1.17.2–23.22 (Kaster 1.206–306). Listeners' reaction: 1.24.1. Admiration only for Praetextatus's learning: Cameron, *Last Pagans* 266, "the other interlocutors treat Praetextatus's exposition first and foremost as a display of *erudition.*" W. Liebeschuetz, "The Significance of the Speech of Praetextatus," in P. Athanassiadi and M. Frede, eds., *Pagan Monotheism* (Oxford: Clarendon Press; New York: Oxford University Press, 1999), 185–205, esp. 200–202,

rightly argues that the speech is "neither pagan propaganda nor anti-Christian polemic."

9. Identity of Apollo and Asclepius: *Sat.* 1.20.4, *Aesculapium eundem esse atque Apollinem . . . hinc probatur quod ex illo natus creditur.* Christian view of sun: e.g., Arnobius, *Against the Gentiles* 1.29.7, *solem deum cum esse credatis, conditorem eius non quaeritis?;* Zacharias of Mitylene, *On the Creation of the World, PG* 85.1043–1058. Christian view of Asclepius: A. Cameron and S. G. Hall, *Eusebius' Life of Constantine* (Oxford: Clarendon Press, 1999) 304: "Asclepius was, like Apollonius [of Tyana], an obvious analogue for Jesus." Christological debate of the 420s and 430s: W. H. C. Frend, *The Rise of Christianity* (London: Darton, Longman and Todd, 1984), 752–758. Eternity of the universe: *Commentary* 2.10.5–16, cf. n. 3 above.

10. Julian, *Hymn* 141 D-142 A (Helios an emanation of the One), 143 B ("there are gods"), 136 A (oracle, cf. Macrobius, *Sat.* 1.18.18), 156 B–C (Invincible Sun). Sol at Rome: M. Beard, J. North, and S. Price, *Religions of Rome* (Cambridge: Cambridge University Press, 1998), 1.258 and Index s.v. Sol. Cameron, *Last Pagans* 269, suggests that Macrobius omitted Mithras from his list of gods because "he may not have realized that the abbreviation *PP* [in Praetextatus' funerary monument, *CIL* 6.1779, and *CIL* 6.8.3, pp. 4757–4759; *ILS* 1259] stood for *pater patrum,* the highest grade in the Mithraic hierarchy," but this does not seem consistent with Cameron's view of Macrobius's antiquarian expertise. Cf. Nock, *Essays* 453: "Mithras never acquired civic status or a place among the *sacra publica* . . . The Mithraism which reached the western world was a new thing, created by fusion in Asia Minor."

11. Macrobius's son: above, n. 2. Earlier Eustathii: *PLRE* 1.310, Eustathius 1 and 5, suggesting that the two are possibly identical, but if related, they are more likely father and son.

Index